AN

**Diamonds
Dispossession
& Democracy**   **in Botswana**

AFRICAN ISSUES

AFRICAN ISSUES

Diamonds
Dispossession
& Democracy

in Botswana

Kenneth Good

JAMES CURREY

JACANA MEDIA

Transferred to digital printing

James Currey
www.jamescurrey.com
is an imprint of Boydell & Brewer Ltd
PO Box 9, Woodbridge, Suffolk IP12 3DF, UK
and of Boydell & Brewer Inc.
668 Mt Hope Avenue, Rochester, NY 14620, USA
www.boydellandbrewer.com

Jacana Media (Pty) Ltd
10 Orange Street
Auckland Park 2092 SA
www.jacana.co.za

A caralogue record is
available from the British Library

ISBN 978 1 84701 312 5 (James Currey Paper)
ISBN 978 1 77009 646 2 (Ohio University Press Paper)

Typeset by
Saxon Graphics Ltd, Derby
in 10/12 Melior with Optima display

This publication is printed on acid-free paper

CONTENTS

               the Realities

          8
Appendix   A Case of the President,   **146**
               High Court
               & Public Opinion

          Bibliography   167

               Index   175

ILLUSTRATIONS

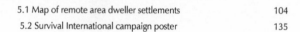

ABBREVIATIONS & ACRONYMS

i

ACHPR	African Commission on Human and Peoples' Rights
AG	Attorney General
ANC	African National Congress
APRM	African Peer Review Mechanism
ARV	Anti-retroviral
ATSIC	Aboriginal and Torres Strait Islander Commission
BCC	Botswana Council of Churches
BCP	Botswana Congress Party
BDC	Botswana Development Corporation
BDF	Botswana Defence Force
BDP	Botswana Democratic Party
BDVC	Botswana Diamond Valuing Company
BHC	Botswana Housing Corporation
BIDPA	Botswana Institute for Development Policy Analysis
BMWU	Botswana Mining Workers Union
BNF	Botswana National Front
BOCCIM	Botswana Confederation of Commerce, Industry and Manpower
BOCONGO	Botswana Council of Non-Governmental Organizations
BTv	Botswana Television
CERD	Committee on the Elimination of Racial Discrimination
CKGR	Central Kalahari Game Reserve
CMI	Chr. Michelsen Institute
COSATU	Congress of South African Trade Unions
CTB	Central Tender Board
CUZs	Community Use Zones
DCEC	Directorate on Corruption and Economic Crime
Debswana	De Beers Botswana Mining Company
DIS	Directorate of Intelligence and Security
DPP	Director of Public Prosecution
Ditshwanelo	Setswana for Botswana Centre for Human Rights
DTC Botswana	Diamond Trading Centre Botswana
DWNP	Department of Wildlife and National Parks

EIU	Economist Intelligence Unit
FAP	Financial Assistance Programme
FDI	Foreign Direct Investment
FPK	First People of the Kalahari
HATAB	Hotel and Tourism Association
HDI	Human Development Index
HDR	Human Development Report
ICCPR	International Covenant on Civil and Political Rights
IEC	Independent Electoral Commission
IMF	International Monetary Fund
IPACC	Indigenous Peoples of Africa Coordinating Committee
IPM	International Project Managers
JSC	Judicial Service Commission
LO	Swedish Trade Union Confederation
MFDP	Ministry of Finance and Development Planning
MISA	Media Institute of Southern Africa
MLGLH	Ministry of Local Government, Lands and Housing
MP	Member of Parliament
MST	Landless Workers' Movement
MTST	Homeless Workers' Movement
MWU	Manual Workers Union
NDB	National Development Bank
NDTC	Namibia Diamond Trading Company
OCPB	Owens Corning Pipes Botswana
PAP	Pan African Parliament
PEEPA	Public Enterprises Evaluation and Privatisation Agency
PI	Prohibited Immigrant
PPP	Purchasing-Power Parities
RADP	Remote Area Development Programme
RADs	Remote Area Dwellers
SBF	Small Borrowers Fund
SDP	Social Democratic Party
SGLs	Special Game Licences
SPIL	Society for the Promotion of the Ikalanga Language
SWAPO	South West African People's Organization
TAC	Treatment Action Campaign
TGLP	Tribal Grazing Land Policy
TI	Transparency International
TIBOT	Transparency International Botswana
UB	University of Botswana
UDF	United Democratic Front
UMC	Upper Middle Income Country
UNCTAD	United Nations Conference on Trade and Development
WIMSA	Working Group for Indigenous Minorities in South Africa

This book focuses on five main elements in Botswana's political economy: diamond production, presidentialism, predominance, social weakness and the subordination of the San people. All of these are in reality closely interlinked, and the demands of diamonds and the power of the president are deterministic, active and intrusive into all other areas. Diamonds are accorded two chapters, the second of which considers the broad social costs of this salient commodity, while the presidency, the ruling party and the dispossessed San each have a chapter of their own. Not all the issues were neatly classifiable into discrete chapters, however, and certain of them, such as growth, poverty and elite corruption in its various aspects and consequences, are referred to in more than one section. The realities overlap, reflecting the fact that the romanticised Botswana is actually a tightly organised and hierarchical place with big gaps between power and popular weakness. These overlaps also reveal the inadequacies of my analytical skills. My apologies to the reader.

The sources for the book are chiefly the extensive scholarly literature on the country, various official reports, both national and international, and the print media. Local newspapers are extensively used in some sections, and no apologies are offered for this. The independent press only came to life in the 1990s and it remains weak and dependent on advertising. It is occasionally sloppy and ill-informed, and sometimes fails to provide an author's name or even the date of publication in online editions. However, this book could not have been written without the *Guardian*, *Mmegi*, the *Gazette*, and the newer *Sunday Standard*. For all its faults, the independent press is at the front of democratisation in the country, and its investigative reporting was what revealed the corruption of the early 1990s. It publicised hidden malpractice, the strong public reactions to which forced the government to appoint the Kgabo and Christy commissions of inquiry. With increasing difficulties, some journalists have continued to scrutinise executive power, and in the case of Outsa Mokone and the *Botswana Guardian*, Justice Isaac Lesetedi affirmed in 2001 that a free and critical media was indeed vital for democracy. To the extent that the truth is known in Botswana it is largely newspapermen who reveal it.

The press also offers an invaluable window into public opinion which, in my case, supplemented the views of my students and colleagues on what was occurring in the country.

Email correspondence has been utilised in places. It was the vehicle for discussion within the university community as my Prohibited Immigrant (PI) process began on 18 February 2005. Discussion on the Mopipi net was then open and lively, and provides a record of what my colleagues were thinking, to supplement what many were saying in the newspapers. Some, I believe a majority of those who spoke out, expressed support for me and for the principles of academic freedom, but others, in the management and my own department, did not. My relations with my students then and earlier were at once warm, active and distant. I liked teaching Botswana politics to a hundred or so noisy second-year students, but I was conscious that I was more critical than many of them and that some were, I thought, a bit lazy; nevertheless I learnt quite a bit from them and we got along. Four women students came to my office to discuss their work at the beginning of my High Court hearings, one of whom turned back to say, as they were leaving, 'We all love you, Prof'. Also warming was the email I eventually got from another when the court's decision had been read, which said 'You are who you are'.

The book is an analysis of power and weakness in a flawed African democracy, and it is personal in places; but not, I hope, at the expense of the facts and some degree of objectivity. Pula!

Kenneth Good
RMIT University and University of Melbourne

INTRODUCTION

Botswana presents itself and is routinely seen by outsiders as an African 'miracle' of growth, governance, stability and democracy. When apartheid and one-party dictatorships characterised the region and ethnic conflict, military coups and collapse occurred elsewhere, the image claimed some credibility. In a continent full of bad news, success stories shone brighter, and exaggerations readily occurred and acquired permanency. It is true that the country's growth rate was the world's highest over thirty years into the 1990s, and that it has held regular parliamentary elections judged free on polling day since the eve of independence in 1965. But change has now been afoot in southern Africa for over a decade, significantly in Namibia and South Africa, more hesitantly in Zambia and Tanzania. And Botswana's growth and electoral regularity, like Mussolini's trains, are only part of the full story.

Revealingly, Botswana's rulers are never stinting in their claims. The country's growth, stability and democracy and their own leadership, were the best in Africa and even further afield. President Ketumile Masire entered the 1994 general election campaign with a typically triumphalist statement. Every previous election had been won by the ruling Botswana Democratic Party (BDP) because of its 'unity, cohesion ... visionary and mature leadership, well-conceived and implementable policies', born of 'goal directed and sure-footed leadership' and 'unparalleled achievements ... of resource and fiscal husbandry'.[1] As corruption scandals reverberated around his government and factionalism rose in the ruling party in early 1995, the president stood firm. 'I will resign when I will – period. We are running a competent administration. The

---

[1] Election Manifesto 1994, quoted in Good (1996a) 'Towards Popular Participation in Botswana', *The Journal of Modern African Studies*, 34, 1, p. 53. In the results, the BDP received its lowest share of the popular vote to that date although its parliamentary domination remained strong.

best in Africa, if not in the developing world.'[2] The claims continued regardless of domestic realities and of external change. Botswana receives 'international accolades for its economic prudence, pro-business policies, low levels of corruption, and commitment to democracy', President Festus Mogae claimed in May 2006, 'making it a recognised success story among the nations of the world.' He also described Botswana as 'one of the world's longest established multi-party democracies, as well as the oldest on this continent with an uninterrupted record of good governance'.[3] Experiencing fast growth, Botswana came to be seen as 'a remarkable state with high principles', upholding both liberal democracy and non-racialism, he believed.[4] The legacy of founding president Seretse Khama was the development, stability and 'the perpetual democracy' which Botswana now enjoyed.[5]

Rather than offering an informed critique, the international Africanist academy has provided the lead chorus to this song of self-praise. From a narrow and uncritical reading of the record, Botswana has been showered with accolades and repeatedly dubbed 'Africa's great success story' (Randall, 2005) and the 'African Miracle' (Thumberg-Hartland, 1978; Samatar, 1999). The bulk of the literature on Botswana is profoundly imbued with both a celebration of this story and a side-lining or neglect of conflicting evidence. The novelist Alexander McCall Smith adds his voice in stories which sell in their millions, and persuasively meld fact and fiction about a 'most remarkable' society where people are well intentioned and elitism, poverty and inequalities hardly exist.[6] The considerable scholarly literature is only slightly less positivistic, mostly economistic, and highly assumptionist. Foreign academics assume that Botswana is indeed a model for success, and assert that the country's distinguishing characteristic

[2] Quoted in Good (1996b), 'Authoritarian liberalism: a defining characteristic of Botswana', *Journal of Contemporary African Studies*, 14, 1, p. 31.

[3] *Tautona Times*, number 16, 21 May 2006, the Weekly Electronic Press Circular of the Office of the President. The *tautona* or 'great lion' is the president.

[4] *Tautona Times*, 21, 2 July 2006.

[5] *Tautona Times*, 9, 19 March 2006.

[6] McCall Smith had written seven books on Botswana by June 2006 and planned to write eleven. His books were intended to offer 'a positive portrayal' of this peaceful, loving and humanistic society. He was aware that his stories had 'a big effect on tourism in the country', and was partly conscious of the contrived and fraught association between his proclaimed sincerity, and the appreciation of the government. Interview with Gazette Entertainment, 'Best selling author visits Mokolodi', *Botswana Gazette*, 30 June 2006. and *Tautona Times*, 5, 18 February 2007.

is its 'prosperity' (Leith, 2004).[7] The negatives of the chosen growth strategies and the working politics of the government are consistently downplayed. Recent scholarly work by Acemoglu et al. (2001, 2002, 2003) which recognises the depth of inequalities and the elitism in the democracy, still claims that diamond wealth shielded the ruling elite from corruption, that the inherited political culture facilitated dissent, that ethnic homogeneity is a reality, and overall celebrates repeatedly 'An African Success Story'.[8] The academic market remains unsaturated by these stories.

Exaggerating the significance of the growth and ignoring the realities of the democracy, the 'miracle' image stimulated a pervasive arrogance and complacency among the country's rulers.[9] What actually exists under this deceptive image is an acute over-dependence on diamonds, the centralisation of power in a strong presidency and preponderant ruling party, and the weakness and dependency of parliamentary and judicial institutions and civil society. Sovereignty in the elitist democracy lies not with the people, as it does constitutionally in neighbouring Namibia, for example, but with the unelected president of 'enormous powers', constitutionally entitled to decide alone, and 'act as he pleases',[10] with all levers of state power to his hand. Parliamentary elections are free in the sense of open, but the ruling party has regularly won all such contests over 40 years. When succession occurs it is through direct transmission from an unelected president to his self-chosen vice-president, automatically so since 1998. High growth and wealth accumulation through the 1980s and 1990s actually facilitated corruption within the ruling elite, assisted by cultural norms legitimising the symbiosis of wealth and power and the deference due to elites. High secrecy practised as a norm

---

[7] Indicative of the established academic literature are the following: Vengroff 1977; Thumberg-Hartland 1978; Picard 1985 and 1987; Holm and Molutsi 1989; Harvey and Lewis 1990; Danevad 1993; Steadman 1993; Dale 1995; Samatar 1999: Leith 2004; Werbner 2004.

[8] Daron Acemoglu, Simon Johnson and James A. Robinson, 'An African Success Story: Botswana', CEPR Discussion Paper 3219, February 2002, reviewed in *The Economist*, 30 March 2002, as 'The African Exception'.

[9] Uncritically absorbed and supported by insufficiently autonomous civic groups which are otherwise aware of the dangers of complacency and critical of policy in specific areas. *Ditshwanelo*, the human rights group, began a recent book on the death penalty with the unsupported and undefined assertion that Botswana 'is recognised as a model of democracy and stability around the world.' (*In the Shadow of the Noose*, 2006, p. 19, discussed in chapter 4 below.)

[10] Bojosi Otlhogile (1998) 'The president: his office, functions and powers', in W. A. Edge and M. H. Lekorwe (eds), *Botswana: Politics and Society*, Pretoria: Van Schaik Publishers. He added perceptively that despite the president's great powers, 'very little is known about the office,' pp. 213, 219 and 224. Discussed in Chapter 2.

in corporate diamond mining contributed further. The process began, it is argued here, with the coupling of diamonds, presidential power and the preponderant ruling party, and through the growth economy led directly to the debilitating social consequences for the bulk of the population which are examined in Chapter Four. The chosen economic trajectories maintained poverty and deepened inequalities in this relatively wealthy African country.

Autocracy and irrationality have increased recently under President Mogae and his vice-president General Ian Khama. The expulsion of the deeply subordinated San people from the Central Kalahari Game Reserve (CKGR) was relentlessly enforced in 1997 and again in 2002. Decision-making has become more idiosyncratic, and free speech has come under increased attack. The ruling party has not yet re-established the ideological bases for the predominance it enjoyed under Seretse Khama and for a time under Ketumile Masire, and the succession to General Khama is both imminent and, on many indications, unpopular with a poorly organised people. Overall conditions of 'negative peace' or tacit underlying conflict exist in the inequitable society, and 'cultural genocide' is referred to by informed participants like Reteng, a multi-cultural association, and the First People of the Kalahari (FPK).

Botswana's distinctiveness lies in part in its 'trail-blazer' modelling of the duopoly of presidentialism and ruling party preponderance in the southern African region, which first Namibia and then South Africa after 1994, adopted. Mauritius is the outstanding exception of an established, consolidated liberal democracy, where three changes of government have occurred through the ballot-box.[11]

Botswana today is in a fix of its rulers' making. Growth and state building were prioritised, and popular organisations capable of changing the status quo are currently weak or absent. President Thabo Mbeki of South Africa is in a not dissimilar situation, but that country has a diversified economy and a strong civil society capable of transcending the impasse. Botswana is without a popular nationalist heritage and electoral participation under unchanging predominance is conspicuously low.[12]

---

[11] More than one successful transfer of power through elections is an essential initial criterion for the consolidation of a liberal democracy. See Samuel P. Huntington (1991), *The Third Wave: Democratization in the Late Twentieth Century*, Norman: Oklahoma UP.

[12] Turnout by some 40 per cent of eligible voters was the recent norm, and it was much lower before 1994. At elections in Mauritius in 2005 the comparable figure was 80 per cent.

Re-examination of the elite-fixated 'miracle' model is long overdue. It is a prerequisite for constitutional and economic reform. The Botswana success story is another example of foreigners getting Africa badly wrong, and placing great conceptual barriers in front of ordinary people. Half of the country's population endeavours to get by on less than two dollars a day, but is nonetheless told by foreigners and complacent rulers that the country is exemplary and that they have never had it so good. The 'miracle' story has weakened popular forces and blunted the just anger of the people. The government has suggested to Batswana and other African people that elections are the be all and end all of democracy, and it has culpably ignored the inequalities which are the consequences of an unregulated growth strategy.

A liberal model of democracy is dominant in the world today, and often amounts to a system where elites of money and status effectively get themselves elected. But this existing ubiquity does not alter the fact real democratic alternatives exist, both in concrete, historical reality and recurrent impulse and aspiration within various societies during times when change seems possible. The so-called Levellers within and around parliament's victorious New Model Army in England articulated basic democratic principles in the late 1640s which are relevant still. All, including the monarch and grandees of wealth and power in parliament itself, are subject to the law (and King Charles was charged with 'tyranny' for making war on his own people). An effective instrument for the defence of individual rights against the state was trial by jury, 12 sworn men of the neighbourhood, as 'the great stronghold of our preservation'. A free press, critical of the powerful, was a striking feature of popular agitation in a time when the world was literally turned upside down, 'whereby all treacherous and tyrannical designs may be the easier ... prevented', and 'liberty' maintained as 'greatest concernment to the [new] Commonwealth'. Government accountable to all citizens, not just to property owners, accompanied equality before the law, as enunciated by Colonel Rainborough at Putney on 28 October 1647: 'the poorest he that is in England has a life to live, as the greatest he ... [and] the poorest man in England is not at all bound in a strict sense to that government that he has not had a voice to put himself under'.

Freedom was being understood as self-determination, and as the reduction of poverty and inequality. Severe inequality, as Rousseau later stressed, undermined citizenship and thus democracy. And the achievement of truth and democracy demanded unending struggle. In early 1649, with kingship and the House of Lords abolished, and the people and the Commons declared the origin of all just power, Colonel John Lilburne told parliament that the republican regime was itself placing 'new chains' on the people. But 'our cause and principles do through their own natural truth and lustre get ground in men's understanding; so that where there was one, twelve months since, that owned our principles, we believe there are now hundreds: so that though we fail, our truths prosper. And posterity we doubt not shall reap the benefit of our endeavours whatever shall become of us.' This petition circulated in London and attracted 40,000 signatories. But the people lacked independent organisation, and within weeks he and the other leading Levellers were arrested (Levellers, 2007: xxiii, 105, 114–15, and 124).

Athens created democracy for the first time in history, and maintained it against great odds for almost two centuries. Certain values and institutions stand out in their enduring relevance. One was a belief in the wisdom of mass assemblies, and the associated practice that all citizens were eligible for public office; growing up in democratic Athens was deemed to be an education in itself. The status enjoyed by free labour was without precedent, and 'peasant-citizens' were able to use their political power to resist the exploitation and domination of the rich. Tight restrictions on the political power of elites of wealth and education were another key element in this highly participatory system. Another was the criticism of elections as an elitist method of selection for public office (Good, 2002: 168–70).

With advanced capitalist development opening new possibilities for democratisation at the beginning of the twentieth century, two interrelated ideas were current. One was the saliency of organisation as 'the weapon of the weak in their struggle with the strong', and as an essential characteristic of real democracy. The other was the recognition that organisation offered fertile ground for elitism within organs of popular power – 'who says organisation says oligarchy'. While this notion reflected conservative presumptions that the masses were incapable of self-government – hence that popular democracy was an impossibility – it also contained a kernel of truth.

The dual problem of democratic organisation and of elitism within it was addressed within the internal movement in South Africa in the 1980s. The new black trade unions and the United

Democratic Front (UDF) aimed at broad-based self determination. In Murphy Morobe's words in 1987: 'By developing active, mass-based democratic organizations and democratic practices within these organizations, we are laying the basis for a future democratic South Africa.' What was aimed at he added was 'direct as opposed to indirect political representation, mass participation rather than passive docility ... a momentum where ordinary people can do the job themselves' in their classrooms, workplaces and neighbour-hoods.

To these ends, the UDF developed an exemplary notion of 'organizational democracy', with these key principles: 1) Elected leadership, periodically re-elected and recallable; 2) Collective leadership; 3) Mandates and accountability; 4) Reporting and reporting back; 5) Criticism and self-criticism. These were, said Morobe, 'fundamental weapon[s] of our struggle'.

But the popular movement faced enemies on two fronts; not only the immediately heavy oppression of the apartheid state but also in the longer term from the 'Aristocrats of the Revolution' (Mda, 2000: 197) in the vanguardist, long established African National Congress (ANC), on the eve of its incumbency.[13] The latter did not doubt its right to rule within a conventional parlia-mentary democracy, and brooked no competition from the UDF. The transformation option floundered, and within a year of Mandela's release, the UDF was disbanded amidst regret and dis-gruntlement in its ranks. The Congress of South African Trade Unions (COSATU), however, remained embedded in the advanced capitalist economy, as did a diversified civil society. As majority rule was succeeded by presidentialism and ANC predominance by the end of the 1990s, the values of criticism and self-criticism, and the principles of organisational democracy, regained their rele-vance (Good, 2002: 176–90; Feinstein, 2007).

Brazil is another prime site of the participatory impulse today. The Homeless Workers' Movement (MTST) broke off in 1997 from the Landless Workers' Movement (MST) in response to the fact that some 85 per cent of the country's population lives in urban areas, and to link the struggle for land with that for housing in the towns. MTST has mobilised thousands of families to occupy and

---

[13] Founded in 1912, its activities for the next 30 years rarely extended beyond an annual con-vention of African 'gentry and notables', and thence to 'the first substantial cohort of African middle-class professionals'. The iconic image of Nelson Mandela contained 'an ambiguity' combining personal charm and modesty with 'authoritarian forms of charismatic authority' (Lodge, 2006: 188 and 202–3).

improvise housing on waste and unused sites. One large-scale action beginning in March 2007 involved 5,000 homeless people in the Joao Candido community in Sao Paulo. After the occupation was effected, the squatters organised themselves into groups of between 100 and 180 families, responsible for discipline, infrastructure and health, and for establishing collective kitchens. Meetings were held daily among group coordinators to discuss community organisation, publicity, and ways of increasing pressure on the authorities, while political education and cultural events also occurred. After some weeks, some coordinators reported that squatters were shaking off their lethargy and acquiring new dignity and pride in being part of a shared and meaningful project.

Helena Silvestre, a member of the MTST collective leadership, described squats as both a school for participatory democracy and a training ground for future community leaders. The long view is taken. The Joao Candido community was finally evicted on 18 May, but federal and state governments had by then given written undertakings to build houses for all the squatters. MTST remained an informal movement without offices of its own or payment for staff. 'Our strength lies in our ability to mobilise the favelas,' Silvestre said, and the process of struggle strengthened the movement and attracted recruits.[14] This was not unlike Morobe's participatory notion of people doing the job themselves but was in stark contrast with the entirely non-participatory, presidentialist democracy of Botswana.

[14] Philippe Revelli, 'Brazil: the squatters won't go away', *Le Monde Diplomatique*, November 2007.

1
Diamond Dependent Economic Wealth

From the outset, diamonds, the De Beers corporation, economic growth and the government have been closely interlinked in Botswana. De Beers had begun exploration work in the protectorate in 1955, and 'shortly before independence', corporate chairman Harry Oppenheimer told Seretse Khama 'in confidence' that viable diamond deposits existed at Orapa in Central District. This potentially momentous news was not publicly announced, however, until 1967 (Masire, 2006: 204). The De Beers Botswana Mining Company (Debswana) was established to develop the site in 1969. Production of high quality, kimberlite gems, in low-cost, open-cast operations, began in 1971 and expanded further at that site in 1979. Another mine opened at Letlhakane in 1979, followed by Jwaneng, the largest and richest in 1982. By the turn of the century Jwaneng was reputedly the world's richest and most profitable diamond mine. A fourth, Damtshaa, came on stream soon afterwards. Diamonds also existed at Gope, inside the Central Kalahari Game Reserve (CKGR), from where San/Bushmen have been uprooted, in 1997 and in 2002.

The value of diamond exports rose from $43 million in 1976 to some $1400 million in the mid-1990s, when minerals, mostly diamonds, represented around 35 per cent of GDP (Jefferis, 1998: 303).[1] In 2002, Botswana's total diamond sales amounted to $1.8 billion and it typically produces around 25 per cent by value of the world's rough diamonds (*The Ecologist*, 2003). There is no doubt that diamonds were 'the main driving force' behind the country's very high growth, averaging some 11 per cent a year, between 1974 and 1989 (Jefferis, 1998: 302). Diamonds moved Botswana from an underdeveloped country with a per capita income of some $70 per annum at independence into an Upper Middle Income Country (UMC) with a GDP per head (in PPP terms)

[1] US dollars throughout.

of $8,244 in 2002. Diamonds dominated the economy across the board, representing that year 45 per cent of GDP, 65 per cent of government revenue and not less than 80 per cent of export earnings (World Bank, 2004: 310). Some 90 per cent of all foreign direct investment (FDI) entering the country went into mining (Clover, 2003: 9).

It is also conventionally agreed that Botswana has managed diamond revenues well, in fiscal terms especially and in infrastructural development, both physical and human. Diamonds bought roads, railways, airlines, telecommunications, education and health facilities. They abolished aid dependency in the government's recurrent expenditures by 1972 and introduced overall budget surpluses by 1983, even while total government expenditure was rising by some 11 per cent a year between 1970 and 1995. From 1976, diamonds brought a strong currency – the Pula, 'the Swiss franc of Africa' – and high foreign exchange reserves, commonly worth some two years of import cover. Outstandingly, no significant foreign debt was acquired in doing so (Jefferis, 1998: 302–3).

Following an orthodox comparative advantage strategy, diamonds clearly represented a tremendous boost to government revenues, through a range of instruments, notably royalty payments, profits tax, withholding tax on remitted dividends, and the state's 50 per cent share in Debswana. These were followed by big profits earned on the management of foreign-exchange portfolios by the Bank of Botswana (Hope, 1996: 55–6).

These fiscal and infrastructural factors, gainful in themselves, might represent nonetheless the extent of the government's success in diamond-based development management. While diamonds also bought imported food and manufactured goods from efficient neighbouring producers – because the planners deemed this the financially preferable alternative to the task of stimulating domestic agriculture and manufacturing – this choice severely narrowed openings to economic diversification and transformation which still elude the country today. Botswana's growth, as some recognise, was 'mainly driven by capital accumulation', rather than by improvement in productivity and growth in employment (Limi, 2006: 8). Wealth was accumulated on a very narrow base with structural transformation ignored.

Directing capital accumulation, public and private

The task of directing capital accumulation was given to a specific institutional array. The country's leading developmental ministry, indicatively, coupled finance and development planning (MFDP). Established in 1970, it was described by Samatar (1999: 85) as 'the institutional brain' of economic policy-making, which 'dominated all other ministries'. Its political importance accorded with its economic preeminence and its leadership produced both President Masire and his successor Mogae. The position of minister of finance and development planning was associated with that of vice-president until the elevation of General Ian Khama in 1998. Under the MFDP's direct responsibility stood the National Development Bank (NDB), 'a pillar of our financial system', and an 'essential vehicle for channelling loan financing', according to Mogae in 1991.[2] The MFDP supervised the Botswana Development Corporation (BDC), and in turn the Financial Assistance Programme (FAP) introduced in 1982 and portrayed by Samatar (1999: 147–55) as 'the most important initiative' for industrialisation.

The operations of both these key instrumentalities, the BDC and the FAP, misjudged from the start by Samatar, soon proved defective. The former, consistent with the government's chosen strategy, prioritised profitability over structural development and diversification, and when a path-breaking but shortlived car assembly venture in Gaborone collapsed in 2000, the BDC's prime concern was not to protect a new and productive resource, but to secure its financial investment. The failure stemmed from South African hostility to 'independent development on [its] periphery': this was perceived as such by both Masire and Mogae, but neither rallied to defend car assembly (Good and Hughes, 2002: 54–8). Further, FAP essentially operated as a source of easy money for under-capitalised citizen-based companies, and footloose 'cowboy capitalists' from outside who took their loans and left soon after. Some five billion pula was laid out over twenty years till 1998, and all that was achieved, according to Mogae himself, was self-sufficiency in chicken production.[3]

The emphasis on monetary policy in the booming economy and

[2] Budget Speech 1991, quoted in Good (1994), 'Corruption and mismanagement in Botswana: a best-case example?', *The Journal of Modern African Studies*, 32, 3, p. 509.
[3] *Mmegi Monitor*, 3 May 2004. The rate for the pula was approximately four to the dollar through the 1990s, declining to five in the early twenty-first century.

a self-serving administration by the ruling elite produced corrupt and wasteful practices. The signs became glaringly manifest between 1991 and 1994 with the near failure of the flagship NDB, owing to unpaid loans totalling more than P60 million. Some of the largest debtors were government ministers, holding direct responsibility for the security of the NDB. The resulting scandal soon became cumulative and it is discussed below.

To his credit, Leith recognised fairly clearly the consequences of the country's diamond-based monetary and financial policy: it 'allowed borrowers access to commercial bank funds at negative real interest rates until late 1993'. Thereafter, as Leith details, government programmes 'continued to provide cheap capital' through FAP. A further adverse incentive was the capital available through the NDB and BDC. Additionally, big cattle owners, located in the socio-political foundations of the BDP, 'continued to be favoured in the tax code'. State-owned financial institutions saw their role as providing funds to important personages, frequently the members and supporters of the ruling elite, and they were ineffective in evaluating and monitoring projects. A 'haemorrhage of funds to unproductive investments' went on until the end of the decade (Leith, 2004 and 2005).

The stress on capital accumulation during very high growth induced broad distortions and weaknesses. Between 1991 and 1997, Botswana was expending some 5.2 per cent of its GDP on the military, a very large sum in both regional and world terms (World Bank, 2000 and Leith, 2005). At much the same time, a former governor of the Bank of Botswana, Quill Hermans, observed that the bureaucracy's development planning was no longer coordinated, that development management capacities had 'diminished', and policy implementation had become 'lamentable'. Government had become the second largest sector of the economy after (diamond) mining, and diversification, he firmly noted, 'ha[d] not occurred' (*Mmegi*, 30 June 1995). A decade later, when diamonds reached 45 per cent of total production, government expenditure represented 35 per cent of GDP, and the state sector remained the country's largest employer (*Financial Times*, 20 June 2006: 3).

Prioritising growth and accumulation left other sectors such as agriculture virtually unattended. Between 1970 and 1980, when diamonds were entering production, agriculture grew by 8.3 per cent, in the next decade by only 2.2 per cent, and then 'contracted by an average of 1.2 per cent per annum', due in good part to 'relatively low investment' in the sector (Clover, 2003: 7–8). Inflowing diamond revenues rendered a problematic domestic agriculture redundant to the financial development planners. By 2003 to 2004, agriculture, where around half of the country's people endeavoured to make a living, was only 2.3 per cent of GDP. The significance of this fall for rural people is indicated by data showing that agriculture had represented 33 per cent of GDP in 1970 but only 6 per cent in 1993, while comparable average figures for sub-Saharan Africa were respectively 27 per cent and 20 per cent (Siwawa-Ndai, 1997: 343). Though manufacturing displayed big annual variations in growth rates (Mpabanga, in Salkin, Mpabanga, et al. 1997: 371), the longer trend was also downwards, from 6 per cent of GDP in 1970, to some 4.8 per cent from 1998 to 2000, when Hyundai cars were produced and exported, and 4.1 per cent in 2003 (World Bank, 2004 and Republic of Botswana, 2003). Although tourism was beset by Zimbabwe's collapse and the expulsions from the CKGR, it was bigger than either of these, generating some five per cent of GDP.

Diamonds and slow growth

For almost three decades from 1970, Botswana had enjoyed the highest rate of growth in per capita GDP in the world.[4] But in the early 1990s, Botswana's growth rate had slowed dramatically, leading to rising unemployment, and what Jefferis (1998: 300) referred to as other economic hardships and social tensions. Limi (2006: 7) considered that future growth might not be sustainable. Recent figures show that GDP per capita rose by just 4.2 per cent between 2001 and 02 and 2002 and 03 (Republic of Botswana, 2003), little different from previously weaker neighbours like Zambia and Tanzania.

Moreover, it was officially recognised that production from the country's existing diamond mines was nearing its upper limits and that production would plateau soon, according to Minerals Minister Charles Tibone, in December 2005. Impressive output was achieved at the blue-chip Jwaneng mine that year, but work at Orapa and Letlhakane had experienced repeated setbacks, and Debswana's new managing director, Blackie Marole, announced in May 2006 that the company was moving to what he called a

---

[4] Botswana had achieved a cumulative rise in GDP per capita over twenty-seven years of almost 500 per cent, above East Asia in second place, and double Mauritius in third. World Bank (2000: 9).

new long-term strategy, applying better methods of gem recovery, and aiming at improvements in profitability and the lowering of costs. By the end of the year, the finance minister's budget speech acknowledged that diamonds continued to experience uneven growth.[5]

Serious social tensions were already evident among Debswana's miners. 461 men, around one-twelfth of the total workforce, were sacked in August 2004 for initiating a two-week strike for improved wages and conditions. According to the secretary-general of the Mine Workers' Union, Jack Tlhagale, the dismissals were meant to instil fear in the workers. Two years later, the union did not regret their action: the aftermath only exposed the ills of the unjust system in place, where miners who had escaped the dismissals were being retrenched as part of Debswana's 'unfolding' plans.[6]

Silence and prevarication had long surrounded Gope. Some 15 years of largely secretive exploration work had gone on before it was publicly announced by the minister for minerals, energy and water resources, Boometswe Mokgothu, in July 2000, that diamonds existed in quantity at Gope. The mine was expected to cover an area of 45 square kilometres and have a lifespan of 18 years (*Botswana Gazette*, 5 July 2000). Both the Hotel and Tourism Association (HATAB) and the Botswana Christian Council immediately voiced their shock and consternation at both the government's failure to inform the nation earlier, and at the likely impact of a mine on San/Bushmen communities in the area.[7] Ambiguity continued. Chairman Nicky Oppenheimer announced in March 2002 that De Beers had no plans to mine at Gope 'for the foreseeable future', but in November a spokesperson added, 'We can't say we will never mine it,' and the company kept its retention rights (Good, 2003: 18–19). In November 2006 it was revealed that TH Drilling of Gaborone had crews in the area of Gope at work on 15 test pipes on behalf of Petra Diamonds,[8] and in June 2007 Gem Diamond Botswana announced its purchase of Gope Exploration

---

[5] *Mmegi Online*, 8 May and 12 June 2006; *Mining Weekly Online*, 1 June 2006, and *Budget Speech* 2007: 3.

[6] *Mmegi Online*, 7 August 2006. Diamond mining is classified as an essential service, where all strike action is illegal. It is in any case almost impossible to stage a legal strike in Botswana.

[7] In unusually strong statements, HATAB called for compensation to be made to the San, and the Christian Council sought an official apology. Alphonse Moroke, 'Do you Trust This Government?', *Midweek Sun*, 12 July 2000, discussed in Good (2003: 16–17). This came after the first expulsions of San from the CKGR in 1997.

[8] Tom Price, 'Kalahari diamond search rekindles Botswana's Bushmen dispute', *Business Day*, 24 November 2005.

Company for $34 million. It said that kimberlites at the mine represented a significant ore body, and that it was committed to engaging with San/Basarwa communities on the sustainable development of Gope. Such consultations were claimed to be consistent with Gem's existing operational policies in Angola, Congo (DRC) and elsewhere.[9] But they were not consistent with De Beers' secretive and non-consultative operations in the CKGR. The Botswana government remained silent about the development of Gope.

Immediate prospects in the global diamond market were not without difficulties. De Beer's managing director, Gareth Penny, expected 'a continuing wave of challenges' would confront the Diamond Trading Company, the group's marketing arm, in the second half of 2006, based on higher fuel prices, interest rates, and extensive global instability. While sales had been marginally up in the first quarter by one per cent, Penny anticipated a decline in sales of rough stones ahead (*Mmegi Online*, 31 July 2006).

Debswana and the new future

Debswana's saliency remained as the prime domestic agency for diamond development. Established in 1969, it had remained under the operational control of Anglo-American Services Ltd until as late as 1992, before creating its own management structures.[10] Reflecting the chosen growth and accumulationist strategies of the government, Debswana had eschewed all nationalisation measures, favouring instead joint ventures, profit-sharing agreements, and the expansion of production through effective negotiation. On Jefferis' sanguine assessment, this approach 'worked to the mutual benefit of Botswana and De Beers, harnessing the know-how of the multinational, while enabling the government to take full advantage of its [diamonds] resource'.[11]

While the fullness of that advantage is highly questionable, the mutuality conspicuously exists. Under agreements between De Beers and the Botswana government of 2006, each appoints five

[9] Kgomotso Kgwaripane, *Sunday Standard Online*, 23 June 2007.
[10] De Beers and Anglo–American have controlling shareholdings in each other, and share the same chairman. The Oppenheimer family has a controlling fifty per cent interest in the corporation. Botswana is the other significant shareholder, having fifteen per cent of De Beers today. It also appoints two directors to the boards of De Beers and its marketing subsidiary, the Diamond Trading Company.
[11] Jefferis (1998: 303–4 and 306).

directors to Debswana's management board, and those appointed by President Mogae in July were among the country's topmost officials. The chairperson's position would in future rotate biannually between De Beers and the government. Nicky Oppenheimer remained as chair until the expiry of his current term, and Dr Akalang Tombale became his deputy and next chair in succession.[12]

The relationship is as personal as it is close. Debswana's earlier and long-term director, 1992–2004, Louis Nchindo, was a known close friend of Mogae. He worked for Anglo-American until 1992, and retained a position on its board. At his retirement he was described as being not only a prominent businessman but 'probably one of the most powerful individuals in the country' (*Mmegi*, 23 February 2004).

When long-awaited renewal agreements were signed between De Beers and Botswana in May 2006, mutual admiration was high. 'It gives me enormous pleasure', exclaimed Oppenheimer: 'Enduring relationships are rare in today's world [and] like diamonds something to be valued and cherished.' The minerals minister, Charles Tibone, declared that 'this is an incredibly successful – arguably the world's most successful – business partnership.' It was a symbiotic relationship between Siamese twins. And they were now at the 'start of the next chapter', which would 'change the future of this country' (*Mmegi Online*, 24 May 2006 and *Mining Weekly Online*, 1 June 2006). An enhanced 'miracle' seemed at hand.

About seventeen months of protracted negotiations preceded the agreement, and it accorded De Beers twenty-five years control of Botswana's entire diamond production, with the high-value Jwaneng now included in the same overall arrangement as the other three. Though diamonds' exploration was proceeding intensely,[13] nothing was said publicly about control over possible future mines. Permanent Secretary Tombale admitted that certain agreements remained confidential, while other details were still being worked out (*Mmegi Online*, 19 May 2006). The uncertain relationship between Blackie's long-term, cost-cutting strategy announced two months' earlier, and the expansionist New Future, was among other matters not addressed publicly.

[12] Membership was: the permanent secretary to the president, Eric Morale; the attorney general, Dr Athaliah Molokomme; the governor of the Bank of Botswana, Linah Mohohlo; the permanent secretary for the ministry of minerals, energy and water resources, Dr Akolang Tombale; and the permanent secretary to [MFDP], Serwalo Tumelo.
[13] De Beers was spending some pula 500 million on exploration in Botswana in 2006, according to Gareth Penny. *Tautona Times*, 16, 28 May 2006.

In return, De Beers would, partially or wholly, relocate the Botswana Diamond Trading Centre (DTC) from London to Gaborone. The aggregation and marketing of a large percentage of De Beers' diamonds would be carried out at a new Diamond Trading Company Botswana from 2009.[14] Beneficiation, or the adding of value through cutting and polishing of the rough stones, and in jewellery manufacture, was anticipated. Minister Tibone expected that 3,500 jobs might be created, many of which would be skilled. Considerable skills and technology transfers were anticipated.

Nevertheless, serious problems existed at both the international and regional levels. Other countries already had established cutting and polishing industries, Gareth Penny noted, with relatively cheap labour costs in some cases too. It would be 'expensive to cut and polish diamonds from here', he admitted (*Tautona Times*, 28 May 2006). India was outstanding, being by far the world's largest diamond-manufacturing centre, processing some half of all rough diamonds by value, in an industry worth $12 billion in 2004. Belgium and Israel were also prominently placed in this special field, and a long list of other countries – Armenia, Canada, China, Costa Rica, Mauritius, Russia, Sri Lanka, Thailand and Viet Nam – supported their own cutting and polishing sectors (Global Witness, 2005: 25). Nicky Oppenheimer also conceded that it would be difficult to create significant employment in diamonds manufacturing in southern Africa, simply on the basis of the cost structures and productivity that were entrenched in India and in China too. With some one million people employed in the sector in India, he noted, its domination was set to continue.[15]

Regional diamond producers also presented big competitive problems in themselves. Botswana's relations with South Africa remained broadly and critically important. While Botswana was by far South Africa's leading market on the continent, as President Mogae informed that country's parliament during his state visit in October 2005, the trade was hugely unbalanced: Botswana's exports to South Africa were worth R 2 billion in 2004, but its imports of goods and services from there totalled R 17 billion (*Tautona Times*, 29 October 2005). Asserting that South Africans

---

[14] Obscurities abounded. For a critique of the arrangements see Shiela Khama, 'The De Beers-Botswana-Namibia Venture', *Mmegi Online*, 9 March 2007.

[15] Polishing a carat in India cost, he said, $15 to $20, but in South Africa it cost $60–$80. *Mining Weekly Online*, 1 June 2006.

and Batswana were like one family divided by a fence, and that 'our future prosperity should be indivisible', the president was at pains to present the new Botswana DTC in the most attractive, potentially collaborative, even nationalistic light. Its establishment was 'an historic turn for the industry, the world's largest diamond producer by value ha[d] broken De Beers' control over the distribution of 50 per cent of the world's diamonds ... bringing its diamonds back home.'

He had therefore a 'major request', that you 'permit your diamonds to be aggregated by the DTC in Gaborone instead of London'. Given the existing unequal relationships, South Africa's trade was bound to benefit from the venture: 'as we all know, 80 per cent of any income generated [through development projects] by Botswana would be spent on South African goods and services'. But he finished his appeal with the admission that 'we need you more, much more than you need us', and noted the Setswana saying that 'a child who doesn't cry risks dying on its mother's back unnoticed' (*Tautona Times*, 29 October 2005).

Even when presented in such ingratiating and humble terms, Mogae's proposal was not guaranteed success, given the Hyundai precedent. News of the DTC Botswana came amid growing pressure among other diamond-producing countries in southern Africa for greater local beneficiation (*Mining Weekly Online*, 1 June 2006). South Africa was the world's fourth-largest diamonds producer by value, and Pretoria was insisting that diamonds must support the people of that country more fully. It was considering imposing an 8 per cent tax on exported rough gem stones, and the creation of its own State Diamond Trader. De Beers extracted some 90 per cent of the country's diamonds, but it questioned the cost-effectiveness of the government's proposals and pointed out that only two of its South African mines were profitable. In this fluid context, Pretoria was reportedly unattracted by the prospect that its diamonds would be taken by De Beers for aggregation in Gaborone.[16]

When an agreement to create a new Namibia Diamond Trading Company (NDTC) was announced at the end of January 2007, the immediate reaction of Akolang Tombale in Gaborone, who had clearly been kept in the dark, was consternation. On 31 January he said, 'from the little we have been able to gather' we believe that 'this is not a good thing for us as a diamond producer and

[16] *The Economist*, 29 October, *Mail and Guardian*, 1 November 2005, and *Mmegi Online*, 27 May and 19 July 2006.

aggregation outlet'.[17] De Beers and Namdeb, Windhoek's Debswana equivalent, would sell up to five per cent of the country's rough diamonds to local cutting factories, aligning, in Gareth Penny's words, 'all activities from exploration and mining to evaluation and selling until 2013'.[18] Though the deal had been kept secret until its announcement, Sheila Khama, CEO of De Beers (Botswana), insisted that '[this would not materially affect] the agreements between Botswana and De Beers'.[19] Tombale appeared to accept that the NDTC posed no immediate and substantive threat, but he noted that pressures from Windhoek to expand its gem polishing activities were ongoing.[20]

Angola too was intending to process its diamonds domestically on an independent basis. A new polishing plant opened in Luanda in November 2005, built by Lev Leviev of Israel. It planned to cut and polish at least $20 million worth of rough gems monthly and to lift its production to almost $2 billion in value within a year.[21] Angola and Congo both had, additionally, considerable untapped diamond resources. The latter represented a particularly strong potential challenge to Botswana's plans. It held an estimated 30 per cent of the world's diamonds' reserves, which big mining companies were actively competing to exploit.[22]

Through Debswana, Botswana had committed all of its diamonds to De Beers for a quarter of a century and substantially extended its dependency on the gems. The diversification absent in the broad economy would now supposedly take place, to a limited but not insignificant extent, within the diamond sector itself. But major constraints affecting economic development were unrecognised in Debswana's New Future.

The absence of diversification and FDI

Foreign investment in the country and regional competition especially from the South African economic hegemony, were two of

[17] Quoted by Moabi Phia, *Botswana Guardian*, 2 February 2007, who also said that Mogae's efforts to have all of the region's diamonds aggregated in Gaborone might be 'flung through the window'.

[18] Representing sales of up to $300 million by 2009. *Mmegi Online*, 1 February 2007.

[19] 'De Beers Concerned as Windhoek Deal Sours Botswana's Mood', *The Sunday Standard*, 5 February 2007.

[20] According to Stryker Motlaloso, valuing, sorting and polishing would be handled through the NDTC while aggregation would be done in Botswana. *Mmegi Online*, 9 February 2007.

[21] *BBC News Online*, 4 November 2005.

[22] Joseph Winter, *BBC News Online*, 24 July, and Raf Custers, *Le Monde Diplomatique*, July 2006.

the constraints. Botswana's FDI had been fairly consistently parlous since the end of the 1990s, both in total terms – in a purportedly successful economy – and by regional comparisons. Botswana's investment inflows totalled only $37 million in 1999; rose to $57 million in 2000, plummeted to just $22 million in 2001; jumped to $403 million in 2002; then dropped again to $86 million the following year, according to official UN data. Worse still, in an economy that had long stressed capital accumulation and strict financial and monetary policy making, investment inflows were dwarfed by profit remittances. Over the period 1995 to 2003, a total of $943 million entered the country as FDI, while the sum of $5,621 million flowed out as remitted profits, a negative differential of some 600 per cent.[23]

The region generally performed better as UNCTAD's 2005 data shows. South Africa's FDI's receipts were, for example, $1,502 million in 1999; $6,789 million in 2001; and $762 million in 2003. Even weaker neighbours attracted more FDI than diamond-rich Botswana. Tanzania over the same period received FDI worth in total $2,396 million, and it lost only $50 million in remittances, while in copper-dependent Zambia the two figures were respectively $1,158 and $362 millions. Mozambique had been attracting FDI in steadily rising amounts since 1997, and total investments over the eight years came to $1,855 million against just $96 million in outflows. On UNCTAD's data for 21 countries in continental Africa, no country had a comparably negative ratio of low FDI inflows to high profit outflows like Botswana's.

The underlying weaknesses became more apparent as growth slowed. According to the Economist Intelligence Unit (EIU), the country's diversification into manufacturing was partly constrained by the smallness of the domestic market – though this patently did not prevent Mauritius, with only 1.2 million people, (a half-million fewer than Botswana), from acquiring a manufacturing capacity of 20 per cent of GDP – but also by what it termed Botswana's excessive bureaucracy (EIU, 2005).

The country's organised business saw things similarly and were specific in their criticisms. Botswana lagged behind completely in attracting new FDI to the country, and the government bore the responsibilities. 'Our businesses are in an intensive care unit', said Iqbal Ebrahim. A number had closed shop only to reopen in

---

[23] United Nations Conference on Trade and Development (UNCTAD) (2005: 8 and 85–86). Alternative 'Greenfield FDI inflows' were sometimes lower, for example, $325 million in 2002 and $66 million in 2003.

neighbouring countries, he said, and the government was failing to rebuild their waning confidence. State-owned utilities like water, power and telecommunications were too expensive, and current bank interest rates of 16.5 per cent were the region's highest, save for Zimbabwe, and more than treble those in South Africa.[24]

The finance minister, Baledzi Gaolathe, admitted that only meagre growth of 1.9 per cent was experienced outside mining in 2005, and the Bank of Botswana noted weak performance in many sectors. The private sector economy, according to an unnamed Gaborone banker, was actually 'standing still, if not moving backward' (quoted in *Financial Times*, 20 June 2006). According to the Bank of Botswana, on the big fundamentals of competitiveness and productivity, the country's performance, was 'embarrassingly low'.[25]

Preliminary data at the end of 2006 indicated a decline of 4.4 per cent in real GDP in mining, and similar declines of 3 per cent in agriculture, manufacturing and construction. On the judgement of the finance minister, the country's need to attract and then to retain FDI was 'critical' (*Budget Speech 2007*: 2–3).

Well before the New Future, Botswana's diamonds dependency was already huge in world terms. Michael Ross has endeavoured to measure resource dependency, especially that concerning minerals and oil. Taking commodity exports as a percentage of GDP, he sees its effects 'peaking with exports of around 30 per cent of [GDP]'. On a table of 20 of the world's most mineral-dependent countries, Botswana showed a figure of 35.1, as early as 1995, above Sierra Leone with 28.9, Zambia with 26.1, Mauritania at 18.4, Bahrain at 16.4, and Liberia on 12.5. On this calculation, Michael Ross noted that Botswana was clearly the most mineral-dependent country in the world. He also noted that heavy minerals reliance tends to foster atypically high poverty rates and corruption (Ross, 2003: Chapter 2). Nothing that the government has done since 1995 has lessened this acute dependency.

Resource dependency with few alternatives

The government and Debswana have seemingly locked Botswana into diamond dependency. The limiting inter-relationship has

---

[24] President of the Botswana Confederation of Commerce Industry and Manpower (BOCCIM), *Mmegi Online*, 30 June 2006.
[25] The governor, Linah Mohohlo, making reference to the Bank's own research, *Mmegi Online*, 23 August 2006.

grown out of the size and profitability of Botswana's diamonds, De Beers' monopoly control over the world market, and the large and easy money which Botswana obtained in consequence. The initial mine at Orapa proved so profitable that De Beers' net earnings covered its original investment in less than two years. A new agreement between the two parties in the 1970s increased the government's stake in Debswana from 15 to 50 per cent – though full details, characteristically, 'have never been disclosed'. Estimates of Botswana's total share in the profits from diamonds, royalties, taxation and dividends, rose from 50 to about 75 per cent. The corporate-governmental linkages widened beyond Debswana itself as Botswana increased its shareholding in De Beers from the 1980s to the present level of 15 per cent. Botswana acquired in the 1980s 'a pivotal role' in the world industry, particularly in De Beers' marketing cartel, the Central Selling Organisation (Jefferis, 1998: 304–6).

Here lies the restrictive mutuality between De Beers and the Botswana government. The former, Jefferis believes, 'could not afford to take the risk of losing control of the marketing of Botswana's output, for in doing so it would risk a collapse of world diamond prices'. The world market demanded monopoly control and all that accompanied its maintenance. One of De Beers' main claims, to both buyers of the jewellery and to sellers of the rough stones, is that 'Diamonds are Forever', and prices never fall. They have 'historically fluctuated around a long-term upward trend', taking costs of production into account. Botswana's high-value, low-cost mining brought 'gross profit[s] of about 80 per cent' into the 1990s. Diamond producers receive prices far higher than they would outside of the cartel, and its successful buffer-stock arrangements, long-term agreements, and advertising – the masquerade of scarcity and high value.[26]

Botswana's sustained commitment to diamonds and De Beers is dangerous far beyond the economic dimensions. 'Much of the diamond industry' operates in a 'secretive and non-transparent manner', that 'makes it difficult for their activities to be effectively regulated by governments' (Global Witness, 2005: 1). Specialist observers believe that the industry is 'secretive to the point of paranoia ... contracts and written codes are virtually unheard of' (quoted in Good, 2003: 17). De Beers' *modus operandi* and result-

---

[26] De Beers' operational techniques were summarised as follows: it uses its near-monopoly to restrict supply and hence force prices up; it maintains a 'monopoly of information about the industry' disadvantageous to potential competitors; it is highly 'aggressive in its marketing techniques' towards the buyers or sightholders of its rough diamonds (Jefferis, 1996: 306).

ing pre-eminence, as already noted, contributed powerfully to this general practice. The De Beers marketing cartel, according to Pallister et al. (1987: 105–6) has 'always been notoriously secretive'. Nicky Oppenheimer is pleased to be 'known as a man of discretion and few public words'.[27]

Secrecy and deception is of special importance as the issue of conflict diamonds gains in importance. In 2001 the United Nations reported that to date 'not a single parcel of illicit Angolan diamonds has been intercepted anywhere'. The Kimberley Process was intended to stop this illicit trade, but when Global Witness carried out a wide-ranging examination in 2005, it found that conflict gems were 'finding their way into the international trade', and that 'gaps in oversight' in cutting and polishing factories, and in other areas, enabled this to happen.[28] De Beers had the capacity to move diamonds along secret international trails utilising its established practice of concealing the facts about production in individual countries (*The Ecologist*, 2003: 13). Oppenheimer admitted in mid-2006 that an international black market in diamonds still existed some six years after the launching of the Kimberley certification process. He declared it 'unacceptable' that 'we as an industry are failing to live up to our commitments'. He acknowledged that 'research carried out by the DTC demonstrated that the findings of the NGOs were very largely correct.'[29]

Debswana's linkage to this single secretive, non-accountable and powerful corporation is greatly important,[30] compounded further by the position which De Beers has come to assume in the country's domestic political economy. The government failed to stimulate small and medium-sized companies, paternalistic policies stifled entrepreneuralism, and agriculture was left to wither. Over almost forty years the government and this corporation have promoted a situation where the country's room to manoeuvre is now severely limited. 'Its not apparent to me', says Sennye

[27] Interview by Terry Macalister, *Guardian* (London), 2 July 2005.
[28] Conflict diamonds were entering the pipeline and the Kimberley certification process in all countries with artisanal activities. They believed that Botswana was an example generally of best practice, but in an inspection in June 2004 they found that authorities 'only checked weight and parcel count' of stones, without applying 'a regime of physical inspection, including valuation.' Global Witness (2005), pp. 15 and 33.
[29] Speaking at the World Diamond Congress in Tel Aviv, *Mmegi Online*, 4 July 2006.
[30] Non-accountability is the elephant in Botswana's living room. It was highlighted by HATAB and the Christian Council with regard to Gope, and soon after the New Future was announced, *Mmegi's* editor asked – after two years's of protracted negotiations, and the grant of 25 years' monopoly control to De Beers – 'What Else did De Beers and Botswana Agree on?', *Mmegi Online*, 27 May 2006. It is discussed further below.

Obuseng, programme economist for the UNDP, 'that we have planned consciously for the post-diamond era' (conclusions of the *Financial Times*, June 2006).

An autocratic and corruption-prone government has instead enmeshed the country still further in diamond dependency through aggregation, processing and marketing. President Mogae eagerly anticipated Botswana's supposed diamond-studded future. Early in 2007, he targeted a 17-fold increase in its fledgling cutting industry within five years, representing 'at least half-a-billion dollars worth of diamonds per annum'. Addressing industry representatives in Antwerp, he declared: 'We can and will graduate from a diamond-producing country to a world-class diamond centre' (quoted in *Mmegi Online*, 18 January 2007). While the president apparently entertained few doubts about the feasibility or desirability of this commitment, and its consequences, Debswana's Blackie Morale recognised the country's acute dependency and something of the consequent dangers. Addressing a Kimberley Process plenary meeting in November 2006, he noted that as the world's most diamond-dependent country, Botswana was highly vulnerable to adverse developments in the global diamond market. Its leading position also entailed a large degree of responsibility for the world jewellery market and for what he called the integrity and image of diamonds.[31] It was now embroiled in marketing the gems and inter-linked more tightly with De Beers in maintaining the myths of high-value, scarcity and permanency intrinsic to diamond selling. Secrecy was being further entrenched in government; the minister of minerals, Ponatshego Kedikilwe, informed parliament at the end of 2007, that the full details of the 2006 agreement with De Beers involving Jwaneng and the relocation of the DTC to Gaborone, would never be made public.[32] Further wealth accumulation might well result, but the global hazards were rife, and economic transformation did not exist.[33]

---

[31] Morale was known as a 'reticent and studious former civil servant of abundant intellectual reserve', according to Spencer Mogapi, *Sunday Standard*, 11 March 2007. For a similar concern about integrity and image, see Sheila Khama's comments, *Mmegi Online*, 18 January 2007.

[32] In a routine statement he said that 'the agreement entails, among other points, that [DTC] Botswana will be established, the Botswana Diamond Valuing Company (BDVC) will be wound up, [and] new sorting and valuation processes and procedures ... will be adopted from DTC International'. Staff Writer, 'Govt-De Beers Agreement Secret—PHK', *Mmegi Online*, 14 December 2007.

[33] For a substantive critique that Botswana's diamonds represent 'pre-modern growth without development' see Ellen Carlsson Hillbom, 'Diamonds or development? A structural assessment of Botswana's forty years of success', *The Journal of Modern African Studies*, forthcoming.

2

Presidentialism

As with the linkage between the government and Debswana in the economy, an accompanying duopoly exists between presidentialism and the preponderant ruling party in Botswana's government and politics. This authoritarian state system was legitimised by the past, quickly established in the nation-state at independence and extended thereafter. Presidential successions have occurred smoothly on two occasions, over the heads of the people. Regular parliamentary elections have never produced a change of government and are equally notable for their low turnout of eligible voters. This unusual quasi-democratic system has passed for normalcy in Botswana, until it was first challenged in the mid-1990s. A second automatic transition in the presidency occurs in 2008.

The characteristics of Botswana's politics were emulated by Namibia after 1990 and by South Africa four years later. While the southern African region is both the most developed economically and the most democratic in the continent, such duopoly represents regional democracy at the state level. On its record to date, it is a system which discourages opposition and delays change

Autocracy then and now

State power is centralised in Botswana in the person and office of the executive president. He is at once head of state, head of government, leader of the ruling party and commander-in-chief of the military. The main levers of state power the (bureaucracy, the military, police, information and broadcasting, and the anti-corruption agency) are to his hand in the office of the presidency, where he is served by a highly influential minister of presidential affairs and public administration. His control of the military – the Botswana Defence Force (BDF), comprising army and air-force – is both direct and active: he appoints its commander and chief of staff.

An outstanding example was set by President Seretse Khama when he appointed his eldest son, Ian Khama, aged only 24, as a brigadier and deputy commander of the BDF on its formation in April 1977.[1] The president can appoint, promote and dismiss any officer and can determine the operational usage of the BDF, as President Mogae did when he alone ordered what was a bloody and destructive intrusion into Lesotho at the end of September 1998.[2]

The president is also ready and able to deploy military force against civil unrest on the streets at home. When rioting took place in central Gaborone on 16 February 1995, military force was immediately utilised. President Masire announced on Radio Botswana on 19 February that 'stern action has been taken' to 'stamp out' all unruly behaviour: heavy police action was overt and active against protest, real and imagined, over many days, in Gaborone and adjacent areas.[3] Though a young man was killed, many more injured and schools remained closed for weeks, no official inquiry followed. Whether the spontaneous rioting had precipitated the disturbances or the ready use of military force, remained unknown.

The president is not elected by the people and holds no popular constituency whatsoever. Since 1998 he is effectively chosen by only one person, his predecessor, by the act of his appointment as vice-president. Contemporary presidential powers are powerfully buttressed by the norms and practices of the past. Formerly, the chief or king had control over the use and allocation of land and labour, and cattle, the third main productive resource in the growing pastoral economy in the nineteenth century, was privately owned. Acemoglu et al. (2001, 2002, 2003) would suggest that a distinctive indigenous institution like the *kgotla* made dissent easy and gave commoners a voice, but Wylie (1990: 23–7 and 82), more realistically, saw 'silent discontent' constituting the strongest form of popular protest at such meetings. Competition and conflict readily occurred of course, contained entirely within

[1] His paramilitary experience then totalled no more than four years, and the president bypassed older and more experienced officers in the then Police Mobile Unit when he promoted his son. Mike Mothibi and Kagiso Sekokonyane, 'Khama reluctantly sheds his uniform', *Mmegi*, 27 March 1998; Dan Henk, Air War College, Maxwell, United States, pers. comm., February 2007.
[2] For further detail see *Mail and Guardian*, 9 October 1998; *The Botswana Guardian*, 25 September, and 2 October 1998.
[3] Good (1996: 69–72).

the ruling elite of the king/chief, with other aristocrats and wealthy men. Reciprocal economic relations existed extensively between the king, notables and commoners, but with no semblance of equality accompanying them. She noted that all of a client's property and labour 'could be appropriated by the chief', in an 'obligation [that] never ended' (Wylie, 1990: 23–7 and 82). Iliffe (1987: 71) similarly concluded: 'reciprocity disguised inequality'.

The interdependence of power and wealth was another key legacy of the past to the autocratic present, typified by the interchangeable usage of the keyword, *kgosi*, for both chief and wealthy man. Chiefs accumulated wealth through inheritance and wideranging privileges including court fines, gifts, loot in battle and tribute from subordinate communities. Khama III, in 1875, for example, enjoyed an annual income of around £3,000, owned around 8,000 cattle and invested his wealth developmentally in improved breeding stock, transportation and trade (Wylie, 1990: 27, 39 and 42).

The British colonial protectorate functioned overall as benign neglect, but it also 'help[ed] chiefs to establish independent fortunes'. From 1885 no distinction was drawn between the Ngwato chief's (in today's Central Province) personal revenues and the coffers of the state, and a chief like Khama used his tax revenues to establish a cadre of salaried bureaucrats answerable to him. British justice and elite, royal rivalry worked together to render communal property private. By the mid-1920s, the personal property of Tshekedi (son to Khama III), for instance, was estimated at 50,000 cattle and thousands of pounds in cash (Wylie, 1990: 50–2 and 72). Tribal chiefs in Botswana enjoyed great powers over their subjects, amassed wealth through free labour, herding and related activities, while enjoying 'near omnipotence'. The much romanticised *kgotla* system was actually a forum where 'the chief had the final say, and modern practices, [like] decision-making by majority vote, played no part'(Fawcus and Tilbury, 2000: 50 and 213).[4]

The transition to independence, when it eventually came, was both smooth and swift, occurring entirely at an elite level between top British administrators and an established and rising indigenous leadership. Seretse Khama (nephew to Tshekedi) had entered politics 'hesitantly and with some reluctance' in 1962, but what attracted British administrators like Fawcus was that 'he owned

---

[4] Additionally: 'The inherited Tswana political culture limited public discussion to adult men: women, youth or ethnic minorities were silent or dependent on others to convey their thoughts to the elite.' John Holm, Patrick Molutsi and Gloria Somolekae (1996: 43 and 47).

large herds of cattle and, as a substantial owner, was concerned that the right steps should be taken' to develop the cattle economy. He and the other creators of the BDP in the same year, like Ketumile Masire, were experienced in public life and big cattle-men. The BDP was immediately established as a party of govern-ment, and won 28 out of a total of 31 parliamentary seats in the founding elections in 1965. Voting occurred among an 'entirely apolitical electorate', and on Fawcus and Tilbury's accurate assess-ment, 'there could hardly have been a more painless transfer of power' (2000: 87–8, 182 and 187). It was just so: a transfer at the national level, to an elite in Lockean terms of truly responsible men, cattle barons and bureaucrats with a stake in the economy. No equivalents here to Kenneth Kaunda, teacher and used-clothes peddler, in pre-independence Zambia; *Mwalimu* (teacher) Julius Nyerere in Tanzania; or to Kwame Nkrumah and his Verandah Boys in Ghana. Their engagement in accumulation through cattle production was thus readily extendable with state power and cor-porate collaboration into diamond wealth and the growth economy.

The Botswana constitution conferred powers on the president worthy more of a despotic chief than a truly democratic leader. He 'decides alone [and] shall not be obliged to follow the advice ten-dered by any other person or authority', Otlhogile noted. He is supported by both prerogative and immunity powers, and as long as he remains in office, 'he is above the law'. In formally demo-cratic Botswana, the president is entitled to act as he pleases (Otlhogile, 1998: 218–21 and 224).

Presidentialism, parliament and people

The president appoints and dismisses all significant office holders in government, including the vice-president and cabinet ministers – who must all, unlike himself, be elected (or appointed) members of parliament – as well as the chief justice and judges of the high court and the attorney general. Appointment of the chief justice is particularly significant since he may act in an administrative-cum-political way as returning officer in the indirect presidential appointment process, and his determination therein is final (Otlhogile, 1998: 214). The president alone has the power to appoint and constitute a commission of inquiry into any matter, to determine whether it sits in public or in private, and whether or not its report is made available to the public.

These are actively exercised powers, sometimes with very negative effects. An official police inquiry was launched into the apparent ritual murder of a 14-year-old girl, Segametsi Mogomotsi, in Mochudi, near Gaborone, in November 1994. Spontaneous protests and heavy police counter-action followed in January, as the murdered girl's school friends angrily informed visiting dignitaries point-blank, in unprecedented scenes, that they felt unprotected against killers (children have traditionally been expected to be almost as passive as San/Bushmen). As the protests soon focused on the unresponsiveness of government, it was announced that Scotland Yard was being brought into the inquiry. The British police submitted their findings on 10 May 1995, but the report 'was never publicised' (Molomo, 2000: 98).

The Independent Electoral Commission (IEC) was established as part of a number of belated reform measures in 1997,[5] but its autonomy is incomplete; the president appoints the commission's secretary, its chief executive officer, who possesses overriding responsibilities. It is the President similarly who appoints periodically a delimitation commission with the power to vary parliamentary constituencies in relation to demographic trends.[6] This body increased parliament's size dramatically just before the 2004 elections, from 40 to 57 elected MPs, without public debate about the import of the change, which seemingly impacted negatively on opposition parties. In 2004 only the BDP fielded a full slate of candidates.

Empowered constitutionally and, by a governmental ethos 'predicated on an effective executive president', Seretse Khama, according to his biographers, quickly initiated the strengthening of his office (Parsons, Henderson and Tlou, 1995: 271). The president nominates and thus effectively appoints four specially elected MPs. All three presidents to date have frequently utilised these powers to entrench their positions and that of the ruling party – sometimes against the expressed democratic preferences of the voters – and overriding existing constitutional provisions. When Vice-President Masire was twice rejected by his Kanye consti-

---

[5] The lowering of the voting age from 21 to 18 years, introducing absentee voting, and the creation of the IEC were passed in referenda in 1997, and became effective at elections in 1999. When President Masire first announced these proposals in April 1995, he made plain that he acted without prior consultation with cabinet or party. *Mmegi*, 5 May 1995.

[6] 'Brochure of the [IEC]', 4 November 2004 and IEC's chief education officer, Barulaganyi Chacha, *Mmegi Online*, 27 July 2006.

tutency, in 1969 and 1974, defeated by former chief Bathoen Gaseetsiwe of the BNF, President Khama specially appointed him to parliament and re-promoted him as his deputy. He also introduced the constitutional requirement that a chief had to have resigned his chieftaincy for a period of five years before seeking parliamentary election.[7] This provision was then ignored by President Mogae when he made General Ian Khama, paramount chief of the Bamangwato, a specially elected MP and then his vice-president in 1998.[8]

The same specially elected provision facilitated the cooptation, for example, of Lt-General Mompati Merafhe, commander of the BDF, and Festus Mogae, as permanent secretary to the president, first into parliament and then to cabinet office in 1989. When Vice-President Peter Mmusi was forced to resign in 1992 after his involvement in corrupt land transactions, Masire made Mogae his deputy. In 1998, after further constitutional change which removed parliament from the presidential appointment process, Masire passed the presidency to him automatically, in a smooth, undemocratic progression from senior bureaucrat to parliamentarian, and thence ministerial and even presidential office. Mogae only obtained an elected parliamentary seat in October 1994 which he resigned from less than four years later.[9]

The practice of subordinating the preferences of the voters in parliamentary elections to those of the president is a norm in Botswana. In October 2004, Margaret Nasha, an old ruling party stalwart, was defeated in a prominent campaign in her Gaborone Central constituency, only to be immediately returned to parliament and to her ministry of local government by Mogae. A month later, Minister Nasha announced the names of nominated local government councillors nationwide. Out of 101 such nominees, only three came from the opposition. Given that the total opposition vote at the general elections was 48 per cent, while the ruling party's support had dropped to 52 per cent, the nominations were described by *Mmegi*, 29 November 2004, as a 'monstrosity' – the

---

[7] Parsons, et. al. (1995: 283–4) and C.J. Makgala (2004: 6–8), 'Calling a spade a spade: New dimensions in internal democracy in the BDP, 1991–2003', paper presented to the Politics Seminar, University of Botswana, 11 February.

[8] General Khama had been installed as chief of the Bamangwato in 1979, and when he accepted senior political office in 1998 he made plain that he had no plans to relinquish his role as *kgosi*, and expressed his view that chiefs must be given a significant role to play. See *Mmegi*, 27 March 1998.

[9] Titus Mbuya, 'Profile: President to Be', *Mmegi*, 14 November 1997, and 'Biography of President', *The Botswana Gazette*, 8 April 1998.

'greatest loser in the whole [specially elected] circus is the people.'

The president exerts his power directly and personally over the legislature. He is constitutionally empowered to call and to prorogue parliament. He is, moreover, an *ex officio* member of the national assembly, unlike in South Africa, where a new president holds neither a seat nor an automatic right to appear in parliament. The Botswana president is entitled both to deliberate and to vote in the assembly and is invested with veto power.

Such wide-ranging domination over the popular chamber inevitably encourages arrogance. Facing questioning about corruption and his possible retirement plans, in December 1996, Ketumile Masire declared that he would answer that question 'when the need to answer it comes', and added: 'I can dissolve parliament tomorrow or any time' (*Botswana Guardian*, 13 December 1996). During the ground-breaking 2004 general elections, Mogae repeatedly announced in public that he would dissolve parliament if it rejected his re-nomination of Khama as deputy. He made clear his determination to have a vice-president of his choice; if parliament did not endorse his nominee it would be, as he put it, punishing him, and he would retaliate. 'I am their leader, so they have to follow their leader. If they do not endorse [Ian Khama] then I will dissolve parliament' (*Botswana Gazette*, 3 November 2004). That a president without popular constituency would sack a just recently elected legislature highlights the fragility of Botswana's democracy.

An articulate BDP MP, Boyce Sebetela, said that the intrusion into Lesotho showed that 'the executive regard[s] parliament as a rubber-stamping institution' (*Mmegi*, 9 October 1998). On issues of national importance it is often simply silent. When the country's military expenditure almost trebled between 1992 and 1995 the national assembly failed to discuss the matter and even a parliamentary question about a particularly controversial purchase of heavy equipment was brusquely dismissed.

No debate on the military occurred then or later, owing to timidity and coercion. As debate on budgetary allocations for the BDF began in 1996, more than 48 uniformed army officers marched into the public gallery in parliament, in a clear act of intimidation (Molomo, 2001: 54). Debate is yet to take place in parliament on the highly important issue of the removal of San/Bushmen from the CKGR, enforced in 1997 and 2002, and none has occurred on the related issue of the Remote Area Development Programme, in existence for 30 years, and embracing today more than 40,000 impoverished people. No debate took place either on automatic presidential succession prior to 2008. That this was an issue of clear constitutional and public concern was shown in a survey conducted in mid-2005, which found that 63 per cent of those interviewed supported constitutional amendments to create a popularly elected president. This majority embraced not only over 70 per cent of opposition party respondents, but also 55 per cent of BDP members. 'Widespread' support for the abandonment of automatic succession was similarly reported; 57 per cent favoured the election of presidential successors, located in both urban and rural areas, and across the supporters of all parties (Afro Barometer, August 2005: 1, 3 and 6).

While sovereignty in Botswana is vested in the president, things are outstandingly different in Namibia. Its constitution of 1990 placed all power in the hands of the people. Members of the national assembly were described as being the 'servants of the people', and they were endowed with significant powers to allow the people to 'influence the composition and policies of the government', as the constitution stated. Cabinet ministers were required to attend assembly meetings, and to respond to any queries and debates on the legitimacy, wisdom and effectiveness of government policies. Parliament could require any senior official to appear before any of its committees and to account for and explain their acts and programmes. The president too was required to report on government policies annually and to respond to questions. Executive power, unlike in Botswana, was vested in both the president and the cabinet, and the former was obliged to act in consultation with the latter. Further, the constitution required that the president be directly elected by the people and obtain 50 per cent or more of the votes cast. He could dissolve parliament, but in this event both president and assembly would face national elections within 90 days (Good, 1997: Chapter 4).

The Namibian parliament has not utilised these powers effectively to date, but that does not gainsay their importance. The sovereignty of the people remains enshrined, although parliament's enforcement powers have succumbed in practical politics to precisely the same institutional forces that hold sway in Botswana – the predominance of the ruling party and presidentialism. The South West African People's Organization (SWAPO) won 53 out of a total of 72 assembly seats in 1994, and President Sam Nujoma gained 77 per cent of the vote at the same time. Within four years, MPs became servants not of the people but of the president and his party machine.

In establishment terms, parliament in Botswana is located within the office of the president, dependent on the executive for its finances and the approval of its budget. The member for Okavango, Joseph Kavindama, noted in 2004 that 'all powers rest with the executive'; the reason why civil servants refuse to appear before parliament was because parliament had 'no teeth and cannot bite'. MPs unanimously affirmed that it was wrong for parliament to have its budget presented by the minister for presidential affairs rather than the speaker. But the impact of these deliberations was weakened by the fact that similar criticism had been voiced ineffectually before. In 1988, the assembly had 'strongly urge[d] government ... to ensure that parliament ... becomes an independent institution detached from the [presidency]'.[10] It is the president who appoints both the leader of the house and the Clerk of the National Assembly.

An outstanding example of independent parliamentary action occurred in early 1996. In the wake of the corruption scandals swirling around President Masire and other leading governmental figures, a nominated MP, Joy Phumaphi, proposed a motion on 28 February calling for 'the president, vice-president, ministers and assistant ministers and members of parliament [to] declare their business and financial interests, including farming interests and fixed assets, which shall be entered into a register, which shall be open for inspection by members of the public on request.' She appealed to her parliamentary colleagues to 'provide specific binding requirements which could be enforceable'. She said that an open register would dispel public suspicions rife against leaders, and noted that the success of a democracy depended on the confidence and trust people placed in those leaders. The motion came amidst reports claiming that Masire owned twenty farms in the Ghanzi area, and that the minister for presidential affairs, Ponatshego Kedikilwe, held disputed property holdings.[11]

The motion quickly heightened factional rifts within the ruling BDP. While the Mompati Merafhe faction supported the proposal in the party's parliamentary caucus, it was 'vehemently opposed' by the Daniel Kwelagobe camp, including Kedikilwe and President Masire. Kwelagobe favoured the watering down or outright rejection of the motion (*Botswana Gazette*, 6 March 1996). On 22 March parliament passed an amended motion which severely restricted

---

[10] Letshwiti Tutwane, 'Parliament Demands independence', *Mmegi Monitor*, 15 March. Spencer Mogapi, 'Parliament has no Teeth – MPs', *The Botswana Gazette*, 17 March 2004.

[11] Keto Segwai, *Mmegi*, 16 March 1996.

the openness and transparency of the register. Contravention of the secrecy of the register, rather than illicit wealth accumulation by ministers and MPs, was the focus of the new measures. A parliamentary committee would oversee the register – not the criminal code and courts of law – and it could impose a fine of P5,000 and imprisonment for two years on anyone contravening tight inspection rules (*Botswana Gazette*, 6 March 1996 and *Botswana Guardian*, 7 February 1997).

Opposition to Phumaphi's motion remained strong within the BDP, and a cabinet meeting in March 1996 was reportedly in chaos. The Minister for Home Affairs, Bahiti Temane, was quoted as saying that the BDP was 'in crisis ... only four people are in control of both the party and government'.[12] Minister Kedikilwe informed the assembly on 22 March that he would implement the aim of the motion within one-and-a-half months. But in debate in August 1997 Phumaphi said that the purpose of the bill was 'not to catch thieves, and [identify] millionaires' but to protect the reputation of MPs (Good, 1999: 60, and *Botswana Guardian*, 15 August 1997).

The bill resurfaced in parliament between April and July 1999, and was again postponed. Kwelagobe, as minister for presidential affairs, said in April 2002 that consultation was proceeding on the contents of the bill, and in February 2005, his successor, Phandu Skelemani, declared that 'plans [we]re afoot to have this bill resubmitted in ... July/August' that year (*Botswana Guardian*, 19 April 2002 and *Mmegi*, 16 February 2005).

Phumaphi became an assistant minister and then minister for health, and she went on to be assistant director general of the World Health Organization. In late 2005, the editor of *Mmegi* (20 October 2005) endeavoured to make sense of the decade-long saga of the register of members' assets. MPs, 'particularly those from the ruling party, showed unparalleled reluctance and hostility even to consider the bill.' After a lot of cajoling and the fear of public wrath, 'a watered down version was half-heartedly considered, [but] never saw the light of day.' It remained in presidential limbo in 2006, as noted further below.

Yet this was not the first time that parliament had endeavoured to enforce ministerial accountability in their business affairs. Following the recommendations of the presidential commission on economic opportunities, chaired by Peter Mmusi, parliament resolved that all public officers must register their interests,

---

[12] Prof Malema, *The Midweek Sun*, 20 March 1996.

covering their assets, liabilities and employment of his/her spouse and children, annually in a central record, and that ministers should register their interests in the same way as members of the public services. Responsibility for the implementation of the register of ministers' interests, should rest with the president. The commission's recommendations appeared in a government white paper, and were fully approved by parliament on 22 December 1982.[13] The president failed to implement these proposals, and parliament learnt nothing, in 1996 or since, from the executive's sustained failure of responsiveness and enforcement.

Parliament's subordination is extensive. Most MPs only obtained parliamentary office accommodation for the first time in 2006. The speaker in the same year, Patrick Balopi, was as usual a former minister, and the leader of the house, Lt-General Mompati Merafhe, was a senior serving minister. Reflecting the mood of the country, MPs today are more restive, and with a parliament of 57 elected members since 2004, more BDP parliamentarians are without ministerial office and free to criticise, should they want to do so.

When parliament ended its winter session on 31 August 2006, Bame Piet assessed its performance. Seven bills were presented by the government and all passed. Some 300 questions were asked, including one from the BCP MP for Gaborone Central, Dumelang Saleshando, asking about the vice-president's piloting of BDF aircraft and the ombudsman's recommendation against this. The minister for presidential affairs and public administration, Phandu Skelemani, replied that General Khama could fly BDF aircraft when necessary as the president had allowed it.[14]

Throughout the session, most MPs from the ruling party and the opposition, had complained bitterly, according to Piet, about poor implementation of government projects. This was an area where the vice-president held direct responsibility, since 2000, as coordinator of ministries, programmes and projects while, unlike all previous vice-presidents, holding no other ministerial responsibilities. Complaints were also frequent, from BDP as well as opposition party MPs, about Khama's consistent failure to participate in parliamentary affairs, and even, as one experienced journalist phrased it, 'the president-designate's seeming contempt for

[13] 'Gazette Opinion', *The Botswana Gazette*, 11 March 1992.
[14] 'Focus on Parliament', *Mmegi Online*, 1 September 2006.

parliament'.[15] Another question from Saleshando on whether it was appropriate for General Khama to offer periodic briefings to parliament on his progress with implementation, elicited further insight into the realities of presidential-parliamentary relations. Skelemani stated that the vice-president was not obliged to report to parliament as he reported directly to the president and had done so regularly since 2000.[16]

Presidentialism and the judiciary

The judiciary, the other main institution of liberal democracy in Botswana, is in much the same weak and dependent position. Judges of the high court do not enjoy uniformity of tenure, and conditions and are thus dependent on the executive for the terms and salaries they receive. Judges on contract appointments are particularly affected as they near retirement age. The existence of contractual differentials was publicised in 2005 when, as *Mmegi* reported, the public witnessed unsavoury exchanges between judges over pay, taken further when a civil case was initiated by a judge over his inequitable terms. Eventually he settled out of court leaving the problem unaddressed.[17] In effect, the president appoints all judges on non-uniform conditions of service.

In September 2006 the high court accepted a donation of P100,000 from De Beers. According to the registrar and master of the high court, Godfrey Nthomiwa, the money would be used to buy reference works for the court's libraries. He offered immediate assurances that the gift could not 'compromise our integrity'. Six days later, Sheila Khama of De Beers Botswana said that the donation had been made in response to a request from the high court to assist in their fund-raising activities for the library. She stressed that De Beers had donated in good faith and in public, and pointed out that the corporation did not have a case before the Botswana courts at that time.[18]

---

[15] Stryker Motlaloso, *Mmegi Online*, 25 November 2005. See also the editorials, 'Who is Khama Accountable to?', and 'Khama Must Respect Parliament', *Mmegi Online*, 25 November 2005 and 3 March 2006.

[16] Bame Piet, 'Khama not obliged to report to parliament', *Mmegi Online*, 24 August 2006.

[17] For full details see *Mmegi Monitor*, 6 June 2005, and editorial, *Mmegi Online*, 7 February 2006 and 23 January 2007. See also the attorney general's rebuttal, *Mmegi Online*, 15 December 2006.

[18] Bame Piet, 'High court registrar defends De Beers' donation', *Mmegi Online*, 14 September, and Letter to the editor, *Mmegi Online*, 20 September 2006.

But Debswana, in which De Beers and the Botswana government held joint ownership, was involved in a court case, as already noted. The Botswana Mining Workers Union (BMWU) had an on-going case against Debswana in the high court concerning the sacking of the 461 workers in 2004, and it voiced its apprehension that the gift might be detrimental to their case. Furthermore, there were on-going disturbances between the union and Debswana, including possible further dismissals. This was not the only issue: a decision was awaited in December in the high court in the long-running case against the expulsion of San people from the CKGR, and De Beers had been mentioned. BMWU secretary-general, Jack Tlhagale, said the donation had the potential to influence the court's decisions, and threatened the judiciary's independence and the country's democracy (*Mmegi Online*, 18 and 21 September 2006). De Beers' gift was thus a questionable act, as was the failure of the government to increase its funding to the court or, given its close relations with De Beers/Debswana, to prevent the donation from going ahead.

Circulation of office occurs between top legal positions in the state and the judiciary, advantageous to certain preferred individuals but highly predjudicial to the independence of the high court. Ian Kirby moved between the attorney general's office and the high court bench not once but twice, and Athaliah Molokomme moved from the court to being attorney general in replacement to Kirby. As this latest shift took place, the chairman of the Botswana Law Society, Omphemetse Motumise, expressed fear that the essential boundaries between the executive and the judiciary were being eroded. He noted too growing disquiet in legal circles that certain key positions were being reserved for preferred people.[19]

As already noted, appointments to the high court are made by the president. Recommendations are made by the Judicial Service Commission (JSC), the chairman of which is the chief justice, himself the appointee of the president, as are all other members of the JSC but one.[20] The process of appointment, according to Motumise in early 2005, was shrouded in secrecy. The legal profession never knew when there was a vacancy on the bench, what steps were being taken to fill this vacancy, and what the desired

[19] Gideon Nkala, 'Kirby for the high court?', *Mmegi Online*, 17 March 2006.
[20] Ndulamo Anthony Morima, in *Mmegi Monitor*, 6 June 2005, noted further below.

qualifications were.[21] It is worth noting that the chief justice in 2007 was Julian Nganunu, a known close friend and indeed business partner of President Mogae.[22]

Changes affecting the attorney general's chambers initiated in 2004 to 2005, were both problematic and highly consequential. The creation of a new post of Director of Public Prosecution (DPP) impacted upon the Attorney General (AG), and it was deemed by some to be influenced by the awaited presidential transition. The latter was the established principal legal advisor to the government, but the DPP was also appointed by the president, with ambivalent role and powers.[23] Tensions reportedly existed between the two officials over the identification of issues of national importance – when the DPP was supposed to consult the AG – and over who had the final say when consultation occurred.[24] A third senior official, a 'legal advisor to the president', also existed from 2001; President Mogae had appointed Sidney Pilane to this post, allegedly without following normal public service procedures and without clarifying either the future relations between Pilane and the then attorney general, Phandu Skelemani. The latter stated that he did not know Pilane's job description and was not aware that he was supposed to work closely with the new legal advisor. After 2002 it was apparent that Pilane's work was almost entirely focused on the high court, presenting, sometimes abrasively, the government's case on the expulsions from the CKGR.[25]

The establishment of the DPP was followed by resignations among experienced senior legal officials, and widening repercus-

[21] Morula Morula, 'Bench appointments made under the table?', *The Botswana Guardian*, 4 Ferbruary 2005.

[22] Chief Justice Julian Nganunu, Debswana's Louis Nchindo, and two other men were 'Botswana king-makers', and Mogae 'bounces most important decisions off [these men] before adopting them in cabinet.' No author, 'The President's Men', *The Botswana Guardian*, 16 June 2000. The president and the chief justice, in addition, were shareholders in Motswedi, a citizen-owned company, which in turn was a major shareholder, along with the Botswana Development Corporation (BDC), in Owens Corning Pipes Botswana (OCPB), the latter contracted to supply pipes to the state-owned Water Utilities Corporation. The president, and presumably the chief justice, were 'among Batswana investors who benefited from [this] controversial government black empowerment deal.' Deeply controversial in fact, because Motswedi had also benefited from a soft-loan from OCPB; public money had facilitated personal gain; and the pipes supplied to the government proved faulty. Outsa Mokone, *The Sunday Standard* (Gaborone), 6 March 2005. The BDC was a leading developmental institution, and the money it injected into OCPB had helped keep that company afloat financially. *The Midweek Sun*, 8 December 1999.

[23] Constitutional amendments of 2005 gave the DPP autonomous powers, but also said that in exercising them he or she should consult the attorney general in matters of national importance.

[24] Batlhalefi Leagajang, *The Botswana Gazette*, 22 September 2006.

[25] Tuduetso Setsiba, 'Who is advising the president?', *Mmegi Online*, 1 September 2006.

sions. While 20 out of a total of 42 magistrates in the country in 2004 were foreigners, this number was expected to rise. According to a Motswana officer who had resigned: 'The justice system will [soon] be run exclusively by foreigners from Banana Republics where the rule of law does not exist.' An unnamed state counsel added: 'These foreigners want to ensure that their contracts are renewed and their impartiality is doubtful.' By early 2007 a spate of resignations of Botswana magistrates was reported, many frustrated by their conditions of service and especially by the numbers of Zimbabweans taking over.[26]

Problems escalated within the judiciary. *The Gazette* revealed in March 2007 that it was common knowledge in criminal circles that some magistrates could be bribed. The director of the DCEC, Tymon Ketlholo, confirmed that the agency was investigating a number of magistrates.[27] The editor of *Mmegi* noted on 7 March 2007 that 'Botswana's law enforcement agents and not just the justice system are under attack for perceived corruption', and Chief Justice Nganunu confirmed that big problems existed. He disclosed to a meeting of magistrates at Phakalane that his office was investigating alleged unethical behaviour in the judiciary: 'All of us must expose [the bad eggs] so that we can restore the system to its good name.'[28]

Other problems affecting the judiciary and referred to by the Law Society and others, concerned the lack of separation between the high court and the court of appeal, the country's final chamber, and the particular need for constitutional revision to ensure that its provisions accorded with international legal trends and Botswana's associated treaty obligations. Botswana was falling behind in 'human rights practice and discourse', Motumise noted, and soon 'we will be reduced to reluctant followers as everyone around us becomes ever more innovative in the development of more modern constitutions' (*Botswana Guardian*, 4 February 2005 and *Mmegi*, 17 March 2006).

Presidentialism and society

Presidential powers are not least important where democratic process is concerned, since an array of legal instruments accords

[26] Lekopanye Mooketsi, 'Frustrated magistrates quit en masse', *Mmegi Online*, 23 February 2007.

[27] *The Botswana Gazette*, 'DCEC Investigating magistrates', 3 March 2007.

[28] Stryker Motlaloso, 'Corruption out, warns Nganunu', *Mmegi Online*, 13 March 2007.

the president direct and sometimes personal control over opinion and information. The Immigration Act confers wide powers on him alone in declaring, for example, that a resident foreigner is a prohibited immigrant. These powers were utilised by Seretse Khama against John K. Modise (whose father was a Botswana citizen), who was declared an 'undesirable immigrant' in September 1978, and handed over to South African police. Modise was prominent in the BNF and seen as a possible contender for the state presidency, an office reserved for natural-born citizens.[29] The same powers were used by Festus Mogae to expel this author from Botswana in May 2005 after 15 years' work and residence in the country.

The Penal Code encompasses sedition, defamation and contempt, and can be invoked against published and depicted information and against citizens and non-citizens alike. The president is also empowered to restrict the movement of citizens of Botswana, despite the enshrinement of freedom of movement in the constitution. In 1978 Seretse Khama seized the passports of BNF youthwing members on route to a cultural festival in Cuba (Otlhogile, 1998: 222).

The National Security Act of 1986 best expressed the authoritarian and secretive elements at the core of this purportedly democratic state. Its usage in the 1990s indicated that almost all news concerning the BDF was a matter of state security, while even trade union activities and governmental wages policy came within its ambit. Penalties range up to 25 years' imprisonment regardless of public interest. Nevertheless at the end of 2006, a far more totalitarian system of surveillance and presidential domination, a directorate of intelligence and security, was before parliament (as will be considered below).

Simultaneously, presidential powers are unrestricted by the existence of any right-to-know or freedom of information legislation, or by any whistle-blower protections for ethically-minded public servants. The latter are prohibited from speaking to the press and are limited further by punitive confidence laws introduced following the corruption scandals 1991–1994. Those in the Botswana Housing Corporation, for instance, imposed a fine of P5,000 on an employee breaching confidentiality. Ombudsman

---

[29] Modise suffered severe and prolonged difficulties, until the African Commission on Human and Peoples' Rights (ACHPR) found in his favour, and called on the government of Botswana to recognise him as a citizen by descent, in November 2000, noting that his appeal process had been wilfully obstructed by the government. 'John K. Modise v. Botswana', ACHPR, Comm. No.97/93 (2000), Human Rights Library, University of Minnesota, pp. 2, 7 and 14–15.

Lethebe Maine called for the enactment of a freedom of information act in 1999. Attractive words about the ombudsman as a pillar of democracy meant very little, he emphasised, unless the right to complain and raise issues was fully available to all sectors of the public (*Botswana Gazette*, 3 November 1999).

The ombudsman was first appointed by the president in 1995, to consider matters of 'injustice' experienced by members of the public. He or she was required to report annually to the president, and the report had to be laid before the national assembly. His investigatory writ was tightly circumscribed, the proceedings that followed his investigations were vague and indeterminate, he had no independent powers to prosecute, and the penalties he might impose were slight – a maximum fine of P200 and/or imprisonment of one year.[30]

After receiving a written complaint from the Botswana Congress Party about the vice-president piloting military aircraft, Lethebe Maine submitted a report to the president in April 2001.[31] More than two years later, after president Mogae failed to respond to his report, he passed the matter to the minister for presidential affairs, Daniel Kwelagobe, in the expectation that the report would be taken to parliament, but still no action was taken. In late 2003 the ombudsman declared publicly that there was no more that he could do (*Mmegi*, 5 December 2003).

The long and silent saga was a testimony to autocracy in Botswana and the confident implicitness of its expression. On 16 March 2004 the assistant minister for presidential affairs, Olifant Mfa, announced in parliament that Vice-President Khama was free to fly BDF aircraft. Cautioned by the deputy speaker, Bahiti Temane, that what he was saying was wrong, Mfa stressed that 'the President has given him permission and he will continue to use it' (*Mmeg*i 17 March 2004). Shortly after, the press secretary to the president, Jeff Ramsay, wrote an open letter to GabsFM radio station saying that the president had given his permission to the vice-president before the ombudsman's investigation and 2001 report, and he also said it was notable that the ombudsman 'did

---

[30] 'The Ombudsman Act, 1995', *Botswana government extraordinary gazette*, 21 April 1995.

[31] Ombudsman, Republic of Botswana, Report in terms of section 8 (1) of the Ombudsman Act of 1995, 'Report into the alleged irregularities with regard to: a) Public officers accompanying his honour the Vice-President Lt.Gen. Seretse Khama Ian Khama on political party activities; and b) his honour the vice-president flying Botswana Defence Force aircraft', 4 April 2001. Essentially the report found that that the flying of BDF aircraft by the vice-president, a person not bound by the BDF act, and outside the BDF command structure, constituted a violation of that act.

not bother to approach H.E. the president for his own explanation' (*Tautona Times*, 29 March 2004). Six months later, President Mogae wrote a letter to the press stating that it was as commander-in-chief that he had authorised the vice-president to continue to pilot Government aircraft.[32]

Although MPs sometimes raised important questions in the house, much like good journalists did with greater cogency and frequency in the media, the democratic chamber had failed to act on the ombudsman's report, even when he invited them to do so over some six months. Ombudsman, parliament and people were closely inter-connected politically, and contempt shown to one was as if to all. With information and opinion so restricted, all three were weaker. Accountability was absent and presidentialism both more elevated and exposed. The president was above the law and so was the vice-president when Mogae determined.

Executive-parliamentary relationships are similar in South Africa. Thabo Mbeki quickly emphasised his presidential pre-eminence in 1999 when he succeeded Nelson Mandela. Cabinet ministers were summoned in turn immediately after his inauguration banquet. Derek Hanekom was told that he was axed as minister of agriculture at 2.30 am, and Pallo Jordan learnt his fate thirty minutes later. Significant appointments by president Mbeki were greeted with bafflement in the media, and at a press conference to announce the new cabinet he offered no explanation for his choices. The president soon assumed direct authority over the appointment of ANC provincial premiers. In little over six months, a new entity, the presidency, had come into being with an initial staff complement of 334 people. The role of the deputy president was reduced and refocused away from the broad mandate which President Mandela had accorded Mbeki, to the fulfilling of tasks delegated by the president, and leadership of government business in parliament. Extensive restructuring occurred and the overall results were a lack of accountability to elected representatives and the centralistaion of power in the hands of a few individuals close to President Mbeki.[33]

Presidentialism was strongly at work in Namibia also. The country's 1990 constitution was a landmark for democratic and accountable government, and its Article 29 restricted the tenure of the

---

[32] He added at the end that Khama was to be 'commended for having attained and maintained his skills as a pilot'. Letters to the Editor, *The Botswana Guardian*, 3 September 2004.
[33] Sean Jacobs, 'An imperial presidency or an organised one?', *Business Day*, 17 February 2000, quoted with further detail in Good (2002: Chapter 5).

president to not more than two terms. But half-way through his second term, President Nujoma indicated that he contemplated a third term for himself. In March 1997 he told parliament that he was still young, aged 67, and 'if the people ... want me to continue making a contribution I will continue to do so.' He was said to have made his announcement without consulting his party. But the party effectively established the terms of debate when it called on Nujoma to serve as long as he was medically fit. SWAPO's central committee cited Nujoma's long history of tested leadership and his role as founding father of the nation. Predominant in parliament, the necessary constitutional amendment was soon made (Good, 1997: 561–3). Presidentialism was firmly in place in all three southern African democracies before the 1990s were over.

3
Ruling Party Predominance

The power of the president in Botswana is enlarged by his simultaneous role as the leader of the ruling party. The BDP was, as noted, the governing party from the beginning, and presidentialism and predominance rose rapidly together. For more than thirty years, the state president's leadership position was broadly unchallengeable – 'While the party is in power, the president shall remain president of the party without further elections' (Article 33 (5) of the BDP's constitution) – and the tenure of the state president too was similarly unlimited for 35 years. Seretse Khama died in office, Masire remained unchallenged amid abounding corruption scandals until he chose retirement with statesman-like privileges, and arranged automatic succession to his chosen successor Festus Mogae.[1] Until the late 1990s, the Botswana president was effectively as much a 'president for life' as a Hastings Kamuzu Banda.[2] The ruling party's victory in parliamentary elections confers a democratic legitimacy on the unelected state president.

Supremacy is built upon solid numerical superiority in the legislature. The BDP has comfortably commanded legislative power over every election. No opposition party has come close to challenging the BDP, nor have they done so either in total combination. Over the nine general elections, 1965–2004, the ruling party's predominance was consistent: 1965 BDP 90 per cent, Opposition 10 per cent of parliamentary seats; 1969 BDP 77 per cent, Opposition 23 per cent; 1974 BDP 84 per cent, Opposition 16 per cent; 1979 BDP 91 per cent, Opposition 9 per cent; 1984 BDP 82 per cent, Opposition 18 per cent; 1989 BDP 91 per cent, Opposition 9 per cent; 1994 BDP 67 per cent, Opposition 33 per cent; 1999 BDP 83 per cent, Opposition 17 per cent; 2004 BDP 77 per cent,

[1] Good and Taylor (2006, Chapter 3). See also Botsalo Ntuane, 'The regent who became king', *Sunday Standard*, 4 November 2007.
[2] Zibani Maundeni, 'Life party president undemocratic', *Mmegi*, 4 November 1994.

Opposition 23 per cent (Molomo, 2005: 40). Even when its share of the popular vote fell to an all-time low of just 52 per cent in 2004, and the combined opposition vote rose to a high of 48 per cent it still obtained, under the given simple majority, or first-past-the-post electoral system, 77 per cent of elected parliamentary seats. The party's legislative success also overrode – and probably benefited from – low voter turnout. When the turnout of eligible voters dropped to 37 per cent in 1969 the party got 77 per cent of seats, and when turnout reached its nadir of 26 per cent five years later, they obtained 84 per cent of parliamentary places.[3] Such legislative dominance means in turn patronage via the state president's extensive appointment powers. Throughout the 1990s, almost half of the BDP parliamentary party membership – 40 elected MPs plus the four appointees – acquired ministerial office.

But real predominance under reasonably democratic conditions, with open, competitive elections and freedom of association and expression, means much more than parliamentary numbers. It requires the creation of a distinctive strategy or programme which, encapsulating ideas about the country's political culture, defines the problems the country faces and the steps that must be taken under the guidance of the aspirant ruling party. The strategy mobilises leading social forces behind the party, which serve as its socio-political foundations, much as the BDP quickly attracted cattlemen, traders and the colonial administration, and through whom the party reaches out in turn to the wider electorate. The strategy, or 'political formula', as Mosca termed it, must therefore be meaningful to people, attentive to their sentiments and responsive to their needs. It must also be adaptable to changing circumstances, and open to criticism, as the criteria of both democracy and the successful adaptability of the formula. This is the vital democratic element in supremacy – voters must be persuaded by the value of this formula to continue electing the ruling party with which it is closely identified.[4] For Pempel (1980), a scholar of one-party predominant systems in democratic polities in countries like Italy, Japan and Sweden, what he termed 'uncommon democracies' existed.

[3] Molomo and Wilford Molefe (2005), 'Voters and electoral performance of political parties in Botswana', in Maundeni (ed.) (2005: 102). (Different turnout figures are provided by Adam Mfundisi 2005: chapter 9, Table 9.1, p. 165.)

[4] Mosca's political formula encapsulates the role of ideology or strategy within successful ruling party predominance within what he saw as stable, liberal, essentially elite democracy. Mosca (1939: Chapters 3 and 5).

The Social Democrats and the Swedish Model

Sweden is an exemplar of predominance firmly at work in a democracy. In 2006, the Social Democrats had been in power for 65 of the past 75 years, primarily because their party offered a distinctive form of social democracy expressed in the 'Swedish Model'. The system delivered high growth (5.6 per cent in 2006), moderate unemployment (officially 6 per cent), and high welfare benefits, funded from high levels of taxation (ranging from 30 per cent to 55 per cent), based on traditional values of consensus. Extending back to agreements in the 1930s, systemic decision-making between employers and trade unions, mediated through the state, formed the core of the system. Nearly 80 per cent of Swedish workers were trade union members, a large public sector embraced 30 per cent of employees, and the Swedish Trade Union Confederation (LO) represented some two million blue-collar workers, in a population of nine million. The Confederation of Swedish Enterprises represented 55,000 companies and joined with the unions and the state in considering collectively key issues like wages and benefits, output and profits. The consultative process helped to produce a fairly dynamic capitalism even under intense challenge from Anglo-American globalisation. Corporations like Ericsson, Volvo, Saab and Ikea combined quality manufacturing with exports in knowledge, service and communications industries, and the government ran a comfortable surplus. The Swedish Model was notable for the world's second highest human development index level, high affluence, and innovative design and manufacturing from the likes of Ikea and Saab.[5]

Support for the model and the ruling party with which it has been identified was indicated broadly at the polls. In a large multi-party, proportional-representational system, the Social Democrats garnered 40 per cent of the votes in 2002, making them three times the size of their nearest competitor. Voter participation was also high, with a turnout then of 79 per cent, and averaging some 87 per cent since 1945 – figures which the American democracy could only envy. The main opposition, the Moderate Party, pledged to slash income tax levels – a core element in the model – and got just 15 per cent of the vote in 2002.

Changing the model was nonetheless possible. The moderates, under a new and younger leader, Fredrik Reinfeldt, had moved

[5] GDP per capita (in PPP terms) was $26,000 in 2002, when Sweden's HDI was 0.946.

from the right to a centrist position between 2002 and 2006, advocating reduced unemployment benefits, a freer labour market, and down-playing tax cuts. 'We want to show that we like the Sweden we have', Reinfeldt insisted. Tore Robertsson, president of Skydds, a defence firm in Malmo, said 'there won't be a [neo] liberal revolution' in Sweden, but 'we might change a bit', to promote entrepreneurship and job-seeking. An LO economist, Lena Westelund, believed that the Swedish model was well adapted for tough international competition and could continue delivering growth. She felt that collectively agreed wages have flexibility; a worker needed job security, 'so that he doesn't resist social change.'[6]

After reassuring the electorate that the social model would be safe in his hands, Reinfeldt won a slim parliamentary majority at elections on 17 September 2006 by one per cent of the vote. In his victory speech he said that his party had won power by changing. Prime Minister Goran Persson immediately resigned, simultaneously as Social Democrat leader too: the party's policies were good, he said, they were aiming for a comeback, 'but it is not a comeback I will lead'.[7]

Predominance in Sweden is clearly based on a distinctive model closely identified with the Social Democrat Party, and the success and durability of both spanned 70 years. Affluence, human development and relative equality have been inter-related achievements. The model is open to criticism, adaptable and stronger for those reasons. Its support is broad. The country's main opposition (now new ruling party by a narrow vote) endorses it, while the Social Democrats, still the majority party, re-affirm their commitment.

The BDP and the growth model

The Swedish example highlights the inherent weaknesses in Botswana: the BDP's predominance is different. Here the numerical factors, sustained dominance in the legislature and sole control of the executive, stand out. But the BDP had created a distinctive political formula in the early 1970s, which explained and justified its role and power over almost two decades.

---

[6] *Business Day*, 17 and 18 September 2002; Laurence Peter, 'Beauty of Swedish Model disputed', *BBC News Online*, 11 September, and Nicholas Watt, 'Right tempts Swedes to change course', *Guardian Unlimited*, 15 September 2006.
[7] Nicholas Watt, *Guardian Unlimited*, 18 September 2006.

Constructed by founding fathers Seretse Khama and Ketumile Masire, the BDP's model promised socio-economic growth in one of the world's least developed countries. It would be based on the guiding and enabling role of the political elite, in close collaboration with the bureaucracy and corporate mining, directed at the intensification of cattle production and over the longer term the accumulation of diamond wealth. Returns in goods and services, profits and salaries, would go to those who contributed most to the growth's success. While all might share variously in the enjoyment of the physical aspects of national development, with advances in communications, education and health, the more tangible monetary rewards would go to the big stakeholders. It was an economically rational strategy which cemented the party's socio-political reliance on cattlemen, bureaucrats and corporate miners. It was distinctive, realistic and hard-headed, in pre-Reaganite, pre-Thatcherite capitalist terms, and it worked, in the specific and narrow goal of sustained high growth. It explained and justified the rule of the BDP to the elites in the leading sectors, and to a part of the voting public.

The model was only tacitly and implicitly expressed, and did not appear in cogent economic form in election manifestos. Brief references were officially made around 1990,[8] and Masire made mention soon after to the needs and contribution of venture capital. The model's important corollary was that those who made little or no contribution to growth would necessarily rely on the generosity of those who did – those who had no resources to contribute could expect no returns more than meagre handouts. While neglect of the poor was sanctioned in nineteenth-century Tswana culture, it was best left unclarified electorally in the democratic state. However, it was certainly implied that the poor in Botswana, unlike those in less well-governed African countries, would be bound to benefit, vicariously at least, from the realism of the model and the tangible development it produced.

The model's political dimensions were more explicitly addressed. The growth model strongly emphasised regular and open elections, where many parties might compete. In an Africa of one-party states, with rigged or no elections, the founders showed

---

[8] The Report of the Presidential Commission on the Review of the Incomes Policy, Republic of Botswana, March 1990, and the associated government white paper, explicitly rejected proposals for extending minimum-wages protection to domestic workers and farm labourers as impractical and unworkable, and dismissed evidence of serious and worsening incomes inequalities, as considered further below.

their wisdom in choosing an open liberal model and enjoying the long stability which resulted. All might compete, although the ruling party, advantaged by its solid social base and the resources of incumbency, always won; turnout was low, but those who turned out voted BDP. That only the legislature was popularly elected went largely unnoted especially by foreign friends. Democracy was defined as parliamentary elections.

Through the 1970s and immediately beyond, Botswana, as Alice Mogwe observed, became the 'darling of the North',[9] in consequence of its combined growth and regular elections, and the miracle of the model was unquestioningly upheld.

But the adulation of foreign countries eager to find an African success helped to disguise important weaknesses in the model. Makgala points to the 'subservience enjoyed by the founding [BDP] president...from 1962 to 1980', which 'continued during the tenure of his successor', Masire. The same deference was accorded to the BDP leadership from other party members. Subservience furthered political stability: 'for a long time, once in parliament, MPs and position-holders in various party organs hardly ever faced competition from other party members, [and] were only replaced following their retirement or death.'[10] .

The other major weakness was the narrowness of the ruling party's electoral base. As turnout figures graphically indicate, the hard-nosed exclusionist growth model never succeeded in attracting majoritarian popular support. The turnout of eligible voters only passed 50 per cent in 1965 and 1984, and then but narrowly.[11] In 1974, when diamond production was about to begin, turnout was only 26 (or 24) per cent, and when necessary electoral reforms were put to referenda in 1997, only 17 per cent of voters bothered to participate, in part owing to the fact that some BDP leaders, fearful of the youth and for their own positions, opposed lowering the voting age to 18 (*Botswana Gazette*, 8 October 1997). The Botswana model said far more to the relatively rich and influential and to the imaginations of outsiders than it did to the poor majority at home.

[9] Director of Ditshwanelo, speaking in an interview with Connie Scanlon, and reported in 'Educating for Peace and Human Rights in Botswana', paper presented to the Politics Seminar, University of Botswana, 27 March 2002.
[10] C.J. Makgala (2004), 'Calling a spade a spade: New dimensions in internal democracy in the BDP, 1991–2003', paper presented to the Politics Seminar, University of Botswana, 11 February, pp. 2 and 4.
[11] Figures in Molomo (2005) are 65 per cent in 1965 and 54 per cent in 1984, p. 102, while Mfundisi (2005) has 58 per cent and 55 per cent, p. 165.

The creation of the miracle also engendered a dangerous complacency among the rulers, seriously limiting or perhaps negating their capacity for change. This became critically important in the early 1990s, when the need for change was apparent to many through a series of scandals embroiling the top leadership. When ministers were questioned about the causes of the failures that had suddenly emerged, their response added arrogance to complacency, alienating many and further exacerbating the elite's problems. As reforms became increasingly necessary – the creation of a strong and independent anti-corruption agency, an effective ombudsman, the register of assets, among others – state and party leaders were more concerned with fighting for party position than with addressing national problems. Competition for leadership positions in the party's organs 'became fierce and dirty', as competitors variously known as 'newcomers' and 'professionals', (such as Merafhe and Mogae specially elected in 1989), 'veterans', 'northerners' and 'southerners', publicly attacked each other with relentless and reckless abandon. Rapid growth, and the prestige and advantages of office – fundamentals of the model – encouraged such in-fighting.[12]

Exposure, protest and inaction

From 1991 a series of public scandals undermined the probity and efficacy of the growth model and shook the foundations of the BDP.[13] Their revelatory impact was detailed, cumulative and sharp. The first in 1991 involved the award of a large contract to a company called IPM to supply teaching materials to primary schools. The firm was virtually just one man with a brief-case, and it saw P27 million dissipated in a series of gross errors of procedure within the ministry for local government.[14] At much the same time, as examination of recent land-grabbing and illegal land transactions in Mogoditshane and other large villages near Gaborone

---

[12] The factionalism preceded the corruption crises of the 1990s by a year or so and certainly they compounded each other. Makgala (2004).

[13] The 'Leno Real-Estates Affair', involving the acquisition of land in booming central Gaborone and its subsequent re-sale to big corporations, had emerged in 1986. It involved some 29 people from the topmost echelons of government, including Kedikilwe, Mmusi, Merafhe and a firm called GM Five in which President Masire had interests, but it was successfully hushed up. Bojosi Otlhogile, 'Leno: The Deafening Silence', *Mmegi*, 15 February 1986.

[14] Republic of Botswana (1991), *Report of the presidential commission of inquiry into the supply of school books etc.*, 16 April.

revealed that vice-president, and minister for local government, Peter Mmusi, used the power of his office to effect the transfer of land to his friend, Daniel Kwelagobe, minister for agriculture: Mmusi was also national chairman of the BDP and Kwelagobe was its secretary-general, respectively numbers two and three in the party hierarchy after President Masire. Many believed, notes Makgala, that 'Masire, Mmusi and Kwelagobe's word was law in the BDP.'[15] But the two individuals had brought the government into serious disrepute in Mogoditshane.[16]

Next came the Christie report near the end of 1992 which exposed gross mismanagement and dishonesty in the Botswana Housing Corporation (BHC) and in the supervisory ministry of local government, resulting in the loss of tens of millions of Pula. Assistant ministers for local government, Ronald Sebego and Michael Tshipinare, were involved in malpractice, the latter most seriously, and Mmusi carried the political responsibility for the massive corruption.[17] These illegal land sales and the BHC scandals came at a time of acute housing shortage in the rapidly growing capital city, and they exposed failures in the entire government system at its highest levels. Housing shortages affected manual workers and the poor most of all. 'Key members of the government knew very well what was happening' in the BHC, noted a close observer, 'but [they] hoped somehow to keep matters quiet'.[18]

Events in the National Development Bank (NDB) from late 1993 were the most explosive politically of this cycle. The NDB was described by Finance Minister Mogae in 1991 as a 'pillar of our financial system', and an 'essential vehicle' for channelling loan financing into 'development activities of high priority.' By late 1993 its near bankruptcy was obvious. Accumulated losses totalled P41 million, outstanding loans amounted to P91 million, of which over one-third were in arrears. The essential problem entangling the NDB, according to Mogae in January 1994, was the near refusal of borrowers even to service their loans.

The leaking of a top debtors list by an unknown NDB employee, in January 1994, after it became known that 50 per cent of the Bank's employees were to be sacked, revealed the identities of those recalcitrant debtors. Among them, the minister for

[15] Makgala (2004), p. 6.
[16] Republic of Botswana (1991), *Report of the presidential commission of inquiry into problems in Mogoditshane etc*, 13 December (also known as the Kgabo report).
[17] Republic of Botswana (1992), *Report of the presidential commission of inquiry into the operations of the [BHC] etc.*, 30 November.
[18] All three commissions of inquiry are considered in detail in Good (1994: 501–5).

presidential affairs, Lt-General Merafhe, owed P47,000; his colleague at commerce and industry, Kedikilwe, owed P640,000, of
which P260,000 was in arrears; the minister for labour and home
affairs, Patrick Balopi, was indebted via an investment company
he owned to the extent of P1,100,000; Sebego owed P1.5 million,
and Tshipinare P600,000, both in arrears; and President Masire
himself owed P546,000. It was estimated that the combined debt
of ministers and BDP MPs to the NDB totalled some P30 million.

Collectively, these were the people responsible for the good
operations of the Bank, who determined interest rates and like
matters, and who had sanctioned at least two generous debt write-
offs in the 1980s. Another NDB source revealed that ministers and
MPs had repeatedly sought loans for which they did not qualify,
and Mogae suggested that creditworthiness had not been a prerequisite for all borrowers. He also revealed that a Small Borrowers
Fund (SBF), administered by the NDB, had actually been utilised
almost exclusively by, as he said, the 'big guns'. The country's
vanguard financial institution had been extensively exploited over
many years by the ruling elite. Their ethos was not one that prioritised national development but one of almost unrestrained, individual self-enrichment (Good, 1994: 509–14).

Ministers reacted to the exposures by claiming that their indebt-
edness was the fault of the NDB or part of the common lot, saying,
as did Masire, that 'I had a problem like all farmers of sometimes
being in arrears.' Others attacked those who tried to investigate
what happened. Masire declared that it was all unethical and
insisted that 'the media should refrain from this witch hunt', while
the minister for foreign affairs, Dr Chiepe, attacked the press,
saying: 'We are breeding ... a culture of mistrust and abuse.' The
president went a little further, in February 1994, when he explained
that the issue had to be looked at in its context. Botswana was a
highly risky area, especially in agricultural pursuits, but 'the
people who venture' were 'the hope of our society' – the generators of the growth. What these generators did not offer, however,
was any explanation of what had happened at the NDB and of
their role in the debacle. No resignations resulted, and no commission of inquiry was held (Good, 1994: 513–15).

Public reaction was extensive. Students demonstrated outside
the assembly in February because 'innocent [NDB] employees are
having to pay [for the ministers' failures] by losing their jobs'
(*Botswana Gazette*, 16 February 1994). People were particularly
angry that bank staff had to suffer as a result of the rulers' failure to

honour their financial obligations.[19] More than 1,000 marched to parliament on 13 March 1994 to register their disgust at the escalating rate of corruption in the country. The Anti-Corruption Campaign Group was made up of church, student groups, trade unions and the BNF, and they called for the urgent establishment of an ombudsman, a declaration of ministers' interests, and a code of conduct for all parliamentarians. Banners carried by the marchers demanded President Masire's resignation, and the prosecution of the minister of labour, Patrick Balopi, while others expressed support for Finance Minister Mogae, whose name was absent from the debtors' list and who was believed to be supportive of reform. Students from three tertiary institutions in Gaborone protested again in November, following the re-appointment of Kwelagobe and Ronald Sebego to ministerial office, opposing a cabinet of 'delinquents who cannot accept political responsibility'(*Botswana Guardian*, 11 November 1994).

When a new directorate on corruption and economic crime (DCEC) was being discussed in parliament in July, Mogae declared: 'We are dealing with a serious matter ... extraordinary measures are needed because we are facing a problem of unparalleled magnitude.'[20] After Graham Stockwell became the first director of the DCEC, in September, he stressed that corruption was much more widespread and serious than the public were aware (*Midweek Sun*, 14 September 1994). Patrick Molutsi believes that after 1990, Botswana entered a time of 'societal re-awakening', that 'pitted the old against the young, the rich against the poor ... and employer against employee' in unprecedented ways.[21]

But the ruling BDP reacted to the crisis reluctantly, divisively and to only a limited extent. When the proposed DCEC was debated in July, Kwelagobe and Sebego were among five MPs who walked out of parliament, and when deferral of the motion was considered, Kwelagobe, Mmusi and Tshipinare were among some ten BDP MPs favouring postponement. Seven others absented themselves (*Mmegi*, 29 July 1994). Given the critical environment, a DCEC was established, but it was located within the office of the presidency, and without independent prosecutorial powers.

---

[19] 129 employees out of a total of 240 bank staff were retrenched. *Mmegi*, 29 January 1994, and T.C. Matsheka and M.Z. Botlhomilwe (2000), 'Economic conditions and election Outcomes in Botswana', *Pula*, 14,1, p. 43.

[20] Quoted by Mesh Moeti, *Mmegi*, 29 July 1994.

[21] Quoted in Makgala (2004: 6).

Rising factionalism, not reform, was the biggest reaction of the ruling party to the scandals.

Popular awareness of the incapacities of the BDP rose considerably through 1994, and Masire's recognition of the threat that this implied prompted him to offer reluctant support for reform. The riots in Mochudi and Gaborone in January 1995 were spontaneous protests against remote and unresponsive government; they came in the wake of October elections when the BNF made its biggest-ever gain in the popular vote.

For Kwelagobe, Mmusi and other established figures, retention of party position was their overriding concern. After the Kgabo report, the BDP became divided into two bitterly opposed factions: Kwelagobe and Mmusi as leaders of the south faction, and Merafhe in control of the north. After Kwelagobe and Mmusi resigned from the government in March 1992 and were suspended from their party positions three months later, they brooked no compromise. They had the numbers. When they were triumphantly re-elected to their BDP positions in mid-1993, they had almost detached the party from its government. Effectively, 'the Kwelagobe block controlled the party whereas that of Merafhe [with Mogae] controlled the government' (Makgala, 2004: 11). Masire utilised his powers of appointment to name five members of the BDP's central committee, and reappointed Merafhe and other trusted ministerial figures. Kwelagobe continued to attack the government in parliament (ibid.).

The BDP remained fixated upon itself. Mogae was made vice-president after 1992, Mmusi died two years later, and Masire remained in office until succession was arranged. By April 1998 factionalism was at its worst in the BDP's history, characterised still by the two big camps of Kwelagobe and Merafhe, locked in intense fighting for control of the party (Molomo, 2000: 96). Automatic succession to Mogae and the elevation of General Ian Khama, both outsiders in party terms, were consequences of the party's weaknesses deepening through this critical decade. Vital institutional and policy reforms were neglected, and elite personalities became the focus as the long period of sustained high growth approached its end.

Demonising the opposition

The BDP's incapacity for change was manifest throughout the 1990s, culminating in 1998 with the return to dynastic politics and the elevation of Lt.-General Ian Khama as vice-president. The country turned back to being, in Kedikilwe's words, 'a demo-feudal state', where many people in the top echelons of the ruling party were 'scared to speak their minds because of the stature of Khama' (quoted in *Botswana Gazette*, 18 June 2003). Dynastic tendencies were affirmed by Khama himself when he announced not long after that he expected his younger brother, Tshekedi, to inherit his Serowe parliamentary seat, destined to become vacant by 2008.[22] Automatic succession was then 'entrenched', said President Mogae, and 'a hallmark of our democratic stability.'[23] With the growth model shattered, and the scope for debate ever more limited, the denigration of the opposition rose as the 'ideological' remnant of BDP predominance.

From the start, when the BDP's supremacy was at its highest, Seretse Khama depicted the BNF as subversive. In the 1960s, this frail opposition was seen by Seretse and his security advisers as a Moscow-controlled communist group bent on indoctrinating the civil service, youth and labour groups. BNF offices were raided by the police, a party newspaper seized and party members charged with sedition. From the 1970s to the 1990s the BDP viewed the BNF as unpatriotic and destructive. The ruling party seized every chance to castigate the BNF leader, Kenneth Koma, especially after his entry into parliament in 1984, contributing thereby to Koma's cult status within the opposition (Makgala, 2005: 306–9). President Masire, on the eve of October 1994 elections, accused the BNF of 'unlawfulness [and] political thuggery', and blamed Koma for this (*Mmegi*, 14 October 1994).

Under unrelenting pressure from the BDP, Koma's BNF embraced its own forms of irrationality and incompetence. Instead of understanding the special features of the ruling party's predominance, it insisted that the BDP was bent on establishing a one-party state, and it approached the elections of 1994, when popular awareness of the BDP's failings was escalating, not through the active mobilisation of its potential supporters, but after prolonged talk of boycotting the polls (Good, 1996a: 64). When the election outcome nevertheless gave the BNF the long-awaited possibility of establishing itself as a credible alternative government, the negativism of the BNF's leadership deepened and the opportunity was wilfully destroyed. Makgala has argued that between 1997 and

[22] *Mmegi*, 15 September 2005. The party secretariat pointed out that the selection process worked differently, without visible effect on the vice-president.
[23] 'State of the Nation Address', November 2004.

1999, Koma's self-compromising relations with the BDP destabilised and weakened the opposition. His failure to keep the BNF
united was capitalised on by the BDP to tighten its grip on power.
As the 1999 elections approached, both the BNF and BDP spent a
great deal of time and resources vilifying each other, and from this
diversionary and de-mobilising activity, the predominant party
was necessarily the main beneficiary. Through Koma's weaknesses
the BDP instigated widespread disillusionment among the masses
about the effectiveness of the opposition.[24] In 1999 the country
reverted to the 'dull elections' which Mogae revealingly said
Botswana prefers.[25]

The incompetence of the opposition inevitably leads to the
invincibilty and indispensability of the ruling party. Merafhe
declared in early 1993 that the opposition would gain power only
when the donkey developed horns (*Mmegi*, 26 February 1993).
Koma's successor as BNF president, Otsweletse Moupo, could
claim the support of the 48 per cent of the electorate who voted for
the opposition the previous year – in a continent where opposition parties are usually very weak this was a high level of public
support – and he was the standard bearer of opposition unity on
his arrival in parliament in 2005. But what Makgala terms 'self-
incapacitating tendencies' again took over in the BNF. Like Koma
before him, Moupo failed to build on this strong foundation. The
absence of national office over four decades, limited financial and
other campaigning resources, the bias of the first-past-the-post
electoral system against smaller parties, the powers and preten-
sions of the party leader, all contributed to the BNF's failure.
Again like Koma, Moupo fell prey to accusations both of incompetence and of having an ambivalent personal relationship with the
leadership of the ruling party (Makgala, 2006: 197–9).

Much scope was conceded to the BDP. Ian Khama declared in
public in June 2006 that the BDP was working with the BNF to
destroy the Botswana Congress Party, and after destroying it, the
BDP would finish off the BNF. He told residents in the Tshwaane/
Dutlwe council electorate in the Kalahari to shun the BNF as it
only made empty promises – should they win, he warned, all
development would vanish.[26] The following month Merafhe

---

[24] In 2001 Koma was believed to have entered a profitable business arrangement with Satar
Dada, multi-millionaire car-magnate and BDP treasurer. Makgala (2005: 303, 313–14 and 321).
[25] In an interview with the BBC just after October 1999.
[26] He flew a BDF helicopter into this poor community, and the BDP's 'resource power' was on
full display in the by-election. Tuduetso Setsiba, *Mmegi Online*, 12 June 2006. The BNF candidate won nonetheless by 329 votes to 304.

reiterated the theme of the hopelessness of opposition, and its lack of both viable policies and the human resources necessary for government. If elected, he said that the BNF would 'reverse the gains made in the last 40 years, and destroy the country' and that Moupo himself was the 'quintessence of blunder and inconsequence'.[27]

The tangible hopes which the opposition represented were expressed on 14 October 2005, on the eve of voting in the parliamentary by-election in Gaborone West North, when *Mmegi* devoted its entire front page to a 'Vote Moupo' exhortation. 'This is the first time that all Botswana's opposition parties rally behind a single candidate,' the editor said. It was also a time when 'ever more people are beginning to voice disquiet over the future of Botswana's democracy. The ruling party appeared intolerant of dissent and impatient with the democratic process. There was concern too about the independence of the judiciary. Botswana needed a strong official opposition, and the outcome in the by-election might be the defining moment in Botswana's political history.' Moupo won by a comfortable margin of 1,400 votes. The BCP, second largest opposition party in parliament, congratulated the voters and noted that this was the first contest by a united opposition since the 'Memorandum of Understanding' that they had signed together on 15 August. It was thus 'a critical litmus test of the endorsement of our efforts by the general public'.[28]

By 2000, the ruling party's predominance was almost entirely numerical. Its 'fatigue and decay', as Molomo termed it, was apparent. On the one hand, a man like Kwelagobe had by then held the post of secretary-general for more than 20 years, while on the other, the resignation of Kedikilwe in the middle of the year as minister of education, a senior figure in both government and party, 'mark[ed] serious dissension regarding the process of governance.' Dissension was deep on leadership. The chairman of the BDP Youth Wing/League, Gomolemo Motswaledi, believed that there was a need for debate on automatic succession: 'The current practice, which was introduced more for expediency than principle, shuts out everyone else ... It is unthinkable that a president who is not popularly elected should enjoy the sole right to choose a future president for

---

[27] Letter to the Editor from Lt-General Mompati Merafhe, *Mmegi Online*, 14 July 2006.
[28] Letter to the Editor by Dumelang Saleshando, *Mmegi*, 19 October 2005. A by-election held simultaneously in a council ward in Ramotswa, a BDP stronghold since independence, went the same way.

the nation.'[29] Khama, for his part, appeared 'contemptuous of established norms of government,' parliament particularly. He was autocratic, he boasted of his managerial, not political concerns, and his unique patriotism (Molomo, 2000: 104–6).

At the end of 2004 the BDP remained paralysed by factionalism as it had been for more than a decade, and the struggles were not about ideas. As Motswaledi (by then the former Youth Wing/ League leader) emphasised: 'Within the BDP factions are not about ideas but about alliances brokered when fighting for positions of leadership.'[30]

Predominance was no longer a distinctive development model of realism and success, but a fact of state power. The BDP dominated both the executive and the legislature and the checks and balances of liberal constitutional government were almost redundant. The powers of the president were virtually limitless, and they straddled all the arms of government, not excluding the judiciary (Molomo, 2000: 95 and 97).

The intolerance of criticism

As Sweden exemplifies, predominance is democratic not just on electoral victories and high voting turnout figures, but chiefly and operationally on the extent to which the ruling party and its programme are open to criticism. This not only ensures that citizens have their say about government and its policies on a day-by-day basis, but it also provides for the steady adaptation of the programme to its changing environment. Botswana's ruling elite fails on both criteria, in its strong hostility to criticism and consequencially in its non-adaptability to change.

Government control over information and opinion had been tight in Botswana over the decades. The silence that effectively shrouded the Leno Affair in 1986 was typical of that period of high economic growth and political stagnation. News about this property speculation, involving high ranking politicians and officials, first appeared in the *Botswana Gazette* in January 1986, after which its editor, Alaudin Osman, a Malawian, received a number

---

[29] Molomo (2000: 102 and 105. Further comments: Makgala (n.d.), 'Arrested development: Some notes on ambition and marginalization in the Botswana Democratic Party', mimeo, University of Botswana, pp. 10–11; *The Botswana Gazette*, 18 June 2003, and *Mmegi*, 3 November 2004.

[30] Interview with Kedikilwe, Kwelagobe and Motswaledi, *Sunday Standard*, 12 December 2004.

of anonymous phone calls threatening violence and deportation. The government's attack on the newspaper was direct and devastating: 'virtually instant financial hardship', according to James Zaffiro, with the loss of 'at least half of its pledged advertising during the first week of the story'. Kedikilwe, as minister for presidential affairs – and one of the leading figures named in the affair – was explicit about the intentions of this action. As he told the government-owned *Daily News* on 5 February: "If the press felt frightened by the alleged phone calls made to them they should also be aware that the government was equally concerned about the way in which the press printed pseudonymous letters attacking the government' (Good, 2004: 14–15).

Leno was an incipient scandal quickly suppressed, but government hostility towards free expression remained constant with only the tactics varying. Managing Director William Jones felt that it was a miracle how he and editor Kgosinkwe Moesi had kept the *Botswana Guardian* running through its first years in the 1980s, 'barely breaking even ... snowed under by letters of demand and litigation'. Then the noose seemed to tighten further. In three years, two *Guardian* editors and a reporter were deported, Mxolisis Mgxashe, Charles Mogale, and John Mukela. 'With every PI [Prohibited Immigrant order], the government seemed to become bolder. [Foreign journalists] Gwen Ansell, Samu Zulu were ... sent packing.' When the paper began to employ citizen editors, the government changed tactics. In the 1990s, 'parastatals conspired to impose an advertising boycott', and this well-used tactic was revisited with stronger zeal in 2001.[31]

Senior bureaucrats and politicians, as well as the government, used various legal devices to control both comment and criticism through the 1990s. Merafhe and four other cabinet ministers made defamation claims of P500,000 against the *Guardian* and the *Midweek Sun* for stories involving them in the factionalism visibly rife in the BDP. Sedition laws were utilised against a University of Botswana student, Busang Leburu, chairman of the Anti-Corruption Campaign in 1994. It was a dramatic period on and around the campus: hundreds of riot police had prevented students from demonstrating in the nearby city centre in February, and in October, during the general election, police raided Leburu's rooms searching for material allegedly intended to bring the President into ridicule and contempt (Good, 2004: 12–13).

---

[31] *Botswana Guardian*, 21ˢᵗ Commemorative Edition, 1982–2003, pp. 3–5.

The rapid rise in Botswana's military expenditure though the 1990s was another big issue where the rulers did not welcome comment and criticism. Khama, Merafhe and Kwelagobe all upheld the secrecy and non-accountability of the BDF, with the party's secretary-general insisting that 'people should always be careful what they say about [the army]'. Trade union matters too were drawn under the prohibitions afforded to the state by the National Security Act. In late 1991, both a freelance journalist, Prof Malema, and the editor of *Mmegi* were charged with wrongfully receiving and publishing a secret document concerning an apparent wage agreement between manual workers and the government. The case touched closely on the realities of the subordinate position of unskilled urban workers within the Botswana 'miracle'. Not until 1995 did the high court dismiss the state's case against the journalists, largely on technical-procedural grounds. That government was on constant readiness to silence criticism was abrasively expressed by Merafhe in March 1992, at a public seminar: 'I warn you that [press freedom] has got its own limitation and none of you should feel that he is above the law. The government shall not hesitate to take action against some of you' (Good, 1997: 14–17).

While a lively independent print media has grown steadily in the towns, the government continues to exercise tight control over its own channels. Botswana Television (BTv) is a clear example. Chris Bishop, short-lived editor of news and current affairs at BTv, provided direct evidence in 2001 of the government's rigidity over programme content. In an affidavit before the high court, Bishop provided first-hand evidence of how vice-president Khama intervened to stop him airing a documentary on the hanging of the convicted murderess Marietta Bosch. Bishop actually heard the vice-president say that he would not permit the broadcast of this feature. There were incidents of harrassment against Bishop, 'including veiled threats directed against me' from Andrew Sesinyi, the director of information and broadcasting, as well as from ministers. Another story which he wanted to broadcast on the Basarwa/San people was similarly suppressed.

Certain ministers, he testified, considered BTv 'as their personal privilege [sic] to use at will.' He was informed that Molosiwa Selepeng, permanent secretary to the president, and the president's office were, as he said, 'at their wits end' about us, and they would be directly controlled from the office of the president. Bishop took the threat seriously because of Selepeng's public statement to the effect that 'BTv does not have editorial independence and is required to portray government in a positive light.' [32]

Bishop's experience in a senior editorial position was in no way unusual, as the government itself acknowledged. Kwelagobe, Minister of Presidential Affairs, declared at a *kgotla* in Molepolole, April 2002, that the Dept of Information and Broadcasting and the radio, television and news-gathering agencies under it, 'should be a lap-dog of government. It belongs to government, and what it does should represent the ideals of the government of the day' (*Botswana Guardian*, 19 April 2002).

Freedom of speech is open within Botswana's democracy if one has nothing serious to say, but the presidency and opposition unity are conjoined issues of high sensitivity in the altered post-1994 environment. Journalists at both the *Guardian* and *Mmegi* were in the firing-line of government intolerance and intransigence from 2000 onwards.

On 7 January 2000 the *Botswana Guardian* devoted its front page to a picture of Vice-President Khama in military uniform towering over a diminutive President Mogae, with the caption 'The Shrinking President'. The editor, Outsa Mokone, said that he believed Botswana to be in a crisis situation and that the country's future was dependent on decisive action from Mogae. The picture may have been disrespectful but it was also appropriate, Mokone explained: 'the situation called for our shock-therapy picture and story' ('Editor's Reply', 21 January 2000).

Scholarly and party-political opinion was in accord. Mpho Molomo wrote in 2000 of the inability of President Mogae to control Khama and of the latter's numerous utterances that only served to undermine the integrity and authority of the president (Molomo, 2000: 104). Opinion on the presidency and presidential powers was suppressed in the BDP but occasionally burst forth. In the previous sitting of parliament, Oliphant Mfa, MP for Sebina/Gweta, warned that Botswana might be a dictatorship after Mogae stepped down.

On or around 23 April 2000 the president issued a verbal directive to the effect that all state and parastatal bodies, and private companies in which the state had a majority shareholding should cease placing advertisements in the *Botswana Guardian* and *Midweek Sun* (a sister paper). As indicated in an affidavit issued by the permanent secretary to the president, the government's

[32] *Botswana Guardian*, 13 July, and *Sunday Independent* (Johannesburg), 15 July 2001. Bishop resigned.

expectation was that the two papers should adjust their editorial policy 'so that it conforms to the views of their advertisers', that is, as Justice Isaac Lesetedi clarified, reportage that met government approval.[33]

Government advertising constituted of course a key income source for the papers, and when it suddenly dried up, the publishers soon began to feel the pinch. Although reluctant at first, the publisher, Jones, eventually agreed to take court action. The editor stood by his guns, explaining his view that Botswana was 'afflicted by the battered-wife syndrome – each time we are short-changed by our leadership, we try to make excuses for them, for fear of appearing disrespectful'. The realities demanded a different response: 'the media in Botswana is the last line of defence ... Botswana ... is a one-party dominant state. The political opposition is fragmented and weak. The parliamentary watchdog role has been eroded by the overwhelming majority of [BDP] MPs ... civil society is small and still developing' ('Editor's Reply', 21 January 2000).

The high court's decision in favour of the newspapers in September 2001 was quite different from the earlier case involving *Mmegi* and national security in 1995, when the substantive issues were avoided. Justice Lesetedi tackled the big issues of freedom and democracy directly. He found that the government ban on advertising was unconstitutional and ordered the lifting of the president's directive. 'Freedom of expression is one of the fundamental cornerstones of every democratic society [and] freedom of the media is but one aspect of that.' Lesetedi argued much as Mokone had done, that the media's role was vital. It is normal that the media forms the vehicle for communication between the governed and those that govern. It is through the media 'that members of the society communicate their ideas and feelings about the way they are governed'. Criticism of government was both warranted and necessary, and it should be understood as such by the governors. Responsibilities accompanied power-holding in a democracy. 'Those who hold power', Lesetedi affirmed, 'should be more tolerant [than ordinary individual members of society] of such criticism' (*Botswana Gazette* and *Midweek Sun*, 19 September 2001).

Lesetedi's arguments were ignored by the BDP when they rushed to condemn *Mmegi's* editor, Mesh Moeti, in the wake of his 'Vote

[33] From the ruling in the high court in September 2001, *Botswana Gazette*, 7 July 2001.

Moupo' recommendation of 14 October 2005. Comma Serema, the party's executive secretary, described Moeti's commentary as 'in bad taste ... unprofessional, biased and irresponsible reporting', and it took the paper to the media complaints committee. The editor explained that *Mmegi* was 'merely exercising our right to express our view', and they 'always give the [BDP's] spokesperson ample opportunity to respond to criticism' (*Mmegi Online*, 19 October 2005). In November the complaints committee found in favour of the paper, saying that what was published was an opinion not a statement of fact, and that a newspaper was entitled to publish opinion on any issue of public interest. *Mmegi* had taken a position on a matter it considered to be of public interest.[34]

This did not save Moeti. As rumours circulated in the media that the government was again about to withdraw advertising from independent newspapers, presidential spokesman Jeff Ramsay visited *Mmegi*, ostensibly to declare that such speculation was baseless. He insisted that there was a distinction between the government and the ruling party and he was reported as saying that the latter could not influence the former in making decisions (*Mmegi Online*, 28 October 2005). On the same day the resignation of Mesh Moeti as editor of *Mmegi*, after 18 months at the helm of the paper, was announced.[35]

The government continues to deny journalists the freedom to write what they choose on grounds of patriotism and national interest. In September 2006 the deputy permanent secretary in the ministry of science, communications and technology, Andrew Sesinyi, instructed all departmental heads in the state media to ensure that what was termed negative reporting on the relocations from the CKGR, was always strongly contrasted with freshly-sought government statements. He insisted that professional journalists were 'first and foremost patriots before anything else.' The government media was 'the sole weapon of the nation in the economic war [that was being] waged via the far more developed media networks of the western world.' He also lashed out, it was said, at the private media, which he accused of rallying behind the enemy: Survival International, he said, had taken the side of CKGR residents and had waged economic war against Botswana (*Mmegi Online*, 26 September 2006).

Not long after this writer's expulsion, at least two journalists whose reporting was critical of the government were also deported.

---

[34] The verdict of the committee, *Mmegi Online*, 11 November 2005.
[35] 'Editor leaves', *Mmegi Online*, 28 October 2005. The two stories were treated separately.

On 27 July 2005, the Zimbabwean journalist, Rodrick Mukumbira, who reported for the *Ngami Times* was expelled, and on 5 August another Zimbabwean reporter was banned from entering the country. The US department of state noted reports of government officials who had discouraged academics from presenting papers, especially in international fora, that were critical of the government.[36] My experience in Sweden, and that of Teedzani Thapelo, (discussed below), testifies to the accuracy of this report.

The government did not rely only on patriotic journalism and coerced journalistic and academic opinion, but waged its own propaganda campaigns on major issues such as the San, the CKGR and diamond production. The Botswana high commissioner in London, Roy Blackbeard, confirmed in February 2007 that his office had intensified the fight against Survival International, a London-based advocacy group which supported the rights of indigenous peoples worldwide. Batswana living in Britain were being asked by the public about the CKGR case, and the relevance of the film *Blood Diamond*, which portrays the problems of alluvial mining in conflict situations in Africa, so 'we found it valuable to help them out'. People were being invited to a series of meetings in many cities, 'to ensure that Batswana living here really understand' the importance of the diamond industry. If the country relaxed, he warned, its international reputation would diminish. The government had to be very pro-active, and the services of British public relations' specialists had been engaged (*Mmegi Online*, 23 February 2007).

The government had a broad campaign for some time targeting so-called 'detractors' like Survival, but also defending diamond production – 'Diamonds for Development' – and attempting to justify the removals of San from the CKGR. Near the end of 2006, the government's operation could be said to be 'costing Botswana a fortune' not only in money, but also in terms of 'the energy and time spent on it by ... senior government officials and ministers'.[37] PR specialists were certainly involved in this wide-ranging public relations/propaganda effort. An employee at the London high commission, Dawn Parr, had given a talk at the London School of Hygiene and Tropical Medicine in March 2007, arguing that the

---

[36] US department of state, Botswana, 'Country Reports on Human Rights Practices – 2005', Released by the bureau of democracy, human rights and labour, 8 March 2006, p. 4. Lord Avebury noted that Mukumbira had been given seven days notice to leave, and that the committee to protect journalists had linked his expulsion to his reporting on the CKGR. House of Lords, debate on Botswana, 13 March 2006, column 1068.

[37] Dan Moabi, 'Whither Botswana?', *Mmegi Online*, 23 November 2006.

government was right to evict San from the CKGR. The *Botswana Guardian* had reported in 2005 that Parr, a British national, had been appointed as communications director in the high commission on a contract for three years and a salary of P500,000 a year. Her role, according to Blackbeard, was to minimise the damage caused to Botswana's image by groups like Survival.[38]

The party is the elective, democratic element in the ruling system, although it has never succeeded in reaching out to the bulk of the electorate. But its role and relevance were reduced as more and more major issues were placed outside the bounds of public discourse. Its predominance was dented by the Leno exposures and undermined fatally by the corruption of the early 1990s. The growth model was the foundation of Seretse Khama's and Masire's rule, but the greed of the rulers showed that the returns went, not to the contributors to national development, but to the political controllers of the system. No replacement model has been devised by President Mogae, and the BDP's rule is bereft of ideas.

The demonisation of the opposition, the silencing of 'unpatriotic' individuals in teaching and the media, and the waging of a propaganda war against external critics, are the active elements remaining in the ruling party's supremacy. Negativism is being elevated and sterility superimposed on stagnation.

[38] Rebaone Odirile, in *The Botswana Guardian*, 11 November 2005, and First People of the Kalahari, Press Release, 'A Lot of Money Can be Wasted on Untruths', 2 April 2007. Researchers at the London School of Hygiene and Tropical Medicine had a project on indigenous peoples and they had published an article on the health and welfare of the San in *The Lancet* in 2006.

4
The Social Consequences of Diamond Dependency

Show us a country that ignores the rural sector and we will show you a country with a high poverty quotient. Show us a country with a high poverty quotient and we will show you a country packed with implosive material.[1]

We thank the Almighty God for granting us the mineral resources that the BDP government has prudently managed and enabled us to transform our fortunes.[2]

Diamond wealth and fast growth, in an undiversified economy where agriculture was withering and manufacturing never growing, produced serious and extensive social consequences. Poverty and inequalities were the worst of them, from which 'chains of inequality-disadvantage' extended through unemployment, hunger, child mortality, crime and punishment, and poor human development generally. On recent UNDP and World Bank data for 1993–2003, 23 per cent of people lived on less than a dollar a day, and some 50 per cent got less than two dollars. The probability at birth of not surviving to age 40, 2000–05, affected 62 per cent of the cohort; adult illiteracy remained at 21 per cent in 2003, and the numbers of people experiencing chronic food insufficiency was approaching 24 per cent in 2001.[3]

Poverty is experienced relative to society and especially to those at or near the top of this comparatively rich country. Diamonds had brought fast growth over three decades and easy money for the small ruling elite administering it and those seeking government contracts and tenders. As already noted, diamond wealth was specifically utilised for accumulation, or as David Magang, former

---

[1] Mokubung Nkomo, University of Pretoria, *Business Day*, 11 December 2006.

[2] President Mogae, State of the Nation address, 13 November 2006.

[3] UNDP, *Human Development Report 2004*, p. 90, 148 and 162, and World Bank (2004), *African Development Indicators*, p. 310. Adult illiteracy was markedly lower in Mauritius, South Africa, Namibia and Zimbabwe.

minerals minister stressed, for investment in cash assets and to support public expenditure and consumption.[4] Severe inequalities were the necessary result of fast growth under such conditions.

While the richest 10 per cent of income earners received 56.6 per cent of national income, and the richest twenty per cent commanded 70.3 per cent, on the same data, the poorest 20 per cent of people received only 2.2 per cent and those in the very lowest decile 0.7 per cent of the country's income. The gap between the top and bottom deciles was 77.6, and this income differential was the third highest in all of Africa – only Lesotho (narrowly), and Namibia, were more inequitable. The Gini coefficient, a comparative measure of inequality (where zero represents perfect equality and 100 perfect inequality and readings above 50 are deemed critical) presented similar data. Botswana's figure was 63, one of the world's worst; it was for instance 59.3 in Brazil; 57.8 in South Africa; and 63.2 in Lesotho.[5]

In terms of wage incomes actually received, the gap between the rich and the poor is gapingly wide. A cabinet minister drew an average gross salary of some P36,800 a month in 2005, (composed of basic salary of P18,300; housing allowance of P11,250; constituency allowance that topped at P6,000; and other perks of some P2,500). A permanent secretary got a basic salary of P24,000 and 'over P35,000' when all allowances were included.[6] At the same time the minimum wage for an unskilled worker was only P432 monthly with no allowances.[7] If P36,000 is taken as the average salary of top governmental people – leaving aside their earnings from associated business activities – the differential between them and the unskilled worker is some 84 : 1.

Such big differentials represent endorsed and durable wages policy. In 1990 the government had firmly rejected proposals for raising minimum wages for unskilled workers in agriculture and domestic service (on grounds of their extreme poverty) as 'unenforcable, and thus impracticable'. But for high-level management new and increased salaries were enthusiastically embraced. Top bureaucrats had to be 'adequately reward[ed]' and their skills retained to 'maintain the efficiency of an increasingly complex

[4] Thato Maribe, 'Magang attacks government', *Sunday Standard*, 19 September 2006.

[5] Cf. Norway on 25.8 and Japan on 24.9. UNDP, *Human Development Report 2005*, Table 15.

[6] 'How fat is an MP's pay cheque?', *Mmegi Online*, 4 November 2005.

[7] Ditshwanelo, 'Shadow Report to [CERD]', 68th Session, Geneva, 3–6 March 2006. p. 22, based on the figures of the Dept of Labour for a 45-hour work week.

public sector'. The unskilled worker contributed little to the growth economy, while senior bureaucrats were 'essential'. Differentials in their favour were to be 'implemented without delay'.[8]

Income inequalities widened over the decade to 2003. The poorest 40 per cent, the near majority of the population, experienced a fall in their income share from a total of 11.6 per cent in 1993/94 to only 5.8 per cent ten years later, while the share of the richest 20 per cent rose from 59.3 per cent at the start of the period to 70.9 per cent in 2002/03.[9]

Emphasising the causality between diamond wealth and poverty, the data show a low and deteriorating Human Development Index (the HDI is a composite measure of progress in terms of length and health of life, knowledge and standard of living). On recent data, Botswana's HDI value was 0.565, and its ranking out of 177 countries examined was only 131 (below Namibia, South Africa and Myanmar). Human development in Botswana was deteriorating during periods of rapid, diamond-led growth. The index was moving downwards over more than a decade; from a high of 0.675 in 1990, to 0.666 in 1995, 0.620 in 2000, to 0.589 in 2002 and 0.570 in 2004. While 21 countries recorded a drop in HDI between 1990 and 2001, Botswana was the only one to do this while enjoying high growth.[10] Poor developing countries with low or negative growth such as Cape Verde and Guyana, enjoyed better HDI rankings, respectively 105 and 107, than rich Botswana. Neighbouring Mauritius, another UMC, enjoyed an HDI ranking of 63, the second-highest in Africa.[11]

Unemployment was estimated in 2005 at between 24 and 40 per cent, with youth unemployment at the top of the range. Unemployment and low wages for the poor were obviously inter-related, and closely related also to diamond dependency. The capital-intensive diamond industry, as Ndzinge accurately recognises, 'does not create jobs'.[12] Infrastructural development had

---

[8] Republic of Botswana (1990), 'The revised national policy on incomes, employment, prices and profits', draft white paper, pp. 26, 36 and 39.

[9] CERD, 'Reports submitted by states parties under article 9 of the convention: Addendum Botswana', 23 March 2005, pp. 14–15, based on household income and expenditure surveys.

[10] Clover (2003: 1).

[11] *HDR Report 2005/6*, and Gideon Nkala, 'Most Batswana Live on P12 a day', *Mmegi Online*, 24 November 2006.

[12] Alphonse Ndzinge (2006) 'Poverty Hand in Hand With Wealth', *Sunday Standard*, 3 October, and Tudetso Setsiba, 'Anti-Poverty Measures Worry Experts', *Mmegi Online*, 18 October 2006.

characterised the high growth of the 1980s, with consequent labour demands, but that phase was apparently over.[13]

An improvement in this situation could not be forecast with confidence. Growth continued in 2005, but the undiversified economy could generate few jobs. Dumelang Saleshando, BCP MP for Gaborone Central, told parliament that effective rural minimum wages were not possible when unemployment remained above 24 per cent and a reserve army of poor Zimbabweans existed precariously in the countryside (*Mmegi Online*, 18 August 2006). The data, informed opinion and everyday experience pointed in the same direction. Over 450 applicants were invited for interview for a single post of office cleaner at the national archives in Gaborone in November, and more than 600 people were attracted to the job of immigration clerk – the list of lucky names covered six pages in the government-owned *Daily News* (*Mmegi Online*, 17 November 2006).

Advantaging the few

The political culture of today's 'demo-feudal' republic, as Kedikilwe has it, remains permeated by the symbiosis between wealth and political power, which contributed to early economic and state development, to the formation of the BDP and to state and national development thereafter. Three stages in governance and development have preceded the present. The first decade of independence was one of path-finding in the poor country and relative probity in government under Seretse Khama's influence and that of disinterested foreign advisors. Things began to change in the second stage in the 1970s, after cattle production was sharply intensified, diamonds got underway, and individual wealth accumulation began to be realised by the rural capitalists and bureaucrats in the BDP and government. Inequalities were officially accepted, but their impact was delayed and muted as infrastructural development brought broad benefits.[14]

The reality of fast growth in the third stage in the 1980s, as shown in Chapters 1 and 2, facilitated increased wealth seeking.

[13] Speaking at a forum on economic diversification in Botswana, *Botswana Gazette*, 29 September 2006. But some 'major projects', in dams, electrification, education facilities and energy, were forecast in the *Budget Speech 2007*, p.3.

[14] Ornulf Gulbrandsen (2007), 'Popular reactions to the hidden exercise of political power: Botswana and Italy compared', Social Anthropology Seminar Paper, University of Bergen, 19 March, pp. 18–32.

The rules were changed accordingly. The private business activities of public servants were accorded official, legal recognition in 1982, the start of a boom period. They could engage in commercial agriculture and in 'the ownership and development of land and other property', and hold a minority of shares in a company if the officer had fully paid for them, as stated in the white paper of December 1982. Elite corruption finally burst into the open in the 1990s when popular forces – trade unions, students, the BNF – intruded into politics for the first time. The ruling elite was forced to accept limited reforms. The DCEC and ombudsman were subordinated to presidential power, but their existence mollified outsiders. Close linkages between business and government continued.

The perception by outsiders that Botswana is corruption-free is a 'myth to displace all myths', Dingake insists, and 'all Batswana know' that corruption is concealed under what he terms the BDP patronage system and executive domination over parliament and judiciary.[15]

Corruption and mismanagement are readily identifiable in contracts and tendering procedures, non-conflicts of interest, and cattle production through the 1990s and subsequently. A prominent individual case concerned Michael Tshipinare, in late 1991, assistant minister of local government lands and housing and a director of the construction company Spectra Botswana. Spectra was associated with a bid to construct a new headquarters for the BHC, and granted Tshipinare an unsecured loan of P500,000. He was subsequently found guilty of corruption and sentenced to one year in jail, but released on appeal four months later, after the high court found that he had been engaged in a perfectly normal business transaction. Such a decision was indicative of a weak judiciary, when a minister could acquire some P1.3 million through the award of a contract from within his own ministry to a company of

---

[15] Michael Dingake, 'As I see it', *Mmegi Online*, 26 September 2006. The index of Transparency International is primarily based on the perceptions of businessmen, with the disadvantage that some might see only the 'miracle' they were disposed to see. Ex-President Masire's understanding is clearer today, and he points to the 'prevalence of poverty and the widening gap' between sections of society, along with 'growing signs of corruption'. 'Democracy in Botswana: Challenges and motivations since 1996', lecture at the University of Botswana, 20 September 2006, pp. 25–26. A corruption survey within the local business sector in July 2005 had found that 74 per cent of respondents believed that corruption was increasing. US Department of State, 'Botswana, Country Reports on Human Rights Practices – 2006', p. 6. The disjunction between outside perceptions of corruption in Botswana and the internal realities is considered further at the end of this section.

which he was simultaneously a director. The state did not appeal against this judgement.[16]

Special tendering and procurement arrangements operated within the military. The BDF responded angrily to allegations in 1997 that General Ian Khama was running the organisation like a family business. Secure government contracts were allegedly the basis for the operation. The BDF was said to have purchased equipment from a company called Seleka Springs whose directors were Tshekedi Khama and Anthony Khama, younger brothers of the General. The military also purchased vehicles, especially Landrovers, from Lobatse Delta, also under the directorship of the Khama twins. Another company linked to the family name was said to be Hot Bread Limited, from which the army was believed to buy some of its food. Another person involved in the running of Hot Bread was the wife of Brigadier Ndelu Seretse, a cousin to the commander.[17]

Apparent irregularities in the BDF's procurement processes remained current in 2005, with investigations involving 'some former senior officers', focusing on the purchase of five Strikemaster aircraft bought from Kenya, and a number of French-made army vehicles purchased through a local supplier. The aircraft were found on arrival to be 'unable to fly', and the vehicles were said to be too expensive to maintain. The procurements were believed to have been 'highly unorthodox'. Investigations may have begun in 2003, but the DCEC refused either to confirm or deny its involvement.[18]

President Masire had consistently refused to disclose the extent of his land and cattle holdings, despite strong suggestions that they totalled between eleven and twenty cattle and ostrich farms.[19] He subsequently admitted that he was among cattle farmers who

---

[16] Justice Gyeke-Dako found that 'the accused [Tshipinare] as a director of Spectra was entitled to promote the interests of his company'. Good (1994), pp. 503 and 520. The building project collapsed in the wake of the scandals at the BHC and the Christie report as considered in Chapter 3.

[17] Outsa Mokone, *Botswana Gazette*, 21 May 1997. General Khama denied any conflict of interest because he was not a director or shareholder in any of his younger brothers' businesses, and he declared that he was not involved in the evaluation of tenders or the procurement processes. Joseph Balise, *Botswana Guardian*, 6 June 1997.

[18] Batlhalefi Leagajang, 'DCEC investigates ex-BDF Top Brass?', *Botswana Gazette*, 6 April 2005.

[19] Jwaneng mayor, Henry Mogapi, and the *Sun* newspaper claimed that he owned nine farms in the Kgalagadi area alone, and the deeds registry reported that he had been acquiring farms since 1973, but it was 'difficult to get the precise number ... since some of them are registered under the names of his companies', such as Atis Ranch Pty Ltd. and GM Five. 'Masire and his farms', *The Midweek Sun*, 29 November 1995.

benefited from new tax concessions introduced when he was vice-president and minister of finance. Mokone reported in 1996 that it was an 'open secret in government circles' that big cattle men 'use[d] the system to dodge tax'. They had paid virtually no tax since independence: in 1992/93, for instance, cattlemen paid only P1.7 million in tax on beef exports worth some P160 million, and among those who benefited here were Sir Ketumile and the former cabinet minister Patrick Balopi.[20]

The former denied axiomatically that there was anything wrong in being, as he put it, 'a successful farmer' while 'holding the office of president'[21] and determining the government's policies towards agriculture thereby.[22] Well before the 1990s the government had put in place a range of state supports and subsidies that made large livestock ownership extremely attractive: funding the building of veterinary fences and water sources; providing generous vaccine and veterinary services; establishing very low rents on new (TGLP) ranches (some P250 a year on a property of eight square kilometres); supporting the cattle barons' practice of 'dual grazing' (on both their own and others' communal land); and maintaining favourable slaughter (as well as taxation) policies. All this brought big benefits to wealthy cattle and borehole owners who were simultaneously highly placed members of the government and party. Subsidies alone were worth around 50 per cent of a rancher's production costs.[23] Seretse Khama had owned about 30,000 cattle, and by the 1980s, on conservative estimates, very large herds were held by just five to ten per cent of all farmers.[24]

Commercial involvements on the part of senior public office holders are commonplace. Mogae came to power declaring his strong opposition to the financially pampered cattle industry, and Ian Khama at the same time was known to have 'a business interest in the tourism industry', as supplement to his environmentalist connections.[25] But President Mogae's own extensive business engagements were confirmed when he admitted at an angry press conference that he was a shareholder in Motswedi, which in turn

---

[20] Outsa Mokone, *Botswana Gazette*, 10 and 31 July 1996, and *Botswana Guardian*, 17 September 1999.

[21] *Botswana Daily News*, 24 November 1995.

[22] Gulbrandsen (2007) notes that that Masire was 'widely reported as greedy and corrupt', p. 34.

[23] A. Cullis and C. Watson (2003), 'Winners and losers: Privatising the commons in Botswana' Briefing Paper, International Institute for Environment and Development and RECONCILE, December, pp. 12–13.

[24] Good (1999), 'The State and Extreme Poverty in Botswana', pp. 189–90.

[25] Mokone, *Botswana Gazette*, 21 May 1997.

was a shareholder in Owens Corning (OCPB), and involved in sup-
plying pipes for the large-scale North-South Water Carrier project,
along with the Botswana Development Corporation (BDC).[26] The
president had rented out his house to OCPB since 1973 at a rent of
P5,115 a month, and had also received a loan from them.[27] He had
been in a joint venture with BDC on at least one previous occasion,
Balopi had acted similarly, and so had Chief Justice Nganunu.[28]
These were matters of fact not allegation.

Other notable business entanglements at the same time involved
Kedikilwe, as minister of finance and development planning, Satar
Dada, BDP treasurer and car magnate, and a textile company
named Haltek Pty Ltd. Dada and Kedikilwe had established relations, which they pictured as friendly dealings, when the former
purchased a share in the minister's Tuli-block farm, and the latter
assisted the magnate in opening a supermarket.[29] Dada had also
purchased Algo Spinning and Weaving, injected some P10 million
into the company, then looked to buyers in order to concentrate
his already successful interests; he owned the Toyota and Land
Rover franchises in Botswana; the latter were the preferred vehicles for the BDF and police. Haltex sought financial assistance
from government, and the size of its needs – some P50 million –
was outside normal FAP limits. President Masire, assisted by his
finance minister, helped push through the award of a special
foreign investment fund specifically to finance Haltek, which was
also negotiating to purchase Algo Spinners from Dada. Kedikilwe
said: 'that I am close to Dada is irrelevant. I have supported and
will continue to support facilities aimed at creating employment
for Batswana.'[30] Dada assisted the BDP in its financial and material
preparations for the 1999 elections, and he became an appointed
MP thereafter.[31]

The Central Tender Board (CTB) fell under the supervision of
MFDP, and Jacob Nkate was both assistant minister there and a
director of ZAC Construction. After speculation that he may have
influenced decisions to award tenders to ZAC, already embroiled

[26] By 2005 some P1.3 billion was reportedly invested in this project. Editorial, *Mmegi Online*, 4
November 2005.

[27] Prof Malema, 'Mogae breaks the ice', *Mmegi*, 14 August 1998.

[28] *Botswana Gazette*, 3 April 1996.

[29] Further details are in Good (2004), pp.126–9.

[30] *Botswana Guardian*, 8 September and 2 October 1998.

[31] Good (2002: 20–21). Dada wanted President Masire to buy shares in his new Mercedes
dealership but, on advice from Mogae, he declined; the dealership 'ended up selling equipment to the mines at Orapa and Jwaneng' (Masire 2006: 242).

in corruption allegations, Nkate resigned. Kedikilwe, a director of the Italswana Construction Company since 1985, refused to step down on similar grounds. He claimed that his directorship was 'common knowledge' and asserted that a minister could not influence decisions of the CTB.[32] This did not stop Kedikilwe, as former minister, from claiming later that Botswana's tendering process was being manipulated by a 'mafia clique' which decided who was awarded which tender (*Botswana Gazette*, 22 August 2001).

A preliminary report by Transparency International Botswana (TIBOT) in late 2001 got closer to the realities than its parent body. It suggested that Botswana was a country where a wealthy ruling elite used their influence and authority to enrich themselves at the expense of the majority of the people. Elias Dewah of BOCCIM noted that bureaucratic bottlenecks and unnecessary regulations created opportunities for officials to abuse their power and for businessmen to seek ways of exploiting commercial opportunities. A representative of MISA lamented the aura of secrecy in which the government cloaked itself, while the Law Society called for laws which strengthened the independence of the judiciary.[33]

The prevailing system is maintained despite the many revelatory events. After cattle-lung disease broke out in Ngamiland in early 1995, some 300,000 cattle were slaughtered to control the disease, and costly re-stocking measures followed. Suspicions of considerable wrong-doing persisted and a commission of inquiry produced a report in 2004 at a cost of nearly P500,000. Against the popular feeling that 'some revered big names cropped up during the commission's hearings', assistant minister Olifant Mfa revealed that the government had decided not to release the findings because it did not see the need to do so. He said, 'it does not mean that if we talk about transparency that everything will be made public.' The commission's chairman, Kgalalelo Monthe, had complained about the delay in releasing his report.[34]

On top of ramifying conflicts of interest and tendering/contracts manipulations, land allocations appear wide open to abuse by those in power and those seeking their assistance. According to the judicial commission of inquiry reporting in 2004, the state land act 'vests the power to make, execute or grant rights in state

---

[32] *Botswana Guardian*, 9 April 1999. Like Kwelagobe and others before him, Nkate was soon returned to office.

[33] Extracts from the report on the National symposium on corruption and transparency, TIBOT, *Botswana Gazette*, 3 October 2001.

[34] Morula Morula, 'Transparency dealt a blow as lung disease report gets thrashed', *The Midweek Sun*, 21 July 2004.

land on the president.'[35] These powers are substantive, and he can make meaningful decisions as to when, to whom and how the land can be allocated. Additionally, the minister of lands and housing has wide powers under the act in dealing with applications for planning permission, including changes in land use, and these decisions are final and cannot be appealed to any court.

The commission found that in a substantial number of applications before them, serious irregularities had occurred in both land allocation and land use, with questionable and improper decisions, which created perceptions of favouritism or worse. The list of files before the inquiry involved Gaborone-based companies such as Universal Builders, Kalahari Gateway and Nina Property Management. Margaret Nasha, current lands minister, and her predecessors Jacob Nkate and Daniel Kwelagobe featured prominently in the hearings. The commission believed that the irregularities they had uncovered probably reflected an even wider picture within urban areas elsewhere. It judged that 'the ministers being the ones who approved the allocations and applications for change of use, bear the ultimate responsibility', but it failed to name the ministerial wrong doers. They also re-affirmed the president's powers to deal directly with any land allocation matter that comes to him either directly or in any other manner, and that his decisions were not subject to appeal.[36] It seemed likely that wrong-doing might well continue.

To note two cases emerging at the hearings. Daniel Kwelagobe appeared to answer questions about the allocation of land on which the Molapo Crossing Mall stood in 2004. Ronald Marsh had been offered the land concerned in January 1998, through his company Hitech Investments. The Khama twins were named as directors of Hitech. The price was set at P734,000, and the land was offered on condition that it was to be used strictly for civic, community and recreational activities. The company soon applied to change the use of the land, however, and it was granted additional land measuring 16,100 square metres. Marsh sought a meeting with Kwelagobe, after which the minister determined that the land in question should be sub-divided with one-third re-zoned for commercial use. Marsh admitted to the Lesetedi Commission that his original concept for the land had thereby

---

[35] Republic of Botswana (2004), *Report of the judicial commission of inquiry into state land allocations in Gaborone* (the Lesetedi Commission), Gaborone, July, pp. ii, v and xvii and 153–71.
[36] The Lesetedi Commission.

been realised. Kwelagobe responded to calls for his resignation with 'that's nonsense'. [37]

Universal Builders also benefited greatly from irregular procedures. It acquired the land on which another valuable Gaborone shopping mall, the Westgate Complex, was constructed without criteria for tender, and at a bid of P36 per square metre, reportedly half the value of a similar serviced plot. It also applied for the so-called Maruapula plot, stating that it wanted the land to provide housing for low-income people. It received the land but claimed to be unable to meet the buying price of P8.75 a square metre. According to the commission's findings, the minister, without checking, halved the price to about P4 a metre, and then 'settled for a figure of P1 million in total.' Universal Builders then used the land to build housing 'way out of reach of low-income earners'. Universal reportedly owned at least 700 plots of land in Gaborone alone. [38] *Mmegi's* editor noted the accomplishments of the Lesetedi commission in laying bare the administrative chicanery employed to rob Batswana of land, and showing that the country's politicians consented to some of these corrupt acts. However, the findings of the commission were largely ignored. [39]

But the Lesetedi Commission's suggestion that a wider pattern of irregular allocations probably existed continued to reverberate. At the end of 2006, 36 small communal farmers in southern Kgalagadi had a case before the Land Tribunal in Tsabong, claiming the improper allocation by the Kgalagadi land board of four large leasehold farms; no fencing feasibility studies had allegedly been done, and the farms had not been advertised. The land board was said to have ignored correct procedures by granting common law leases on two de-zoned ranches to two South Africans, while two other farms were also awarded to W. F. du Preez and H. J. van Romberg, both of whom were supposedly in a joint venture with the former minister of agriculture, Ronald Sebego. The communal farmers claimed that strong indications of corruption existed. [40]

When serious irregularities occurred involving the allocation and use of large plots of land in Gaborone, about 50,000 people were awaiting plot allocations countrywide, according to the

[37] Bashi Letsididi, 'Don't shout at me from rooftops – DK', *Midweek Sun*, 25 August 2004.

[38] 'Universal Builders' irregular land deals', *Mmegi Online*, 29 June 2006.

[39] Editorial, 'Who remembers Lesetedi Commission?', *Mmegi Online*, 5 April 2006.

[40] As assistant minister of local government, Sebego had earlier improperly allocated BHC houses to his friends, and the Christie report found that he bore 'his share of political responsibility for the BHC debacle.' Some 20,000 people were on the corporation's formal waiting-list for housing at this time. Good (1994: 505) and *Mmegi Online*, 14 December 2006.

secretary general of the manual workers union, Johnson Motshwarakgole. Some of them had been waiting for years. Inequalities pervaded land allocation. Most Gaborone residents waited over 20 years to obtain a residential plot of land, but Lesetedi had indicated it was not uncommon to find land board members in many places owning a multiplicity of plots. Poverty was being perpetuated by government policies that favoured the rich, Secretary General Motshwarakgole concluded.[41]

In addition, housing policy largely ignored the poor. The BHC acknowledged the problem of land shortages in the cities, but had nevertheless continued to build houses unaffordable to ordinary Batswana. In an interview with *Mmegi*, the chairman of the BHC, McLean Letshwiti, allowed that it was very expensive to acquire a house, and admitted: 'I don't think we are helping the low income earners.' Over the previous five years, the corporation had only been building 50 to 100 houses a year.[42]

A civil society-based conference in September 2005 also noted that policy-making processes were unfavourable to the poor. Some participants highlighted the government's recent decision to raze the housing of poor and landless people at Mogoditshane, the large peri-urban village adjacent to the capital.[43] Such actions vividly recalled the circumstances highlighted by the Kgabo Commission, noted above, of the malpractice of leading ministers and the disrepute of the government among the landless in the conurbation a decade earlier. The situation in 2000, according to Lands Minister Nkate, was just as it had been in 1988–90. Residents agreed, and claimed that squatting was unavoidable since outsiders were given priority by the land board because they had money to bribe them, and that they obtained residential plots when they intended them for business. Nkate was unmoved and advised long-term squatters to pay the P5,000 that the government demanded to legalise their occupancy, or strong measures would be taken against them.[44] The inequalities in land allocation and usage were patent and connected downwards to the deepening of poverty and upwards to the benefit of the rich and to the presidency.

[41] Editorial, *Mmegi Online*, 21 October 2005. Quotation by Tuduetso Setsiba, *Mmegi Online*, 23 October 2006.

[42] Quoted by Wanetsha Mosinyi, 'BHC to build affordable housing', *Mmegi Online*, 13 December 2006.

[43] Joel Konopo, 'Civil society should be organised', *Mmegi Online*, 28 September 2005.

[44] Further details in Tebogo Mogale, 'Land minister and Mogoditshane residents heading for a confrontation', *Botswana Gazette*, 26 January 2000.

When privatisation was being officially portrayed as a panacea for Botswana's economic malaise in late 2006, observers also noted the increasing control which the government had acquired over many parastatals and government-owned companies, in water, telecommunications, transportation, banking, post and power. The appointment of directors and chief executive officers was a favoured device in late 2006. Convoluted changes within the Public Enterprises Evaluation and Privatisation Agency (PEEPA), in which both Mogae and Ian Khama were directly engaged, were then a case in point. The expansion of the board and the appointment to it of Debswana's Blackie Marole asserted the over-arching control of the ruling elite, but it came with many costs. Loyalty not merit governed choices, and the integrity and reputation of key parastatals suffered.[45] The imminent privatisation programme seemed threatened, since it appeared to follow that cabinet ministers would have inside information about everything to do with privatisation. It was unlikely that the selling of public enterprises could be anything other than corrupt. To all intents and purposes the privatisation process was shaping up to be 'a feeding frenzy by the already well-connected and the powerful' (Dingake and editorial, *Mmegi Online*, 12 and 14 September 2006).

The rulers were simultaneously avoiding international accountability. In September 2006 Botswana had failed to ratify the African Union's Convention on Preventing and Combating Corruption, agreed to by heads of state in July 2003, and effective in August 2006. By then, 15 countries had signed up and committed themselves to implement its provisions. These featured such key measures as providing citizens with information on budget spending, protection for whistle blowers and a declaration of assets by MPs and ministers. Such open government instruments clearly posed problems for the BDP government. It had failed to introduce a freedom of information act despite repeated calls for it to do so, and it had flagrantly refused to implement the register of members' assets legislation over ten years. Elite corruption in Botswana might be recognised for what it was.[46] Those on the spot at this time were already clear in their conclusions. Botswana's relatively small elite community was closely interrelated by blood ties,

---

[45] The events were well covered within the independent press. See for instance Gideon Nkala, 'PEEPA: the End', *Mmegi Online*, 29 September, and Dan Moabi, 'Whither Botswana?', *Mmegi Online*, 14 September and 5 October 2006.

[46] 'Botswana could loose its ranking as Africa's least corrupt', *Sunday Standard*, 18 September 2006. Inaction persisted three months later, 'Botswana loses score on corruption index', *Sunday Standard*, 11 December 2006.

schooling, social interests and public service career trajectories, and Dingake unavoidably concluded that on historic experience and what was volumes of evidence, the cabinet was not only corrupt but arrogantly so.[47]

After a decade of prevarication and inaction, cabinet finally disposed of the register of members' assets in late February 2007. This was confirmed by the minister of presidential affairs, Skelemani, in an interview with *The Gazette*. Ministers were understood to be totally against the register – one of them was reported to have described the register, in Kwelagobe-type terms, as 'absolute nonsense'.[48]

There were other areas where the Mogae government avoided association with international ethical norms and procedures. The African Union had established a voluntary Peer Review Mechanism (APRM) to assist member states in putting their governmental systems and economies in order and display accountability. By late 2006, five states had submitted themselves to this review process, while another 26 out of the 53 member states of the Pan African Parliament (PAP) were awaiting peer review. Botswana was among the 22 outside the review system at the end of 2006. As Skelemani told parliament, Botswana did not see the need to accede to APRM. The country's four representatives to the PAP, however, all encouraged compliance. MP Olebile Gaborone said that assent to peer review was necessary because Botswana could learn from other countries: some were making great strides and surpassing Botswana in many respects, and a model democracy should show that it had nothing to hide.[49]

The possible or likely linkage between mismanagement and corruption, clearly evident in the scandals of the 1990s, was unexplored even as government performance plummeted after 2004, as Sebetela noted in parliament. In the 2005/06 financial year, the government had spent P3.8 billion out of its P4.7 billion development budget; 1,177 projects were planned but only 213 were completed and commissioned. The disparities were similar in the previous

---

[47] 'As I see it', *Mmegi Online*, 12 September 2006.
[48] Editorial, 'What are they hiding?', 3 March 2007. Lucky Mokgatlhe of the DCEC had earlier affirmed that the declaration was essential because of the rising levels of corruption and the fact that many people did not believe reports like those of Transparency International that corruption was low in Botswana. Tuduetso Setsiba, 'DCEC Roots for Declaration of Assets', *Mmegi Online*, 16 October 2006.
[49] He noted that Botswana was viewed as arrogant by other PAP members. Botswana's other PAP representatives were deputy speaker, Gladys Kokorwe, Boyce Sebetela and Gaborone North MP, Keletso Rakhudu. Batlhalefi Leagajang, 'Botswana should agree to African peer review', *Botswana Gazette*, 15 December 2006.

year. Wastage characterised the failures in implementation, as the reports of the auditor general regularly itemised. For example, in the construction of the Boatle–Mmankgodi, Thamaga–Molepole and Molepole–Lephephe road projects, the cost of consultancy services increased by more than 109 per cent against the budgeted amount to P4.1 million, and the construction cost overrun rose 42 per cent to reach P71.35 million. In the Molepole–Lephephe project, consultancy costs overran by 89 per cent, and the costs of construction escalated by 44 per cent to P123 million. The auditor general noted that the road was never completed and was apparently abandoned. Those two undertakings alone cost Botswana around P60 million: unscrupulous contractors and suppliers were having a field day (*Mmegi Online*, 22 February 2007). Implementation was Khama's sole ministerial responsibility, and Mogae had promised parliament that he would crack down on non-performing bureaucrats.[50]

'Showing' or transparency was precisely the issue, whether in regard to presidentialism, predominance, elite corruption, or poverty in a rich country, and diamond dependency was at the heart of the problem. On information supplied by long-time industry insiders, ex-minister David Magang, and former Debswana employee, Todd Majaye, the pseudonymous 'Watchdog' concluded that no other economic sector 'had been run in a more terrifyingly untruthful trajectory than the diamond sector'. The suspicion existed that people in positions of influence had ganged up against the nation to pursue narrow self-serving interests.[51]

The allegations of corruption in Debswana had grown stronger and more detailed at this period. Managers had supposedly lied about dubious payments in a plants rehabilitation programme, worth some P6 billion. Managing director, Blackie Marole, had instituted an internal audit into alleged fraud and corruption in the tendering process associated with this big project.[52]

---

[50] Dumelang Saleshando felt that parliament rather than the president should appoint and oversee the auditor general, but another MP observed that the assembly lacked the power even to appoint its own Clerk. Bame Piet, 'Sebetela Blasts Mogae, Khama', *Mmegi Online*, 28 February 2007.

[51] These were 'the small group of decision makers' in 'De Beers, Debswana and government'. The Watchdog, 'There is need for a truth commission on the diamond industry', *Sunday Standard*, 4 December 2006.

[52] Sunday Standard Reporter, 'Marole Investigates Debswana Corruption', *Sunday Standard*, 22 January 2007. Further allegations of fraud, misinformation campaigns and cover-ups within Debswana were made by Monty Chiepe, executive chairman of Geoflux, whose company had been prevented from participating in the rehabilitation because of 'fraudulent transactions' within Debswana. Monty Chiepe, 'The story Debswana officials tried to kill', *Sunday Standard*, 22 January 2007.

International comparisons are relevant to a proper understanding of elite corruption in Botswana. Britain too is possessed of a rich minerals resource in the form of oil, and it also presents a paradoxical situation on corruption. It ranks very high on the lists of Transparency International, ahead of the United States and France, 'despite the lax rules and the fact that it is neck deep in the arms and oil trades – both especially prone to corruption', and 'many [at home] think it demonstrates that Britain is better at keeping dodgy business under wraps', according to *The Economist*, 23 December 2006. Diamonds are equally or more corruption-prone, and such resource dependency has a 'strong negative impact on democratic development' (Kekic, 2007: 2). Image, and elite interrelatedness, patronage and control, have shielded Botswana's conspicuously dodgy business practice from outside view.

Rural poverty and inequalities

Inequalities in cattle ownership have been severe and hidden. 2.5 per cent of farming households owned 40 per cent of all cattle, according to the conservative estimates of the Botswana Human Development Report 2005, while other analysts suggested that, by the 1990s, over 70 per cent of rural households had no cattle. Denied investment, agriculture was being hollowed out, economically and socially. In the rich but undiversified economy, cattle remained for many 'the only effective means' of attaining income above subsistence levels.[53]

About 29 per cent of rural households were not actually engaged in agriculture in 1981, and 42 per cent of people were in the same position ten years later. Towards the end of the 1990s, many rural families were excluded from agricultural production and obliged to rely on itinerant casual labouring for their subsistence (Cullis and Watson, 2003: 4, 12 and 17). In Ghanzi and Kgalagadi districts particularly, poverty was endemic and structural. Many of the destitute were supported only by meagre handouts from the state.

The foreign minister, General Mompati Merafhe, recently testified to the depth of poverty in a large part of Ghanzi district, the CKGR. He referred to a report from 1996 which described the reserve as a poverty trap, with over 53 per cent of the inhabitants

[53] Good (1993: 223) and Clover (2003: 4).

dependent on destitute rations, and with 87 per cent of those studied having received 'no education at all'. He recognised that landlessness was the primary indicator of poverty, but made no mention of the government's prime role in perpetuating San land-lessness. He noted that absolute poverty was on the increase in the CKGR.[54]

Disadvantaging the many

The inter-relationship between national diamond-based prosper-ity, wealth for the few, and poverty and landlessness for the many has extensive consequences. Hunger, malnutrition and destitution are the worst. The numbers of people facing chronic food insuffi-ciency rose from 18 per cent in 1990–92, to 24 per cent in 1999–01.[55] Much evidence and data pointed in the same direction. 'Poverty has a woman's face', UNICEF in Botswana noted; a lot of female-headed households 'are poverty-stricken'. Children were being deprived of schooling to help their parents in farming, and the rural poor were not getting adequate healthcare. UNICEF's recent figures show under-five mortality rates doubling in Botswana over the period 1990–04, rising from 58 deaths to 116 per 1,000 live births. These deaths were attributable to low gov-ernment expenditure and to the poverty and illiteracy of rural mothers.[56] International comparisons with rich Botswana were invidious.[57] An outbreak of diarrhoea in 2006 caused the death of over 400 children, because of an ineffective response from the minister of health (*Botswana Guardian*, 22 December 2006).

HIV-AIDS obviously impacted severely, but other factors were also at work. Priorities in public spending did not favour poverty reduction. Expenditure on education (as a percentage of GDP) dropped from 6.2 in 1990 to 2.2 in 2000-02, and that on health remained level at 3.7. However, spending on the military contin-ued high and constant at 4.1.[58] Such priorities were not atypical;

[54] In making this unusually frank assessment of developmental policies, the minister was endeavouring to justify the enforced removal of San people from the reserve before an audi-ence of foreign diplomats in Gaborone. *Tautona Times*, 29 October 2005, pp.16–20.

[55] *Human Development Report 2004*, pp.148 and 162.

[56] Tuduetso Setsiba, *Mmegi Online*, 10 May 2006 and Joel Konopo, 'Why Botswana's children are dying', *Mail and Guardian Online*, 2 July 2007.

[57] Among 18 developing countries, Zimbabwe, South Africa and Botswana were the only ones to experience a rise in child mortality then, and Botswana's deterioration was the worst of all. *The Economist*, 23 December 2006.

[58] *HDR Report 2005*, p. 286.

as Ross notes, mineral-rich governments enjoying high revenues from resource-exports, 'generally spend large sums on their military forces' (Ross, 2002: 25).

The Global Hunger Index, released by the International Food Policy Research Institute in late 2006, showed that Botswana not only had a serious hunger problem, but that it had worsened over the past decade of high to good growth. The Index was a composite based on three indicators, child malnutrition, child mortality, and people with calorie deficiencies; it provided an enhanced picture of the food supply situation of the total population which took into account the special vulnerability of children to nutritional deprivation. The hunger index also showed that in 2006 Botswana's condition was more serious than that of other regional countries like South Africa and Namibia, and worse than would be expected for an Upper Middle Income Country (UMC).[59]

'Destitution' is a deeply stigmatised status in Botswana, connoting individual failure, isolation and abandonment, officially a person 'without any form of asset', and 'physically or mentally incapable of working' – or 'those who own nothing but head-lice'. But while the country's population grew by some 60 per cent between 1980 and 1996, a period of high growth and no (or low) AIDS infections, the number of permanent destitutes rose from 5,000 to 15,597 people. The number of the officially impoverished was two-and-a-half times larger than those employed in mining. In 1995–6, the rate of permanent destitution per 1,000 of population was highest in Ghanzi, at 59.9, and the next most severe was in Kgalagadi, at 46.2.[60]

Poverty's impact on destitutes, more so perhaps than for other sections of the country's inequitable society, was compound. While possession of some cash income is widely recognised as a prerequisite for citizenship of any meaningful kind, only goods-in-kind, that is 'rations', were offered to destitutes by the government. This contrasted sharply with other aid and welfare programmes such as the small old-age pension (only introduced in late 1996). Destitute rations are intended for mere physical survival not for a semblance of normal social life. On BIDPA's assessment the ration basket was extremely frugal, and fell short of

[59] Doris Wiesmann, IFPRI researcher, quoted in 'Hungry and scared', *Sunday Standard*, 16 October 2006.
[60] The figures were almost certainly underestimates being based on the false premise of the isolated individual destitute, when many family members or a whole household was impoverished. Good (2002), pp. 57–9.

minimal food needs to provide for healthy subsistence (Good, 2002: 58–9). Not only was so little offered to the very poor, but only a few received even that. On data for Gaborone, for instance, 30 people qualified for social assistance in 1999, when its population was 180,000, and when by very conservative estimates, the number of impoverished recipients 'should have been at least 100 times higher'. Official policy failed many of the very poor completely.[61]

In 2002 a revised national policy on destitutes was introduced. An impoverished person was redefined as an individual with 'insufficient assets and income sources' and unable therefore to engage in sustainable economic activities. Insufficient assets and income was interpreted as possession of not more than four livestock units, or earning or receiving an income less than P150 per month with dependents. Other criteria involved mental or physical disability and terminal illness as before.

The revised policy introduced for the first time a tiny cash component. Permanent destitutes became entitled to a ration package valued at some P210 a month, with P55 in cash for 'personal items' included in that sum. This amount was notably below the poverty level of $2 (or about P12) a day affecting about 50 per cent of Batswana (P360 monthly). The condition of temporary destitution was recognised, for which a poor person was entitled to about P180 a month, including the same P55 in cash, with a maximum availability period of six months. Government now recognised that destitutes too had families and dependents, since experience showed that almost without exception, destitute persons shared their rations with family members. Very limited assistance was now to be accorded to the poor on this recognition: for instance, one destitute with three or four dependents would get one additional food component ration package, and one extra food ration would be available for every two additional dependents.

The new policy stressed the obligations of destitutes: to find employment if physically and mentally able; to produce at least part of their own food; and to participate in any rehabilitation activities sponsored by local authority.[62] Overall, the very poor were still required to survive on the most meagre assistance: one

[61] Arnon Bar-On, 'Poverty amid plenty', Paper presented to CROP conference, University of Cape Town, 1998, pp. 17 and 21, and 'Providing so little for so few', chapter in Francis Wilson, Nazneen Kanji and Einar Braathen (2001), *Poverty Reduction,* Cape Town and London: NAEP and Zed Books, p. 259.

[62] BIDPA, *Report on the review of the remote area development programme (RADP),* 19 December 2003, pp. 110–112.

of the enduring fundamentals of the country's development strategy. In the words of the government white paper of 1990: 'It should be emphasised that destitute amounts should always be lower than the lowest minimum wage so as to ensure that such welfare payments do not discourage work effort.' [63]

Ethnic inequalities

Ethnicity is at once an important socio-political factor and a lived experience. It is also interlinked directly with resource dependency, according to Bannon and Collier and Ross: Ethnic dominance exists in societies where the largest ethnic group accounted for 45 to 90 per cent of the population, where they experience a risk of conflict about one-third higher in consequence.[64] Resource dependency plus ethnic dominance, Ross adds, constitute 'drivers of conflict', and through this linkage, he says, 'wealth can make you poor' (Bannon and Collier, 2003: 2–3 and Ross, 2003: 17–21). The role of government was of great importance either in moderating and equalising ethnic relations, or in neglecting and exacerbating them.

Analysing ethnic inequalities is also hampered by the absence of the data – census data are not collected on ethnicity, despite repeated calls from national and international agencies for its introduction.[65] One estimate suggested that the Tswana, measured as a language group, constituted about 70 per cent of the country's total population in the 1990s At that time their numbers were around one million, compared with such minority groups (in descending numerical order) as Kalanga with 160,000, Kgalagadi with 35,000, Herero 31,000 and Yeyi, 27,000.[66] Despite the statistical lacunae, the government has officially portrayed Botswana over decades as ethnically homogenous. While this has some validity when comparison is made with egregious examples of tribalism elsewhere, it tends to erase the cultures and rights of minorities in Botswana. The official perspective was superficially

---

[63] 'The revised national policy on incomes, employment, prices and profits', p. 36.

[64] Taking minerals exports as a percentage of GDP, Ross saw dependency 'peaking with exports of around 30 per cent of [GDP]', and Botswana's figure was 35.1

[65] The Central Statistics Office claimed, in April 2006, that data users had not indicated that they needed this material, but both Reteng, a Botswana multi-cultural coalition, and the UN's CERD had called for the census to include ethnicity. *Mmegi Online*, 24 April 2006.

[66] Ethnologue Report for Botswana, 'Languages of Botswana', 10 November 2003. Reteng's estimates are very different. *Mmegi Online*, 10 May 2006.

harmonising but deeply supremacist in effect. Defining 'tribe'/ethnicity, with the Tswana at the top,[67] was an institutionalised element in the constitution and in the liberal democratic and quasi-feudal system.

Tswana predominance remained above public criticism until the late 1990s, when educated, professional elites of at least two minority communities, Kalanga and Wayei, organised and challenged prevailing relations. An academic, Lydia Nyati-Ramahobo of the Kamanakao Association, a Wayei cultural pressure group, declared at a meeting in Gaborone in May 2002: 'We have a right to talk about our oppression and nobody can [stop us] doing that. We will not stop until we get what we want.' A number of cultural groups came together to press their case for ethnic equality (*Midweek Sun*, 8 May 2002). An urban Kalanga intelligentsia was active and organised in the Society for the Promotion of the Ikalanga Language (SPIL). To counter minority-ethnic agitation, Pitso Ya Batswana arose to maintain a status quo favourable to the Tswana.

Government responded to this new agitation by establishing a commission of inquiry, but its report, of 2000–01, was rejected by Kamanakao.

Tswana domination came under attack too from international bodies like CERD, which recognised significant human rights violations, namely the discrimination enshrined in legislation, the preferences accorded to Setswana speakers in the courts and education, and official cases of discrimination against the San and Wayei in particular. In 2002 the Committee specifically criticised the 'on-going dispossession of San people' from the CKGR.[68] Tswana dominance was an issue in the national elections of 2004, when the BNF attacked the 'ethnic chauvinism' of the ruling party, and promised to create a nation with a shared vision of full equality (*Mmegi*, 2 June 2004). Complacency and hierarchies were shaken as the opposition vote reached its all-time high in October that year.

Ethnic domination is linked with minerals dependency and conjoined with poverty; access to land decreases as its scarcity value increases in specific places. Cullis and Watson reported that

---

[67] Through a Tribal Land Act, Tribal Territories Act, Chieftainship Act, and a House of Chiefs composed until 2006 entirely of Tswana members. The paramount chief of the Bamangwato, the largest Tswana community, General Ian Khama has been the country's president-in-waiting since 1998.

[68] Resolutions and statements issued by CERD on 23 August 2002 and 30 October 2003,

annual market transactions of state and freehold land increased by about 56 per cent, 1996–2001, and tribal land transfers also rose. Mogoditshane experienced an increase of 93 per cent in property transfers each year over this time. Certain sectors of society were marginalised in this process, either because they were insufficiently wealthy or disadvantaged in law. The latter category included women, ethnic minorities, those with HIV-AIDS, and of course the poor. Land Boards in practice allocated land according to a person's ability to use it. Land use conflicts had increased as pressure on land use grew and people were pushed to the margins (Cullis and Watson, 2003: 14–17).

HIV-AIDS

By 2000–02, Botswana was the worst-infected country in the world by HIV-AIDS, with some 280,000 people living with HIV, an incidence rate of almost 40 per cent of the adult population, with life expectancy falling by half. Perceiving the issue as one of national survival, President Mogae responded strongly, revealing what can be done with such a major commitment, and equally what is not being done to address other societal problems.

When the president promised in 2001 to provide free anti-retroviral (ARV) treatment, many physical and human barriers existed. A national AIDS coordinating council was established and since Botswana was known to have relatively good state capacity, large external assistance was forthcoming. Two large American foundations each contributed $50 million over five years, with one offering free ARV medicines and with two pharmaceuticals offering ARVs at cost; the government was still spending $1,000 per patient per year, to deliver the three-drug treatment and blood tests.[69] A gigantic problem had received a powerful response in this wealthy country.

Nonetheless, the scope of the response was not universal. Sixty per cent of beds in public hospitals country-wide were occupied by AIDS-related patients from 2002, when ARV treatment was launched at four centres, with seven more subsequently added. Over 11,450 patients were on ARV treatment at the start of 2004. Seventeen counselling and testing centres were then operating, and about 100,000 people had received these services. The

[69] 'Special Report: Aids in Southern Africa', *The Economist*, 11 May 2002; Festus Mogae, *Botswana Guardian*, 18 February 2000; and *The Sunday Independent* (Johannesburg) 20 July 2003.

Prevention of Mother-to-Child Transmission programme was available in all public health facilities, and some 11,300 expectant mothers had been counselled. By mid-2006, some 256,000 were living with HIV and about 68,400 were receiving ARVs. Recent official survey data suggested that HIV prevalence had dropped from 37.4 per cent in 2003 to 32.4 per cent in 2006, but others such as Indexmundi reported little change: the adult prevalence rate was 37.3 in 2006, and the infection rate was the world's second highest. Discrimination existed in many areas: the epidemic impacted most heavily upon women, minorities and the poor. Children were especially afflicted as the approximate number of orphans from parents dying of AIDS reached 120,000 in 2005.[70]

Understanding the deeper social consequences

A number of theorists have endeavoured to conceptualise the problems faced by the poor and weak in societies like Botswana. Paul Farmer considers inequalities, poverty and discrimination as forms of 'structural violence' upon the poor. In vital areas like health, the poor are doubly jeopardised – they are not only more prone to infectious diseases, but also have limited access to the means of improving their health. The latter is a medical issue but even more a matter of human rights. From this perspective, violence is structured through tribalism/racism, sexism, political domination and poverty, and it constrains the choices which people have or want to make about their daily lives. An asymmetry of power exists in places like Guatemala and Haiti, and it 'generates a kind of quiet brutality' upon the poor. (Farmer, 2003: xvi) In other places like Ghanzi and Kgalagadi something not dissimilar might well occur.

The effects of such constraints, persisting over time, can also be represented as conditions of 'negative peace', or tacit, underlying conflict in society, which is sometimes actualised.[71] The UNDP recognises what it terms 'chains of inequality-disadvantage' operating extensively within a country. Richard Wilkinson (1996, 2005) argues convincingly that inequalities are socially corrosive

---

[70] Iyanda and Keakesitse (2005: 103); *Budget Speech* 2004, p. 11; *Mmegi Online*, 9 March 2007; Indexmundi.com/Botswana HIV/AIDS; *The Economist*, 16 December 2006; US Department of State, *Botswana country reports on human rights practices – 2005*.

[71] The term 'negative peace' originates with Galtung in 1969, and was utilised by Connie Scanlon in 'Educating for peace: politics and human rights in Botswana', paper presented to the Politics Seminar, University of Botswana, 27 March 2002.

and literally kill. A fifth concept, 'cultural genocide', has been utilised by Reteng to interpret the impact of government policy upon vulnerable minorities, especially the San in Botswana.[72] These conceptualisations are relevant and their implications important. Botswana's vaunted stability and its 'miracle' image provide a screen behind which important fault-lines and deep divisions in the society can be hidden, neglected and exacerbated.

'Chains of inequality-disadvantage'

The UNDP emphasises that extreme inequalities 'weaken political legitimacy and corrode institutions.'[73] Inequalities in income and capabilities often reflect inequalities in political power. Disadvantaged groups have a weak political voice and their voice is unheard because of their disadvantages. Such chains operate inside many countries, and those with a Gini coefficient above 50 are in a critical or high inequality category. In Brazil, with a Gini slightly lower than Botswana's, the poorest 10 per cent account, as in Botswana, for 0.7 per cent of national income, but the richest decile receive 47 per cent, that is, 9.6 per cent less than their richer counterparts command in Botswana. Inequalities in Zambia may be described as very large, but the gap between the richest and the poorest quintiles is 42, not Botswana's 77.6. Average income in Brazil is three times higher than in Viet Nam, but the poorest 20 per cent of Brazilians receive an income well below the average income in more equitable Viet Nam. The latter is described by the UNDP as a 'dynamic high-growth economy', indicating the decidedly 'positive benefits' that derive from low inequalities.

Income inequalities both reflect and affect wider life-chance inequalities. In Bolivia and Peru infant death rates are four to five times higher for children of the poorest 20 per cent of people than children of the richest 20 per cent. Inequality deprives people of substantive freedoms and choices, regardless of their formal legal positions.

Comparisons between low-income and high-inequality countries, like the United States and Britain, reveal the heavy impact

---

[72] Reteng points to the government's 'long standing desire to implement a philosophy of cultural genocide on the non-Tswana tribes', and relates this to prevailing conditions of negative peace. Reteng, 'Alternative Report Submitted to [CERD]', Gaborone, January 2005, p. 10.
[73] All quotations in this section are from the UNDP, *Human Development Report 2005*, pp. 55–61.

that inequalities have on people's health. Malaysia, with an average income one-quarter that of the United States, has the same infant mortality rate as rich America, and the Indian state of Kerala has an urban infant death rate lower than that for African Americans in Washington DC.

In Botswana, San people's understanding of their subordination and deprivation reflect the crippling disadvantages afflicting them. A speaker in Dobe[74] comments: 'Illiterate people like us, who earn so little money, feel they can just as well spend it all on alcohol ... their money is anyway never enough to buy the kind of things that would last.' Another reported that 'my mother died in the hospital in Gumare. She was killed by a man who was building the Anwa clinic. My mother was selling traditional beer' when the man started a drunken brawl. He began 'beating and kicking her, with my brother still on her back. She fell down and he left her there and went away.' A person in Tsodilo reported: 'At school we were given clothes and things by the Remote Area Dweller Programme [RADP], and the others said we just belonged to the government ... One of my friends was so ashamed and she would not go and collect her things from the RADP.' Geru Mannanyana of Tobere said that 'today we do not have anything like the life that the government said we could have after ... independence [and our] 'tradition and culture' have gone too. For Kotsi Mmaba of Sekondomboro, impoverishment and inequality was the perceived core of the problem: 'I think the reason why San people have lost their language is what the old people told me: they were poor people and others were rich, and so they started to learn the others' language and culture so that they could get food from them to live.'

On considerable historical and comparative evidence assessed by Wilkinson, extreme inequality produces sickness, violence, depression and death. However rich a country may be, it will be more dysfunctional and dangerous if the gap between the rich and the poor grows very wide. Life expectancy in rich countries correlates closely with levels of equality. With half the per capita GDP of the United States, Greece has longer life expectancy than America. The people of Harlem live shorter lives than the people of Bangladesh. Human development is higher in markedly poorer African countries than in richer but deeply inequitable Botswana. The stress of living at the bottom of the social hierarchy, the stress of disrespect and the lack of personal esteem, produces sickness and death. Cash

[74] Recorded by Willemien Le Roux and Alison White (eds), *Voices of the San: Living in Southern Africa Today*, Cape Town, Kwela Books, 2004.

and land represent status: very low or no pay and landlessness among the San and other very poor groups in rich Botswana tell them just how little they are worth to those above them.

Managing the dysfunctions – enforcing subordination

Scanlon reported in 2002 on how negatively the government viewed civic groups in the broad area of human rights in Botswana. The mere discussion of equality and rights was perceived as endangering authority, wherever it took place: in high-schools, households, work-places, ethnic hierarchies and government. Human rights were undervalued by government and civil society was accorded at best a largely passive and subordinate role. For example, hostility was expressed towards the women's rights group, Emang Basadi, in the House of Chiefs in January 2004, but the women had for years emphasised their collaborative efforts with government at many levels. They took care to work deferentially and carefully within the system (Scanlon, 2002: 8–9; and *Mmegi Monitor*, 26 January 2004). Botswana committed itself to the African Charter on Human and Peoples' Rights in July 1986, but it never presented a Country Report to the African Commission (ACHPR), and by 2002 eight such biannual assessments were overdue.[75] The CERD has noted the absence of 'an independent national human rights institution' in Botswana, and in March 2006 it called for its introduction.[76]

Education for deference and conformity

Education like health has been an area of great national advance; although schooling is not compulsory, some 88 per cent of children attended school in 2005, and 30 per cent completed secondary school.[77] But schooling presented serious problems for both children's rights and democracy.

---

[75] As an under-secretary in the office of the president explained, Botswana simply assumed that our human rights record is fine. The death penalty, refugees and the expulsion of San from the CKGR were just three issues current before the commission which the government had ignored. *Mmegi*, 24 May 2002, and press statement, Ditshwanelo, 24 November 2003.
[76] 'Consideration of reports submitted by states parties ... Botswana', 20 February – 10 March 2006, p. 6.
[77] Recent government statistics noted by US Department of State, Botswana: 'Country reports on human rights practices – 2005', p. 7.

The enforcement of deferential behaviour starts with children in school. It builds upon the belief that corporal punishment is a Tswana societal norm, fundamental and pervasive. A system of 'routinised caning in government schools' has resulted, which is legally sanctioned and widely used.[78]

Headmasters are supposedly required to witness the administration of beatings. But when Thato, an 11-year-old girl at Polokwe Primary, was allegedly beaten on the head with a belt buckle by her teacher, causing subsequent headaches and dizziness, no one in authority queried whether the headmaster had been present. The minister of education, Jacob Nkate, told parliament soon after that corporal punishment was incorporated in domestic law, and his ministry had no intention of abolishing it. Regulations existed to ensure correct application. Nkate was aware of what he called isolated cases of improper punishment, which were investigated. The prevailing system was correct and its aims were reaffirmed: 'Guidance and counselling programmes will fail us if it is not coupled with corporal punishment [sic]. The intention should not be to kill but to make the students understand right from wrong.'[79]

Mino Polelo and other education specialists reported indisputable research evidence on the abusive use of corporal punishment in Botswana schools. Teachers used 'sticks, sjamboks, electric cables, Bunsen-burner hoses and a range of other physically harmful objects' to inflict punishment. [80] The most gruesome incident observed by Polelo was when 'a pupil [in primary school] was lashed all over the body for using a left hand in writing.'[81]

Other specialists reported that punishment recklessly continued and that a few had died. A situation amounting to 'moral indifference to the suffering of children' prevailed in and around government schools. Corporal punishment was being used to enforce learning, and for compliance and silence. It inflicted fear and emotional distress on the children, and ultimately destroyed a child's self-respect and their potential to learn.[82]

Shandulani Vavani wrote from Cape Town at the same time to share his experience in a government school in Botswana, asking,

[78] Mompati Mino Polelo, interviewed by Ephraim Keoreng, *Mmegi*, 12 November 2004.

[79] Chandaoiwa Baputaki in *Mmegi Online*, 28 August 2006.

[80] He referred among others to the work of Willemien le Roux, Elmon Tafa and to graduate students in Education at UB, Mino Polelo, Letters, *Botswana Guardian*, 7 July 2006.

[81] Polelo (2005), 'Inside undemocratic schools: corporal punishment and physical abuse in Botswana schools', *Journal of Sociology and Education in Africa*, 4,2, June, pp. 14, 18–19.

[82] D. Molefe, O. Pansiri and S.Weeks, 'Issues in Education', *Mmegi Online*, 23 October 2006.

'what meaning can an ordinary being ... attribute to a teacher who always comes with a cane for a 40 to 50 minutes lesson? Are students always indisciplined? Can't students learn without being lashed for a day?' Teachers were 'taking advantage of our poor uneducated parents who have been made to believe that corporal punishment was the way to discipline students.'[83]

Polelo also stressed that punishment and abuse assumed discriminatory dimensions in schools of the economically marginalised. This was especially so for those catering for San pupils, as le Roux's research testified. Schooling was a critical phase for young San, when they learnt of their heritage of inscribed backwardness and actual serfdom. Discrimination and subordination was rammed home to them through separation from their parents and physical and sexual abuse. Abnormally high dropout rates resulted, well in excess of 20 per cent in districts like Ghanzi and Kgalagadi, where poverty is severe.[84]

Sexual abuse was a particular problem. Research in the North-West district in the late 1990s by Stefania Rossetti found that 67 per cent of secondary school pupils had been subjected to sexual harassment – touching, patting, pinching, pressure for dates – one-quarter of them on a regular basis. Twenty per cent said they had been asked by their teachers to have sex with them, and almost half of those had accepted, mainly because they feared lower grades if they refused. In Form One, the first year of secondary education, 17 per cent of children wanted to drop out as a result.[85] Although the law in Botswana prohibits defilement, that is sex with a child below 16, no law specifically forbids child abuse.[86]

Highly authoritarian schooling based on violence offered no training or support for democracy. Instead violence was extended through chains of discrimination inside the schools, via bullying between boys of different ages and by boys over girls.

Conformity was being reinforced through pervasive fear. No wonder therefore that Polelo had 'never found any democratically elected students representatives in our schools.' The strong moral indifference surrounding them was not being addressed by civil society, with the exception he noted of Childline and Ditshwanelo.

---

[83] Letters, *Mmegi Online*, 27 October 2006. The widespread acceptance of beating in schools by parents in villages is reported by Polelo (2005), p. 18.

[84] Le Roux (1999: 84, 91 and 95) and Dumelang Saleshando, *Botswana Gazette*, 12 October 2006. See also Polelo's 'School dropout among the remote area dwellers of Botswana', *Pula*, 9,1, 2005.

[85] Caitlin Davies, 'Sexual abuse of students widespread – report', *Mmegi*, 7 April 2000.

[86] US Department of State, 2005, p. 8.

Botswana was clinging to values, laws and practices which negated democracy, and which were incompatible with international conventions to which the country was a signatory.[87] Practices which possibly contributed, moreover, to the levels of criminal violence rising in the country.

Botswana had abolished school fees in 1987, but the government announced their reintroduction at the end of 2005, purportedly as a cost-sharing mechanism, despite the overall wealth of the country and regular budget surpluses. Parents would be required to pay P300 per annum for students at junior secondary schools, P450 for those in senior schools, and P750 for tertiary education. These were significant sums for many people given that about half the population lived on some P12 a day. New systems were being constructed to administer payments. A senior official in the ministry of education said that 72 social workers would be recruited country-wide to asses the ability of parents to pay fees. Parents would be required to sign a payment contract, and those who defaulted in their payments would face legal sanctions (*Mmegi Online*, 27 October 2005).

Both main opposition parties, the BNF and the BCP, immediately condemned the move as hostile to people's welfare and as a burden for the poor. The BCP believed that the country's current economic problems were the creation of the BDP, and did not warrant an imposition on education. Any government with the welfare of its citizens at heart was morally bound to provide free education as a fundamental human right. New school fees, as Dumelang Saleshando stressed, flew in the face of the government's declared plans to create an educated and informed nation under millennium and other goals. And given existing discriminatory school practices, dropout and abstension rates in places like Ghanzi and Kgalagadi could only increase.[88]

In late 2006, the ministry reminded parents that they had signed binding contracts and those who had not paid fees would have their cases turned over to attorneys. Spokeswoman Nomsah Zuzu reported that out of some 157,000 students enrolled in public schools, 24,300 had been granted exemptions, 'with the larger part of that from the central district' [sic]. The Ministry 'had collected

---

[87] Polelo (2005: 4–5, 14 and 24) and interview with Keoreng; the most relevant international norms were the UN Convention on the Rights of the Child (Articles 19, 28 and 37), and the African Charter on the Rights and Welfare of the Child (Article 160), to which Botswana is a signatory.

[88] *Mmegi Online*, 1 November 2005 and *Botswana Gazette*, 12 October 2006.

50 per cent of the P30 million, which was the targeted amount'. Students whose parents did not pay would face difficulties in obtaining a place in tertiary institutions, Zuzu warned.[89]

Protest

Education has promoted deference in Botswana. A chain of influences in the hierarchical society contributes to this end. Students have been 'programmed to dream only of marginal positions in the echelons of the system', Raditlhokwa (1994) wrote, and were 'made to feel inferior and incompetent by political leaders'. Young people constitute a significant numerical component in Botswana society.[90] Until 1999 18–21 year olds were denied the vote, and low electoral participation was a norm within the predominant party system. But occasionally things were very different, as they were in Mochudi and Gaborone at the end of 1994 and early 1995. In the absence of any official inquiry into these events – which saw a young person crippled by security force fire and another beaten to death – they must be understood by their appearances as spontaneous insurrection against unresponsive authority.

Almost every senior secondary school experienced strike action by students between late 1994 and the following March. At one senior school in North East district, students rioted violently in May, against reportedly 'long-standing grievances', including sexual harassment and punishment, and what they called 'the prison-like atmosphere of the school'.

Police responded with teargas and raids on dormitories, and by beating and injuring some students. Ghanzi Senior Secondary experienced similar strike action in November, where staff were said to have used plastic pipes when meting out punishment. When President Masire opened parliament that month, he referred to 'an unprecedented scale [of] riots by students all over the country'. He was worried by the social trends and changing patterns of behaviour of some young persons. But they would not be allowed to continue, he warned, and offenders 'would reap the fruits' of their unlawful actions.[91]

[89] The ministry's public relations officer. *Mmegi Online*, 3 November 2006.
[90] On the 2001 census findings, those between 5 and 19 years numbered 622,000, and those 5 to 24 years totalled 793,000; in the country's total population of 1,681,000.
[91] His words echoed his instruction to the BDF and police in February 1995. Almost his entire state of the nation address in November was devoted to crime and punishment. *Midweek Sun*, 8 November 1995, and Good (1996: 76–7).

Social protest has not completely ceased. Residents of Kumakwane, 30 kilometres outside Gaborone, went on the rampage on the evening of Sunday 26 November 2006, when a man died on the spot after being hit by a vehicle. They blocked the Kanye to Gaborone 'Highway of Death', in protest against the government's failure to erect speed humps on the road, and six vehicles were damaged. Police fired shots in the air to disperse stone throwers and arrested 45 Kumakwane residents. Many of these were young people who seemed aware of their rights and the rectitude of their action. According to Superintendent Andrew Bosilong, while 18 youths, aged between 13 and 18, accepted two strokes each in punishment and were freed, another 21 people, aged between 20 and 25, refused corporal punishment and demanded to be charged and tried under the law. Some of the detainees accused the police of making indiscriminate arrests and using unnecessary force. The MP for the area, Deputy Speaker Gladys Kokorwe, expressed her concern for the numbers of residents being killed by motorists.[92]

Hardly two months later, the 'palpable anger' in Mokolodi, ten kilometres south of Gaborone, saw residents, most of whom were in their 20s and 30s, blocking the road that led into the village to prevent the passage of big tipper trucks from Quarry of Botswana. A tense stand-off occurred over some days which resulted in a new agreement allowing the company use of the road for three months, and the election of a local youth committee, paid for by Quarry of Botswana, to monitor the company's activities. [93]

Capital punishment

Punishment for crime in Botswana can be seriously inequitable especially for crime involving the death penalty. It bears most heavily on those without resources in money and education, and it is administered in ways that can represent the denial of a fair trial and the negation of the accused's rights (as Ditshwanelo documents). Legal representatives lack experience in death trial cases, the resources available to counsel are inadequate, and there is no state legal aid. The president possesses the power of clemency, but the procedures followed by the clemency committee which advises him are without transparency, rushed and secretive. Vindictiveness tends to prevail.

[92] Report by Bame Piet, *Mmegi Online*, 2 December 2006.
[93] Ephraim Keoreng, in *Mmegi Online*, 15 and 18 January 2007.

The injustices involved in this retributive system were displayed in the case of two impoverished San men, Gwara Brown Motswetla and Tlhabologang Phetolo Maauwe, imprisoned for murder in 1995, and condemned to death in two unfair trials.[94] With their death warrants signed by Mogae in January 1999, Ditshwanelo learnt accidentally of the executions scheduled for three days' time, and won an emergency stay of execution. Mogae had refused clemency in secret a month earlier. Against consistent opposition from the state, subsequent hearings up to the Appeal Court, eventually resulted in their sentence being set aside in July 2006.[95] The two men experienced over eleven years incarceration 'a flagrant miscarriage of justice, perpetrated by both the state appointed counsel and a High Court administrator.' Such failings '[could] not be avoided within a system which easily enable[d] miscarriages of justice to occur'.[96]

Ditshwanelo has shown that the failures in the execution procedures are many and serious. The clemency process is shrouded in secrecy. Neither the procedures by which the supposed advisory committee on the prerogative of mercy meets and advises the president, nor the procedure by which the president makes his decision, are clear. When Ditshwanelo wrote to the office of the president, in 1999 and in 2003, seeking clarification, no response was forthcoming. The Prison Act only requires that the prisoner be informed of his or her execution 24 hours before the event. In Botswana it is practice to bury the executed in the prison yard without family participation.

Since Maauwe and Motswetla's case, seven more executions have been carried out without prior notification of the condemned prisoner's family, friends or attorneys. Mariette Bosch was hung

---

[94] Motswetla and Maauwe made confessions under duress to the police, and affixed their thumbprints to documents they did not understand. Only speaking a Sesarwa dialect, they had no interpreter in court, and were pronounced guilty of murder in April 1997 by Justice Gyeke-Dako, who ruled that their statements were a 'tissue of lies', and declared that they had acted out of 'sheer greed'. But Justice Dudley Reynolds subsequently found that the accused had 'suffered from difficulties of communication' and they were 'without resources'. For full details see Alice Mogwe, Maureen Akena and Timothy Curry (eds) (2006), *In the Shadow of the Noose*, Gaborone: Ditshwanelo, 2006, chapter one.

[95] Ditshwanelo believed that Motswetla's and Maauwe's *pro deo* defence counsel had displayed gross incompetence. Skelemani, the attorney general, argued that Ditshwanelo should not be allowed to appear and the poverty of the San was both unproven and irrelevant. Even when their death sentences were set aside, the state demanded a retrial.

[96] Press statement of Ditshwanelo, 10 October 2006, and Mogwe et. al. (2006) Chapters 1–3. In 2006, CERD called on Botswana to 'provide adequate legal aid and interpretation services, especially to persons belonging to the most disadvantaged ethnic groups'. 'Consideration of Reports Submitted by States Parties...', 20 February – 10 March, p. 4.

secretly and hastily despite the government's knowledge that the matter was already before the ACHPR, which represents the final constitutional challenge open to the condemned. In Botswana a condemned person has 'virtually no time' to approach the ACHPR.[97]

There are no known cases, over forty years, of a Botswana president exercising the powers of clemency which he possesses. Repeated calls from various parties for a moratorium on capital punishment in Botswana have been rebuffed. Approximately 40 people had been executed by the state since 1966.

Militarising domination

Today, rich and highly inequitable Botswana experiences an upsurge in violent crime. Researchers at UB suggested that the country's overall crime rate grew by 14 per cent between 2001 and 2002, with robbery rising almost 40 per cent, unlawful wounding by 29 per cent, and murder by 19 per cent. Police reported that murder cases had gone from 110 in 2005 to 154 over the same period in 2006, when armed robbery also increased from 973 cases to 1,111.[98]

The rise in violent and intrusive crimes, such as armed robberies, rape, murder, and the more recent development of home invasions, particularly concerned the commissioner of police, Edwin Batshu, in November 2006. These had resulted not only in heightened feelings of insecurity in communities, but they were also becoming, he claimed, a threat to the country's socio-economic stability. Botswana's international reputation was being undermined and investment and tourism were threatened. The country's prisons were already bursting at the seams,[99] and new measures were necessary.

Two areas would be concentrated upon: an increased role for the military in civil affairs, and an enhancement of intelligence capabilities. The engagement of the BDF with auxiliary special constables assisting them was one way in which stability would

---

[97] Statement by Ditshwanelo before the ACHPR dated 10 November 2003, and press statements of 24 November 2003 and 22 March 2005.

[98] 'Hungry and Scared', *Sunday Standard*, 16 October 2006, and *Mmegi Online*, 25 August 2006.

[99] Conditions were 'poor and possibly life threatening'. With an authorised capacity of 3,910 they were holding one year earlier 6,259 prisoners. Rape occurred. By December 2005, 72 prisoners had died in custody from HIV-AIDS causes. Department of State, 'Botswana' 2005, p. 2.

be regained, and the Security Intelligence Service was the other.[100]

Fully armed BDF troops were already active in wide-ranging military-type operations in many places inside the country. Hotels and lodges had been burgled in Maun, leaving tourists fearful. An army contingent had arrived on 7 August, and patrolling troops and police had quickly rounded up more than 500 illegal immigrants. Drug trafficking was also being attended to in a 'night stop-and-search operation'. Stolen property had`been recovered in house-to-house operations and suspected culprits apprehended. Senior Superintendent Philip Makoba announced that the soldiers 'are here to stay', and he applauded the community for assisting them with confidential information.[101]

Army units moved into Selebi-Phikwe in July, mounting house-to-house searches and road blocks, aimed also at Zimbabwean immigrants. Operations were to cover adjacent cattle posts where many farmers were known to employ highly exploitable Zimbabwean labourers. According to the police station commander, those who had violated immigration and labour laws would get four strokes on the buttocks before being deported.[102]

Intimidation and brutal force accompanied the military's intrusion into internal affairs. Possibly the worst incident concerned five BDF soldiers and two special constables on 'night patrol' in Ramotswa in November 2005, who forced three Zimbabwean men and two Zimbabwean women to perform sex acts on each other. In an Abu Ghraib-like incident, brutality, xenophobia and sadism were compounded. In the words of a defence attorney, both the BDF and the police '[were] on trial.'[103]

The militarisation of society and politics leapt forward in November with the introduction, after repeated denials, of an intelligence and security services bill. The bill asserted that Botswana faced 'a number of threats or potential threats to its national security, political systems and its economy, all of which may be destabilised'. It nonetheless failed to identify any actual threat and referred only to what was termed 'subversive activities from the country's detractors'. To meet these imagined dangers, a

---

[100] As reported by Thato Chwaane, *MmegiOnline*, 9 November 2006.

[101] Nomsa Ndlovu, 'Army, police invade Maun', *Botswana Guardian*, 18 August 2006.

[102] Report by Onalenna Modikwa, *Mmegi Online*, 6 July 2006.

[103] Reports by Lekopanye Mooketsi, *Mmegi Online*, 6 and 7 June 2006. The charges included coercing a number of Zimbabwean men and women to have sexual intercourse while they watched and forcing three Zimbabwean men to masturbate in front of them. Lekopanye Mooketsi, 'Group Sex Trial Resumes Next Year', *Mmegi Online*, 18 December 2007.

complex security edifice built around a Directorate of Intelligence and Security (DIS) would be established within the office of the presidency. It would be headed by a director general, to be appointed by the president, 'on such terms and conditions as [he] may determine'. Its primary role would be to gather information which it would classify and determine who had access to it. It would also protect the president and vice-president, although no known threat had been made against such office holders in the past. Officers of the DIS would be empowered to make arrests without warrant, they would be armed and they could use their weapons when 'necessary and reasonably justifiable.' The ruling elite would themselves oversee the directorate: the president and his top appointees, located within a central intelligence committee, the policy-determining element. An intelligence and security council and a national intelligence community would also be created. The legislature had no envisaged role once they had passed the bill.[104]

Botswana already possessed considerable security capacities for a country of less than two million people. Leaving aside the armed forces, it had been covered since 1986 by the National Security Act, rarely utilised and never against a serious threat,[105] and a plethora of other agencies. Among these were: military intelligence; police special branch; national intelligence agency; criminal investigations department; the security intelligence service; serious crime squad; the diamonds and narcotics squad; and the DCEC.[106] Enhanced security capacities might have been justifiable in association with the establishment of the Diamond Trading Company Botswana in Gaborone around 2008 – unmentioned in the bill – but not with the nebulous 'subversive activities of detractors'.

As discussion on the bill was proceeding in early December, Police Commissioner Batshu announced that the government was in the process of installing a high-tech surveillance network to intercept all cellphone and electronic mail messages without search warrant. The system would intercept calls originating

[104] Republic of Botswana, *Botswana Government Extraordinary Gazette*, v XLIV n. 82, 3 November 2006. The composition of the Central Intelligence Committee is essentially the president, vice-president, ministers of presidential and foreign affairs, PSP, attorney general, BDF and police commanders, and the new director. Comment is found in *Mmegi Online*, 7 and 10 November 2006.

[105] See chapter 2 above and Good (1997: 15–17 and 26).

[106] *Botswana Gazette*, 15 December 2006, *Sunday Standard* 11 February 2007 and *Mmegi Online*, 23 February 2007.

outside Botswana, identify the caller and his/her location, and identify too the friends of the caller. Skelemani soon confirmed that the surveillance system was being acquired.[107]

A number of civic groups expressed strong concern about the DIS in December. A teachers' union representative, Eric Ditau, said that the directorate would be empowered to act without oversight from other authority and the new measures would 'legitimise structures that [we]re currently being used illegally to spy on trade unions.' Johnson Motshwarakgole of the Manual Workers Union noted that the director would be accountable only to the president, and the DIS would greatly increase his already overwhelming powers. He concluded that Botswana's democracy was 'going to the dogs' (*Botswana Gazette*, 15 December 2006).

Sandy Grant, an experienced and informed observer, had earlier attacked the bill for the seemingly great and completely unstated costs of the envisaged DIS structures. It was hard to avoid the conclusion that it was 'to some extent a reaction to Survival International and Professor Kenneth Good'. Grant described it as 'an astonishing, scary and difficult document'. It would ensure that no information about security and intelligence matters would be made available to the public and would expose people to 'arbitrary, armed arrest, seizure of possessions, a life sentence and no right of appeal'. Section 36 was suggestive of what was in store: 'Where a person is guilty of an offence for which no specific penalty is provided under this Act, that person shall be liable to imprisonment for a term not exceeding 10 years.' The bill failed to define clearly key terms like security, espionage and subversion, and was in general both obscurantist and dangerous.[108]

The interlinkages

Mineral-rich countries characteristically outlay money on the military and security. Botswana moved this way through the growth years of the 1990s, but has now escalated its security commitments sharply. This development is part and parcel with the other main characteristics of diamond dependency: the absence of diversification, presidentialism and predominance, top-level corruption, and the failure to provide for human development. The AIDS

---

[107] *Sunday Standard*, 4 December and *Mmegi Online*, 8 December 2006.
[108] Sandy Grant, 'Botswana: Security – But at a Price', *AllAfrica.com*, 13 November 2006. Section 36 is in Part VI of the bill, on General Provisions.

epidemic has been confronted, but poverty and inequalities continue at very high levels in the absence of welfare and taxation policies that have reduced these problems elsewhere. This is accepted with equanimity by the rulers of Botswana. According to a 1972 White Paper: a concern for equality 'must not lead us into assuming that the living standards of all the population can be raised by redistribution of the assets of the few people who are relatively well off.'[109] In his inaugural address in 1998, President Mogae reaffirmed: 'one cannot strengthen the weak by weakening the strong and enrich the poor by simply impoverishing the rich.'[110]

Freedoms of speech and association will be further restricted under the DIS. Its odious stress on security and the subversive activities of detractors threatens democracy and civil society broadly. Given the existing problems in land, housing, jobs, wages, ethnic relations and the subordination of the San, the drivers of conflict seem bound to be exacerbated. Botswana may continue as a wealthy nation for some time, but its near future is one of authoritarianism, suppression and 'negative peace'.

---

[109] Quoted in Liz Wily (1980), *Land allocation and hunter-gatherer land rights in Botswana*, London: Anti-Slavery Society, p. 107. Considered further in the next chapter.

[110] There is nothing pre-ordained about poverty and inequalities. A number of developing countries, for instance Viet Nam and Brazil, have shown in recent years that it is possible to reduce poverty substantially through redistributive action. See the UNDP's Human Development Reports, and *The Economist*, 26 November 2005, 24 June, and 30 September 2006.

5
Dispossession & Subordination of the San

No community in Botswana has experienced subordination so broadly, deeply and for so long as the San. In a country where poverty is widespread, no group of people is more impoverished. The exploitation and discrimination faced by the San involves their very identity as well as the basic material issues of land, income, health, education, and autonomous political organisation.

They are a people without a self-given name. Those that are appended to them – Khoe, Khoekhoe, Khoesan, Bushmen, Basarwa, San, Remote Area Dweller, RAD – are those of their masters, all to varying degrees derogatory.[1] San history was appropriated by outsiders and replaced by stereotypes connoting backwardness, ignorance, incapacity, landlessness – all justifications for their subordination. Even their numbers are uncertain, owing to the refusal of the government to acquire census data on ethnicity. Official estimates of their numbers have remained largely unchanged over decades at some 40,000.

Conquest, servitude and development

Alhough much remains obscure, research in anthropology, archaeology and history through the 1980s and 1990s suggests that the San were not always and everywhere primordial nomads dependent on hunting and gathering. For Wilmsen, San across the Kalahari over the previous millennium were producers of salt, ceramics and ornaments, with settled communities and some engagement in long-distance trade. They were also pastoralists controlling in

---

[1] 'Basarwa' is used both officially and popularly in Botswana. Although it carries the connotation 'contemptible fellow', its usage cannot be avoided. San is considered the least objectionable term.

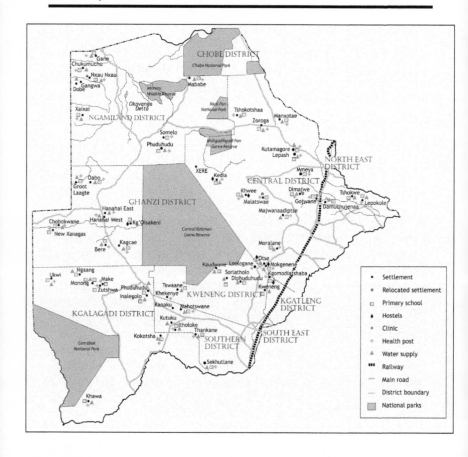

5.1 Map of remote area dweller settlements

different times and places herds of big-horned cattle.[2] The evidence is wide and compelling but not yet entirely substantial: limited archaeological findings, strong eye-witness travellers' accounts, linguistics, and not least important, the continuing resurgence of cattle-keeping by San in Botswana against the opposition of ranch owners and state policies favouring them. Until the turn of the twentieth century, they also possessed their own political organisation and leadership.[3]

Their dispossession began slowly at first. Facing 'hostile and hegemonic settlers' (chiefly Bantu agriculturalists), many San in the Ghanzi area, according to Guenther, offered determined and effective resistance for as long as they were able, that is, for 'about two generations, perhaps from the early decades of the 19th century to the 1870s'. This sustained resistance implied the existence of political organisation, and Guenther has described some large and predatory Bushman groups, up to 350 in numbers, consolidated around bellicose Bushman or Nama 'captains'. He concluded that 'inevitably they were outgunned and outnumbered, encircled and encapsulated, enserfed or proletarianised, defeated.'[4]

It is difficult to underestimate the importance of this process and its outcomes. The land, cattle, labour power and skills over which the San lost control were utilised on a long-term basis by rising Tswana elites. By the 1920s, the system of San servitude, as Miers and Crowder have emphasised, lay at the very roots of the increasingly successful Tswana pastoral economy, 'allowing the masters to build up large herds while freeing them from pastoral, agricultural and domestic chores and enabling them to engage in politics, herd management, trade and wage labour.'[5]

Serfdom contributed powerfully to elitism and development over many decades. At the start of the colonial period, the future Botswana already possessed strong, centralised, and highly

---

[2] See Edwin Wilmsen's path-breaking work of 1989, *Land Filled With Flies: a Political Economy of the Kalahari*, Chicago: University of Chicago Press.

[3] See Good (1993: 207) with reference to the findings of Wilmsen, James Denbow and Alan Barnard.

[4] Mathias Guenther (1994: 11–17 and 22), 'Lords of the desert land: politics and resistance of the Ghanzi Bushmen of the 19th century', paper presented to the conference, *People Politics and Power: Representing the Bushman People of Southern Africa*, 4–7 August, Rock Art Research Unit, University of the Witwatersrand. On banditry see Robert Gordon, in Donald Crummey (ed.) (1986) *Banditry, Rebellion and Social Protest in Africa*, London and Portsmouth, NH: James Currey and Heinemann, Chapter 8, and Breyten Breytenbach (1998: 133-41), *Dog Heart: A Travel Memoir*, Cape Town: Human and Rousseau.

[5] Suzanne Miers and Michael Crowder, 'The politics of slavery in Bechuanaland: power struggles and the plight of the Basarwa in the Bamangwato Reserve, 1926–1940' in Miers and Richard Roberts (eds) (1988), *The End of Slavery in Africa*, Madison, p. 177.

stratified state systems, the largest of which was Bamangwato (or Central District). Wealth was based on cattle ownership, and status was related to birth. Economic and political power lay in the hands of a *kgosi,* who was surrounded by an elite composed of the royal family and rich commoners. Below were ordinary common-ers, and below them were non-Tswana subject and servile groups, absorbed as the kingdoms expanded. It was a society of pervasive inequalities, wherein 'no man was another man's equal'.[6] What Miers and Crowder called the principal servile group, the largest and most exploited, was the San.

Serfdom was almost indistinguishable from slavery, its effects deep and enduring. The power of individual Tswana masters over San serfs increased after 1875 when San became private property. With the spread of the cattle economy whole San families were forced to become the dependents of cattlemen. They were unpaid except in kind, moved and transferred at will, inherited between masters and subjected to arbitrary punishment.[7]

Forced to act on public revelations of their servitude, a colonial inquiry (the Tagart Commission) revealed that property rights existed for San only on the whim of their master, who usually seized whatever they might with difficulty acquire. Tagart also reported that San almost unanimously declared that they wanted freedom, and many called in addition for the cattle, land and ploughs necessary to secure their independence. A subsequent survey by J.W. Joyce in 1936–7, enumerated some 9,500 Basarwa in Bamangwato and another 1,000 in more remote areas, some of whom had virtually emancipated themselves with access to outside wage labour, and ploughed their own lands and held cattle. He also identified 213 masters. The largest serf owner was Tshekedi Khama with 1,395 San dependents, while 24 others owned between 100 and 400 San each.[8] Serf ownership was 'con-centrated in the hands of a few wealthy families who were mainly royals'.[9]

At independence in 1966, the great majority of Basarwa in Bamangwato were, according to Miers and Crowder, worse off than they had been three decades earlier. Cattlemen were depriv-ing them of stock systematically, dispossessing those who still had

---

[6] Diana Wylie (1990: 25 and 27) called this principle 'the core concept' of the Tswana political economy.

[7] See Wylie (1990: 88) and Good (1993: 207–10).

[8] Miers and Crowder (1988), pp. 172, 187–188, and 191–92.

[9] Wilmsen and Rainer Vossen (1984), 'Labour, language and power in the construction of eth-nicity in Botswana', *Critique of Anthropolgy,* 10,1, p. 18.

any control over land or water, and turning San into a landless, cattleless proletariat. This affected the poorer strata of Ngwato too, but San suffered the 'additional disability of being socially despised'.[10]

Colonialism abolished serfdom,[11] but its norms and practices remained strong in the developing cattle economy. A Botswana government report of 1971 stated that the position of San labourers on Ghanzi ranches represented 'voluntary slavery';[12] Gulbrandsen found that San labourers were forced into a new serfdom, in a relationship of utter dependence upon ranch owners, strictly forbidden to keep livestock on the ranch; Campbell Main reported in 1991 that cattle-owners in the Sandveld of Central District treated Basarwa as an underclass conditioned to doing whatever they were told, and that facets of traditional serfdom still prevailed; and Hitchcock and Holm also noted in 1993 that the social status of the San 'remains to the present little better than that of a serf'.[13]

Reconstructing identity: new names and unknown numbers

In purportedly homogenous Botswana, Seretse Khama imposed a new identity on San as 'Remote Area Dwellers' (RADs). This emphasised geography and avoided the issues of ethnicity, though it was clear that the majority of new remote people were San. There was also considerable contiguity among remote people. Campbell, Main and Associates, for instance, found that in the Western Sandveld in 1990–91 they 'could see no apparent difference between the lifestyle of San and other RADs', and in addition, noted that all San spoke dialects which were mutually

---

[10] Miers and Crowder (1988), p. 195.

[11] British administrators knew in the 1870s that the subordination of San constituted 'actual slavery', but only in late 1936 did the protectorate government affirm that slavery had been abolished a century earlier. Margo Russell (1976), 'Slaves or workers? Relations between Bushmen, Tswana and Boers in the Kalahari', *Journal of Southern African Studies*, 2, 1, p. 178.

[12] The Ghanzi Labour Inspection Report, November 1971, quoted by Russell (1976), p. 178.

[13] Ornulf Gulbrandsen, Marit Kalsen and Janne Lexow (1986), *Botswana: Remote Area Development Programme*, Report Submitted to the Royal Norwegian Ministry of Development Cooperation, Bergen/Gaborone/Oslo: pp. 30 and 112; Campbell, Main and Associates (1991) *Western Sandveld Remote Area Development Report*, Gaborone: pp. 14 and 63–5; and Hitchcock R. and John D. Holm, (1993) 'Bureaucratic domination of hunter-gatherer societies: A study of the San in Botswana' *Development and Change*, 24, p. 313.

understandable.[14] Six years later, Ditshwanelo found overriding similarities between San and other contiguous minority communities in the CKGR. When they asked Basarwa and Bakgalagadi people in Kukama whether or not there was a difference between the two groups the response was: 'they had lived together for so long that they considered themselves to be Basarwa,' and in Kikao, where there were two groups with differing languages, they were told: 'we are all Basarwa because we live on this land.'[15] Saugestad agreed that in the difficult environment of the Kalahari, Bakgakagadi and other minority communities had cohabited with the San for centuries.[16] Campbell, Main and Associates defined the reality: what the new term actually connoted was remoteness from power, specifically the lack of political leadership and, in consequence of that, the absence of secure land and water rights.

History and identity are bound up together for the San in Botswana, and intertwined further with enumeration. Not only does the government refuse to collect ethnic data, but the official estimates of Basarwa numbers remain fixed over decades at a low figure of some 40,000. Thapelo has pointed to the stubborn insistence by government officials that the San are insignificant in number.[17] In May 2006 the office of the president offered figures for first-language speakers which suggested that Sesarwa speakers totalled only 30,000 or less than two per cent of Botswana's population, while Sekgalasadi represented 45,000.[18]

Experienced observers offer very different assessments. Hitchcock estimated that there were between 41,000 and 60,000 Basarwa in Botswana in the mid-1980s, and 63,000 San plus 59,000 other remote people in 1990,[19] and the Chr. Michelsen

[14] Campbell, Main estimated that Central District accommodated then some 17,000 out of a total national population of perhaps some 60, 000 Remote people, pp. 32 and 65. Gulbrandsen similarly had found that among the large RAD population in Central District in 1986, 97 per cent were of Basarwa origin, and that in several settlements 'Bakalanga and Basarwa share[d] the same living conditions', Gulbrandsen, et. al.(1986), p. 184.

[15] Ditshwanelo (1996), 'When will this moving stop?', Report on a Fact-finding Mission of the [CKGR], Gaborone: 10 April, pp.15-16.

[16] Sidsel Saugestad (2005/4), 'Improving their lives': State policies and San resistance in Botswana', *Before Farming*, article 1, p. 2. On ethnic differences and rural poverty in the Cape earlier, Breytenbach (1998) observed: 'Nobody can tell whether he is white or brown. When you are poor enough these distinctions fall away with time' p. 35.

[17] Teedzani Thapelo (2002), 'Nomads no more: Public policy and San (Bushman) displacement in liberal democratic Botswana', paper presented at the International Conference on Democracy and Liberation in Southern Africa, Windhoek: 11–13 July, p.16.

[18] Jeff Ramsay, 'Botswana's Ethnic Breakdown – OP', *Mmegi Online*, 9 May 2006.

[19] Hitchcock (1988), *Monitoring Research and Development in the Remote Areas of Botswana*, Bergen/Gaborone/Oslo. In 1988 he had also 'estimate[d] the total population of remote area dwellers to be approximately 180,000 people', quoted in Good (2002), p. 204.

Institute (CMI) noted in 1996 that the Basarwa population could be calculated as between 50,000 and over 100,000.[20] Recently Reteng has begun to construct ethnic data which effectively reverse the official claims.[21] If a figure of some 120,000 San and other remote people in the 1990s is accepted as an informed and moderate base line estimate, the implications are significant. It might be one thing to deny rights to a minority of two or three per cent, but to persist in subordinating ten per cent of the country's people reflects seriously on Botswana's democracy. This is a larger percentage than that of other indigenous peoples in their democratic home countries, for instance, the Inuit in Canada, Aborigines in Australia and Saami in Norway.

Indigenity also constitutes disputed ideological and political terrain in Botswana. This term is particularly important today because it embraces a range of important human rights and the international conventions and agencies supporting them. The concept of indigenous people can be approached, as IPACC suggests, as referring to those who 'occupied a territory before all other peoples and suffer current marginalisation'. It is clear to IPACC that the Khoe and San peoples of southern Africa have occupied the region for at least 20,000 years, possibly as long as 150,000 years, prior to the arrival of black, Bantu-speaking farmers,[22] and San in Botswana have undoubtedly experienced gross marginalisation. The Botswana government, however, rigidly refuses to recognise the San's indigenity, since, as was officially said in March 1993, 'all Batswana are indigenous to the country ... In addition, Government's development programmes and assistance schemes do not draw any distinctions among the country's citizens.'[23]

The recent intervention of the African Commission on Human and Peoples' Rights (ACHPR), a representative, informed and authoritative continental body, may make it difficult for Botswana to continue its obscurantism and denial. The ACHPR acknowledges the difficulties in definitions of indigenous people in Africa,

[20] Chr. Michelsen Institute, *NORAD's support of the [RADP] in Botswana*, a report submitted to the Royal Norwegian Ministry of Foreign Affairs, Bergen, February 1996, p. 22.

[21] Lydia Nyathi-Ramahobo has released data claiming that 'unrecognised or minority tribes in the country' constitute 60 per cent of the total population, while 'the main tribes' represent only 18 per cent. She admitted that Reteng's figures may not be exact, but said they gave a better estimate. "RETENG refutes Ramsay's ethnic report", *Mmegi Online*, 10 May 2006.

[22] The Indigenous Peoples of Africa Coordinating Committee, 'Who is indigenous in Africa?', they also claim that Khoe and San have the oldest genetic markers on the planet and the longest period of exclusive occupation. *www.ipacc.za/who.asp* 5 October 2004.

[23] Quoted in Sidesl Saugestad (1998), *The Inconvenient Indigenous*, Faculty of Social Science, University of Tromso, p. 316.

and notes that, except in a few instances, 'Africans can claim to be aboriginal people of the continent and nowhere else.' But it stresses nonetheless that, within this common heritage of aboriginality, 'African people have for centuries been migrating from various parts of the continent and there have been wars of conquest.' Additionally, communities have mixed, intermingled and inter-married. In order to recognise the unique character of indigenous people, the working group therefore resolved 'to settle for a socio-psychological description of indigenous people', setting out broad criteria, and affirming, as in the United Nations system, the princi-ple of self-definition and recognition of self-identity of peoples. The broad criteria for understanding indigenity were thus history, self-identity and continuing marginalisation through disposses-sion, subordination and discrimination.[24]

The commission's working group noted that African peoples who are facing particular human rights violations, and who iden-tify themselves as indigenous, belong to various economic systems and include hunter-gatherers and pastoralists as well as some small-scale farmers. The San of southern Africa were among these hunter-gatherers, numbering just over 100,000, with the majority located in Botswana. They highlighted the loss of land and other resources by indigenous pastoralists and hunter-gatherer commu-nities incrementally over years. In Botswana, some 1,500 San had been evicted from the CKGR over the past ten years. The evictions and the consequent court case testified 'to the refusal of the gov-ernment of Botswana to recognise that the inhabitants of the area have ancestral rights to the territory.' The government claimed that it aimed to provide 'development' in the forms of schools, clinics, etc. to those evicted. But 'alternative forms of develop-ment' utilising the indigenous knowledge systems of the San, 'appear to be unknown or unacceptable to the government of Botswana,' they observed.[25]

The associated report of the working group's eight-day mission to Botswana firmly stated: 'history has it that the San people ... are the original inhabitants of Botswana' and they remain the single largest indigenous community', economically and politically mar-ginalised and vulnerable to exploitation by their neighbours.[26]

---

[24] ACHPR (2005), *Report of the African commission's working group of experts on indigenous populations/communities*, Adopted by the ACHPR at its 28th ordinary sessions, Introduction pp. 12, 15, and 17–18.

[25] ACHPR (2005), pp. 15–24.

[26] ACHPR (2005), *Report of the working group on indigenous populations/communities in Africa mission to the Republic of Botswana* (2005), p. 12.

Rising growth and deepening inequalities

The details and trajectory of the San's subordination in Ghanzi, an area of cattle wealth and poverty, is well documented. Around the end of the 1960s, San in the district totalled some 10,000, and they were 'third and fourth generation farm labourers'. They were unemployed and underfed, overcrowded on land that did not belong to them, existing by begging along the road that took the cattle trucks out to the abattoir in Lobatse; on their own assessments they had been rendered voiceless and ineffectual.[27]

A decade later, Childers provided a detailed and an unusually sensitive study of the same area and people when the intensification of cattle production was underway. The focus of his study was the 4,500 Basarwa labourers and squatters on or near the 176 freehold farms in Ghanzi in the mid-1970s. New laws requiring the fencing of freehold farms had come in just before independence, the old trek route to Lobatse was being improved, and between 1964 and 1970 the prices paid for cattle at the government-owned abattoir there had increased over 300 per cent. Another 38 freehold properties were due for allocation in 1977. Basarwa were being left with few places where they could live without interference, and rising cattle numbers were destroying indigenous veld (wild) foods.[28]

The average cash wage of Basarwa farm labourers was R6.13 a month (the Pula was introduced in 1976 initially on par with the Rand). But very low wages were only part of their problems. Over 35 per cent of the Basarwa community, 1,475 people, were squatters on land which, in many cases, 'was originally theirs by fact of occupation'. Unemployed Basarwa were dependent for about half their subsistence on begging and increasingly difficult gathering activities. Stock theft was rising, from 23 cases in 1973 to 59 in 1975, and such theft by Basarwa was 'directly tied to the extent of hunger that they experience'.[29]

Livestock raising was a 'subsistence sideline for almost two-thirds of the people.' This was on a very minimum scale for most,

[27] Details in Guenther (1976), 'From hunters to squatters', chapter in *Kalahari Hunter-Gatherers*, Richard Lee and Irven DeVore (eds), Harvard: Harvard University Press, pp. 121 and 123, and Guenther (1996), 'From "Lords of the Desert" to "Rubbish People"', chapter in Pippa Skotnes (ed.), *Miscast: Negotiating the Presence of the Bushmen*, Cape Town: University Press, p. 235.
[28] Gary W. Childers (1976), *Report of the survey/investigation of the Ghanzi Farm Basarwa situation*, Republic of Botswana, Gaborone: September, pp. 2, 12–14, and 19.
[29] Childers (1976), pp. 45–47, and 50–51.

with goats and donkeys figuring prominently. But significantly, cattle too were owned by nine per cent of farm Basarwa. Childers noted three cases where San had been able to raise over 20 cattle each, another two with up to 30 cows, and even one who had raised 57. The Basarwa, he said, 'have the predilection ... for possessing livestock', and he felt they deserved to be given the chance to become pastoralists. They perceived that the ability to have land and water is the first step towards their economic development, and they realised that the economic superiority of all other farm residents was the result of their having 'either village or farm land of their own.'[30]

But they were actually being offered no chance at all. Basarwa were often assaulted for no apparent reason. Terms such as '*O Mosarwa fela*' – You are nothing but a Mosarwa – were commonly used to remind them of their lowly status.

Childers seemed aware that the dynamics of the growth economy underway in the 1970s were against the San. As Russell reported in 1976 small farmers were being eliminated and the number of farming establishments was shrinking as the size of the establishment was increasing. Growth and inequalities were rising together. While 90 per cent of Ghanzi farms held stock worth R9,200 on average, the average of the top ten per cent was R234,528. Ghanzi farmers, Childers noted, had become noticeably wealthier, while the Basarwa were becoming even poorer. The subordinate San were being cumulatively exploited by the state and market: profitable beef production, boosted by fencing, 'meant a decreasing demand for Bushman labour',[31] and the increasing numbers of ranches and cattle meant that the San's access to land, water, and food resources – let alone their pastoralist aspirations – were disappearing.[32]

Mogalakwe takes forward our knowledge of the unrelenting exploitation of the San in Ghanzi into the 1980s. While the 1981 housing census had found some 7,000 people on Ghanzi freehold farms, his study in 1985 enumerated 915 – most San having been relocated in the meantime to the Settlements being established through the 1970s, discussed below.[33] Only 28 per cent of his sample were working, and the wages received by almost two-thirds averaged between P5 and P30 a month, for which they worked long and irregular hours. Consistent with government

[30] Childers (1976), pp. 51–61 and 83.
[31] Russell (1976), p. 195.
[32] Russell (1976), p. 104, and Childers (1976), pp. 50 and 75–76.
[33] Mogalakwe (1986), *Inside Ghanzi Freehold Farms*, Ministry of Local Government and Land, Applied Research Unit, Gaborone: April, pp. 16 and 19.

policy already noted, farm labour was denied minimum wage protection. Denied also the protection of regulated hours: 'most of them work from sun rise to sun set, every single day that passes.'

Living and health conditions for the labourers were appalling. Almost all said they had no access to latrines, and 70 per cent were without refuse pits. On the evidence of the telling photographs included in the report, their housing represented hovels. Few farmers were ready to provide their workers with better conditions, with one retorting: 'Can you teach a dog to use a latrine?'[34]

While the impoverishment of the San was broad and deep, cash wages were near the core of their weaknesses – cattle, land, health, housing and education were unlikely to be acquired without access to wage income.

The Western Sandveld of Central District borders on Ghanzi, and the 1991 study of remote people there reported San cattle labourers getting average wages of about P25 per month with milk and rations. This was an improvement, Campbell, Main said, on 1977, when the wage had been between P2 and P5 per month – thus, even lower than the P6 which Childers had observed in Ghanzi around then. But Campbell, Main still noted that the 1991 wage 'remain[ed] incredibly low' in national terms.

As in Ghanzi, pay was extremely irregular and often delayed: gaps of up to eight months were not uncommon and delays of as much as a year or more were recorded. There were still cases where people worked only for food. Food rations remained as part of the payment package, and they were not regulated in any way as regards quantity and quality. Months went by before food was delivered. The practice of delayed payment of wages and food deepened dependency in itself. San workers recognised that it tied them firmly to the ranch owner; those who complained were fired.[35]

The findings of Gulbrandsen/Mogalakwe/Campbell, Main showed that P30 a month represented top wages for San labourers over a decade of high growth in Botswana. In 1992 GDP per capita in Botswana was P5,886. The statutory minimum wage then was P237 a month, and a top public servant received a salary of P8,216 a month without the sizable allowances associated with such positions (already noted for 2006).[36] In 1990 the government had

[34] For further details of their conditions, Mogalakwe (1986), pp. 22, 24–5, 28, 30 and 39–42.

[35] Campbell, Main and Associates (1991), *Western Sandveld Remote Area Dwellers: Report*, Gaborone: April, pp. 16 and 44–47.

[36] H.K. Siphambe (n.d.) 'Minimum wages in Botswana: Should they be increased?', *Barclays Botswana Economic Review*, 3 (4), p. 6.

reaffirmed both the historically based low wages policy for unskilled labourers, and a highly differentiated salary structure for the well paid. Childers and Russell had recognised that in Ghanzi in the 1970s rich cattlemen were getting much richer while San were getting poorer. In 1992, the gap between the top bureaucratic earnings in nominal terms and the formal wages of a San labourer – which he might or might not actually receive – was some 270 to one. San were the poorest of the poor, inexorably, intentionally.

Ranches for cattlemen, settlements for San

By the mid-1970s a number of trends favouring a wide programme of state-assisted fenced ranching and, in association with that, a settlement policy (or Villagisation: the concentration of people in specially administered villages) for surplus San labourers, came in together in Ghanzi and adjacent areas. The former was highly supportive of ambitious cattlemen, and the latter soon constituted an immense disillusionment to whatever hopes San might have retained for ever obtaining a place of their own with access to cattle.

The move to enclose and allocate individual grazing properties on what were tribal or communal lands developed incrementally 1966–75.[37] The original Ghanzi freehold farms had proved highly profitable. They were expanded in the 1950s and Batswana purchased vacant properties after 1966. Between 1968 and 1973, programmes were developed to assist cattle owners to acquire fenced, watered ranches. Adjacent Western Sandveld land was officially deemed empty by the planners, ignoring the scattered Bakgalagadi settlements and San communities in the area. In 1975 a so-called Tribal Grazing Land Policy (TGLP) was launched, and the true aims of the programme, the privatisation of communal resources, soon became clear.[38]

The other and associated trend focused on the 4,500 San living as squatters on the Ghanzi farms in the mid-1970s, redundant to the changing needs of fenced ranching, and highly vexatious in

[37] Although its origins went back to the 1920s and the introduction and spread of borehole technology in private hands. Good (1992) , 'Interpreting the Exceptionality of Botswana', p. 72.

[38] Liz Wily (1980), *Land allocation and hunter-gatherer land rights in Botswana: The impact of the [TGLP]*, London: The Anti-Slavery Society, Working Paper No. 4, pp.103–04. Wily was the coordinator of the short-lived Bushman Development Programme, 1974–77.

their impoverishment to the ranchers. Cattlemen there, and in control of Ghanzi District Council, were clear that 'they would evict all San rather than pay them [what was due to them as] minimum wages'. They and their counterparts in the Western Sandveld also refused to allow San either to gather or to hunt on their properties.[39] The first new settlement for San and other remote people in Ghanzi, at West Hanahai, 48 kilometres from Ghanzi town, was planned in 1976, supported by Childers as a way – the only way under the circumstances – of according them access to land and water.[40]

The TGLP offered great opportunities to ambitious cattlemen. Rents on ranches of eight square kilometres were sub-economic initially and payment was not enforced. Long and easy leasehold terms amounted in practice to freehold. State policy supported the rising cattlemen broadly. 'Over 12 per cent of tribal land', some 51,000 square kilometres, was zoned for commercial ranches. Commercial land owners could continue to graze their stock in crowded tribal areas – the 'dual grazing', which only the relatively well-off advantageously practised. 'Virtually no land whatsoever', as Hitchcock noted, was actually reserved for the rural poor, despite the policy's earlier assurances to that effect. In less than seven years 700 to 1,000 ranches were established.[41] The TGLP's original social justice expressions were, said Wily, 'a charade'.[42]

Policy implementation towards the very poor went ahead consistent with this firmly pro-rich principle of growth with worsening inequalities, as the white paper of March 1972 had indicated it should; as Wily noted, it was a time when 'democracy found its limits'. Consultation with non-stockholders about their land needs would be brief if it occurred at all. As the district commissioner declared at a meeting of the new Ghanzi Land Board in March 1977: 'All this discussion and planning is getting in the way of development. Bushmen if they are in the way, should be simply gotten out of the way, so we can put up our fences.'[43]

By the following year, official attitudes towards questions of land needs and rights of San had hardened to the point of

[39] Wily (1980), pp. 62–63 and 66.
[40] Gary Childers, Joyce Stanley and Kathryn Rick (1982), *Government settlement or people's community?: A study of local institutions in Ghanzi District*, Republic of Botswana, Ministry of Local Government and Lands, Applied Research Unit, June, p. 1.
[41] Robert K. Hitchcock (1988), *Monitoring research and development in the remote areas of Botswana*; Report, Bergen/Gaborone/Oslo: pp. 2–14, 2–20, 4-2 and 4–8.
[42] Wily (1980), p. 51.
[43] Wily (1980), pp. 84 and 107.

exclusion.[44] Policy direction had been decided 'and it d[id] not bode well for any poor tribesmen, let alone San ... the enclosure of as much tribal grazing land as possible would occur'. The ministry of agriculture was firm in 1978 that the San 'should be made to settle in a village so that they may be developed', and their nomadic lives were to be discouraged in the strongest of terms. Their legal rights to land and to hunting and gathering were extinguished in the attorney general's chambers at this time.[45]

Hunting soon became a severely restricted subsistence alternative for the San. Exclusive hunting rights became the prerogative of the ranchers, readily enforced by the state, and residents, who might have lived there for more than a century, as in Thankana in Southern District, became potential poachers. The introduction in 1979 of unified hunting regulations had 'disastrous effects', according to Egner and Klausen, turning hunting into a perilous and proto-criminal enterprise for the San and the illiterate rural poor in general.[46] Between 10 and 30 per cent of remote people in six settlements claimed during 1990 and 1991 that they had been charged with an offence by police or game scouts, mostly involving poaching or stock theft. In Groot Laagte in Ghanzi, 82 per cent of those so charged received prison sentences averaging four and a half months.[47]

Redundant to the labour needs of Ghanzi ranchers and unable to play a role in the growth economy, the settlement/villagisation programme was the sole option facing San in the late 1970s. Under the Ghanzi Farm Basarwa Project, settlements were seen by a sympathetic official like Childers as providing access to land and water, and in the longer term as sites for the provision of services like health and education, long denied to San. West Hanahai was the first to be established in the district in 1978, on an allocated 20 square kilometres of land surrounding a borehole, and in early 1979 about 150 Basarwa moved to this settlement, seeking freedom from servitude and from being unwanted squatters. Many seemed to harbour both optimism and desperation. As one man said: 'This

---

[44] Thapelo (2002) refers to officialdom's tone of 'indifferent belligerence', p. 23.

[45] Wily (1980), pp. 83, 88, 94 and 98.

[46] A Special Game Licence was available to remote people, on limited and strict conditions administered by a small number of game scouts. E.B. Egner and A.L. Klausen (1980), *Poverty in Botswana*, Gaborone: National Institute of Development and Cultural Research, p. 27, and Gulbransen et al. (1986), pp. 25–6 and 147.

[47] Economic Consultancies et al., *A Monitoring Programme for the Settlements at Thankane, Kokotsha, Inalegolo, Monong, Ngwatlhe and Groot Laagte*, Gaborone, Ministry of Local Government and Lands, May 1991, pp.143 and 152. Four of those were in Kgalagadi District.

is a good place for me because I can now work for myself ... I have no other place to go where I can be free.'[48]

Notably too, over half of them 'arrived with their own cattle (normally 2 to 8 head).' By January 1982, when the residents numbered 300, the total cattle herd on Hanahai had reached over 200, with over half of these belonging to two residents. The district council had provided eighteen cattle to nine new owners since 1979, under a livestock support scheme which Childers said worked well. By 1981, almost 40 per cent of households owned cattle, and 15 per cent of the settlement's income came from that source.[49]

But serious problems were already evident. Food was lacking and hunger was a 'common condition', and the long term viability of West Hanahai, and by implication of the other three settlements awaiting opening, was doubtful. Outside cattlemen were already intruding their large herds on to the settlement, 'over-taxing the low yielding water supply and denuding the surrounding veld area.' [50]

Within a decade, seven settlements were designated in the district, holding near the end of the 1980s, about 5,000 remote people, just over half the district total. Each was approximately 20 by 20 kilometres, containing some 390 residents on average. By contrast, nearly 19,000 square kilometres had been allocated as new ranches to some 250 individuals and syndicates, a share of land about eight times greater than that of some 5,000 remote people.[51] The settlements constituted, not quasi-freehold ownership, but only the loosest forms of access, and the remote inhabitants had to compete unfairly and ineffectively with outside cattlemen for the use of the settlement's resources, if it held any. Water facilities were used by big cattle owners without payment, and with in many cases severe detrimental impact on a settlement's supplies. The land allocated to settlements, moreover, was qualitatively inferior too. In the words of H.W. Korfage, a Ghanzi district official in 1992: settlements were on marginal, infertile land, and in ecologically fragile areas. Chobokwane, for instance, was 'most

[48] Childers, Stanley and Rick (1982), pp. 5–9.

[49] Childers et al. (1982), pp. 6, 10–11 and 77.

[50] Childers et al. (1982), pp. 14–16.

[51] Settlements were quantitatively inadequate on other measures too. Hitchcock (n.d.) considered that some 400 to 2,000 square kilometres were required to sustain a group of 30 to 50 people as foragers in the Kalahari Desert ecosystem, and he noted that the 70 settlements or so that existed in 1998, constituted in total less than one per cent of the country's area. By contrast, 20 per cent was designated for wildlife management and 17 per cent was devoted to national parks and game reserves. 'Indigenous Peoples' Participation, Development, and Empowerment, With Special Reference to the San', mimeo, p. 8.

disadvantaged'; the area around Kagcae was 'devastated'; and the longest established settlements, West and East Hanahai, lacked productive economic activities.[52]

While ranchers had made great gains in the Western Sandveld through the 1980s, the position of San and other remote people was one of near-total deprivation. The area covered in the survey by Campbell, Main was 'vast, nearly 10,000 square kilometres', but where there had been some 1,000 mobile hunter-gatherers in 1978, none any longer existed a decade later. A few San had cattle and donkeys, and in the south, others owned rather more stock. But borehole owners in the area 'charge watering fees for access to their resources.[53] Overall, remote people now owned less stock than they had in 1978.

The whole of the Western Sandveld had been occupied by cattle-men without any regard for the more than 4,000 remote people who lived there, 'the majority' having been born there too. The land they once occupied was allocated for ranching 'without regard for RAD needs'. Most large wildlife species had disappeared with ranching on such a scale, and the San were reduced to little more than beggary. Total insecurity too, for they could be told to move by anyone awarded rights to land by the Land Board.[54]

Nevertheless, resilience, determination and even some degree of hope seemed to remain. Most people opposed, or only condition-ally approved of, relocation by the government to a Community Service Centre in the extreme north-west of the area. One person said: 'We won't move to a [new] Centre unless it is put here, where we are'; another said: 'If we are moved, we want a borehole, school, clinic, fields, tools, donkeys, seeds, cattle and goats'; a third said: 'I can point to more than one hundred graves of my people right here; this is my land'; and another affirmed: 'I was born here and I will die here. I will not move.' While most children in the region left primary school before standard five, and many never went beyond the first two years of school, education was still seen by the people as vital for improving their lives. They just wanted to know how they would obtain it.[55]

---

[52] See Good (1993), 'At the ends of the ladder', pp. 214–16.

[53] On the settlements of Mmiya and Mmakgama in Central District, where there was no perma-nent water supply, outside borehole and cattle owners also charged San for water, or 'simply refuse'. Christopher Ndozi and Elisha Toteng (1989*): A socio-economic survey of selected central district remote area settlements*, Ministry of Local Government and Lands, Applied Research Unit, December, p.70.

[54] Campbell, Main and Associates (1991), pp. 3, 16, 33, 41, and 56–57.

[55] Campbell, Main and Associates (1991), pp. 37 and 59–60.

All the experienced observers referred to above emphasise the paternalism and arrogance with which officialdom approached the San, or the indifferent belligerence that Thapelo rightly detected. Childers noted that officials considered San as children, incapable of making or implementing decisions on their own, and how this in turn perpetuated the 'leadership vacuum' existing in most settlements in the 1980s.[56] Both Gulbrandsen and Campbell Main stressed the broad importance of autonomous political organisation. For the former, settlements without officially recognised leaders had no legal protection against outside intruders,[57] and for the latter the absence of authoritative structures was what essentially defined remoteness.

San political representation improved in the 1990s, affected by the country-wide democratic upsurge, by the demographic leverage which San possess in Ghanzi where they were around half the district population, and by new regional linkages between San peoples. Near the end of the decade all settlements in the district had acquired gazetted (officially recognised) headmen or women. But officials could still manoeuvre to block San candidates at elections, and settlement leaders faced tight limitations. Outside cattlemen might simply bypass a San headman, and go straight to the land board when they wished to reside on a settlement, and the position of an active or outspoken headwoman was undermined in favour of an amenable replacement.[58]

Three settlements, those of Chobokwane, Groot Laagte and West Hanahi, had tried to acquire control over neighbouring leasehold extension farms (those of 164 NK, 154 NK and 173 NK) respectively. It was a long and devious process. Ghanzi District Council had apparently favoured, even agreed to, the allocations, 1989-90, but pressure from within central government intervened against the settlements and a non-governmental consortium assisting the San. The BDP MP for Ghanzi, Johnny Swartz, the serving minister of local government and big cattleman, Patrick Balopi, and a former district commissioner, Anderson Chibua, were also interested in the farms. Michael Tshipinare, the assistant minister found guilty of corruption by the chief magistrate of Gaborone, said that the idea of transferring the farms to Basarwa had come from interfering expatriates,

---

[56] At Xade in the CKGR a headman had existed 'for at least three generations', stemming from a long history of inter-mixing with Bakgalagadi people. The hereditary headman was officially appointed to this position by the Ghanzi District Commissioner in 1976. Childers et al. (1982), pp. 32 and 58.

[57] Gulbrandsen (1986) p. 134.

[58] See Good (2002), pp. 39–40

and Swartz said publicly that the farms should not go to San. Norway was the most generous foreign donor to the RADP, but it withdrew its support in the wake of the 'Ghanzi Farms' issue.[59]

At the end of the 1990s no secure land rights existed on the settlements. Their infrastructure was sometimes good, as were programmes of cattle distribution, but settlements overall remained places of impoverishment.[60]

A refusal to learn from past mistakes, and to profit from even mild and entirely constructive criticism, was a further part of the syndrome of state domination. Campbell, Main referred throughout their report to the prior detailed study made by Hitchcock in 1978; the work was informed, cogent and dispassionate. Nevertheless, 'not a single recommendation' which he made then had been implemented over the subsequent 13 years. The Campbell, Main report of 1991, also thorough, detailed, and properly critical in places, was not just ignored but pointedly rejected by the central district council.[61]

Similarly, when a San/Basarwa regional conference was held in Gaborone in October 1993, it was a promising event, coming soon after the initial conference in Windhoek the previous year. San representatives articulated and debated their concerns, and it was hailed as a success from many perspectives.[62] But a Botswana government report on the conference, with the official proceedings and resolutions, did not appear until three of four years later, and when it did it was a 'clear demonstration of indifference' (Saugestad, 1998: 284).

The remote area development programme

In 1977 the Bushmen Development Programme became the RADP, ostensibly to avoid South African notions of separate development, but actually in consistency with the growth-first, non-

[59] At a meeting in Gaborone between the ministry of local government and Basarwa representatives, NORAD was publicly blamed by a senior officer for 'fomenting Basarwa ethno-political sentiments and encouraging the secession of the Basarwa from the republic'. CMI (1996) *Norad's Support for the [RADP]*, Evaluation Report, Bergen/Oslo: pp. xii-xiii and p. 31. The official's wild accusations expressed the incomprehension of the ruling elite when faced with San calls for political rights and representation.
[60] CMI (1996), pp. 25–6.
[61] Campbell, Main and Associates (1991: 64) and CMI (1996), p. 81.
[62] San spokesmen took clear positions on issues like land rights, mother-tongue education in schools, cultural practices, and the creation of San representative structures to articulate their interests at the national level. CMI (1996), pp. 38–9.

inclusionist development strategy being implemented then. The aims of the earlier programme had been explicitly stated as 'greater self-reliance of the Bushman people.'[63] Suggestions of a rights-based approach to the special needs and problems of the San, and to any possible affirmative/empowerment strategies, associated with the likes of Wily and Childers, were stifled (Wily departing in 1978). An empowerment strategy for the San did not resurface in Gaborone until the early 1990s, when proposals for a revamped and reorientated RADP held brief attention, buoyed up by democratisation in Namibia and South Africa.

Originating in political negativism, the RADP has been small in size, and lacking in political strength and clarity of purpose. While it largely operates as the administrative agency for the settlements, it also provides welfare services because so many San are so deeply impoverished.

The RADP operated in the mid-1990s as just one of 24 other programmes within MLG. It was a decentralised activity which was meant to be planned and implemented at district level. The role of MLG was supposedly overall coordination, left in the hands of the RADP Unit composed then of only one person, appointed at the level of principal administrative officer (RADP) who reported to a deputy permanent secretary in the ministry. The full RADP administrative cadre was very small, with major programme districts, like Ghanzi and Central, having only five and nine RADP staff respectively. No special induction or training courses were offered to staff. The CMI concluded that the status of the RADP within government was 'low' (1996: 75–86).

Nothing had improved when BIDPA assessed the programme in 2003. It was headed as before by only a coordinator working under another bureaucrat in MLG. A specific RADP policy framework was absent, its objectives and goals were unclear, and overall direction was ambiguous.[64]

Where 'clarity' existed was in the deeply negative areas of non-accountability and secrecy. Its current operations were based on a presidential directive (Cab. 28/87) of 1987, which implied, BIDPA

[63] Wily (1982), 'A strategy of self-determination for the Kalahari San (The Botswana government's programme of action in the Ghanzi farms)', *Development and Change*, vol. 13, p. 291.
[64] BIDPA (2003), *Report on the review of the [RADP]*, Gaborone: 19 December, p. 17. BIDPA contrasted the RADP's weak organisation and leadership with that of the Aboriginal and Torres Strait Islander Commission (ATSIC), established by an act of parliament in Australia in 1989. It is headed by a minister who represents it in parliament, cabinet and in budgetary committees. ATSIC formulated and implemented programmes, developed policy proposals, provided advice to the minister, and monitored the effectiveness of programmes for indigenous people.

observed, that parliament had never debated the RADP. The aims of the programme were not well known, either to parliament, the general public, or even the majority of public servants. There was no coordination or collaboration with other ministries, such as agriculture and trade and industry, since it operated on its own terms. It existed in consequence 'outside of the public domain', accorded 'a certain amount of sensitivity that makes it appear rather secretive.' [65]

The RADP's responsibilities were simultaneously huge. It operated in 2003 in 64 Settlements, involving 38,000 people. Thirty-six of these contained more than 500 people each, qualifying them as 'villages' elsewhere in Botswana, and six held more than 1,000 residents, representing ordinarily the higher tertiary two category.[66]

The failures of the RADP were also great. The CMI's overall conclusions stood the test of time. On the infrastructual components, the provision of healthcare and water supplies, for instance, 'the government ha[d] done reasonably well', and it had done 'rather badly with all the rest of it'. The failure to promote income generation in the settlements was the major shortfall, associated with the disconnection between 'investments in infrastructure and the land rights which these investments were indirectly intended to secure'. Money, they also stressed, 'ha[d] not been a problem for the RADP'.[67]

BIDPA noted that the TGLP had led to the displacement of remote people, and 'the costs in terms of landlessness and poverty [we]re very high.' The majority of settlements were located on communal land, and almost all are in the dry sandveld and western regions. Though these areas were normally deemed unsuitable for arable agriculture, the RADP encouraged farming, in particular the growing of maize and sorghum, neither of which were part of the preferred diet of the Basarwa. They liked to plant watermelons, but received no assistance to do so. There was also a general lack of farming implements, including fencing to protect crops from animals. Many residents also complained about the lack of power for ploughing, and that the small numbers of cattle provided by RADP were non-viable as a potential herd. Ineffectualness was conspicuous in this key area. The RADP failed to assist remote

---

[65] BIDPA (2003), pp. 75–86 and 124–5.

[66] In 2001, the two largest were Mabesakwa in Tutume with 1,942 and New Xade just outside the CKGR with 1,442. BIDPA (2003), pp. 26, 32 and 35.

[67] BIDPA (2003), pp. 31, 75 and 77.

people in making land claims to a land board, and land, as BIDPA too recognised, was central to the success or otherwise of the programme.[68]

Problems existed in key areas of infrastructural delivery such as education and health. All settlements had primary schools, but the dropout rate was high. Malnutrition was significantly higher than the national average in western and sandveld settlements – 18 per cent in some cases, in contrast with 11 per cent elsewhere – and infectious diseases were another danger. Heavy alcohol consumption was one of the greatest social problems, with further hazardous consequences.[69]

BIDPA listed the failures: the lack of economic development; poor housing; lack of income generation, and consequent unemployment and poverty; high illiteracy; and weak institutional and leadership structures; community institutions were 'inactive' and participation in them was 'low'. Severe and chronic poverty existed, and weak welfare programmes – in particular the inadequate destitute's allowance and the small old-age pension[70] – constituted the dominant source of income in most settlements.[71]

Proposals to broaden, potentially to transform, the programme's ambit to include land rights, productivity and political organisation for the San, were emphasised by community groups and NORAD in the early 1990s. The ministry of local government announced, in October 1992, that it had completed a review of the RADP that was, in the words of Permanent Secretary Pelonomi Venson, intended to shift the emphasis away from infrastructural elements and towards 'culture, land issues, leadership and community development'. Terje Vigtel, senior Norwegian representative, added that his country wanted 'priority consideration for land requirements and land rights, cultural identity, [and the] representation of RADs in advisory/decision-making fora'. These novel initiatives – a virtual 'empowerment strategy' – perhaps peaked, according to the CMI, with the regional conference in Gaborone in October 1993. They were soon stopped, seemingly

---

[68] BIDPA (2003), pp. 66–8, 70, 78, 86 and 90–1.

[69] BIDPA (2003), pp. 114–20.

[70] BIDPA (2003: xxi and 27–39) An old-age pension was only introduced in 1996, worth then P100 a month, raised to P110 in 1998, and available in cash. The South African pension was then some four times higher while in Namibia it was slightly more. Many elderly Basarwa in Ghanzi had difficulty in acquiring the pension because of their inability to establish their age satisfactorily, their illiteracy and general remoteness. See Good (2002), *The Liberal Model*, p. 59.

[71] CMI (1996), xvii, and pp. 1, 4, and 42.

negated silently at presidential level; the ministry's review is thought to have reached cabinet in about October 1994, but it was sent back to them on the grounds that its proposals went outside their jurisdiction.[72]

The RADP was thus a conspicuous failure to the 40,000 very poor people inside the settlements and the uncounted tens of thousands more outside, and a secretive, non-accountable programme under presidential aegis.

Relocation: the repeated experience

Historically, relocation exists as an icon of the absence of human rights and the fate of indigenous peoples under specific political conditions of a colonial or quasi-colonial kind; including apartheid South Africa, French Algeria, colonial Australia, and the highland clearances in Scotland. The elitist developmental state in Botswana is not totally different in the experience of the despised San and the many poor people. Since independence, 'most San in Botswana have been relocated or dispossessed' (Saugestad, 2005/4: 2). Confident paternalism has normally characterised the ruling elite, but with the removals from the CKGR over the past decade belligerent and contemptuous attitudes have been more clearly exposed.

Vice-President Mogae referred, in 1996, to the inhabitants of the CKGR as 'stone age creature[s]', who were doomed to 'die out like the dodo' if they failed to fall in with official plans for their development.[73] Five years later, the views expressed by Foreign Minister Lt.-General Merafhe, were similarly dictatorial and contemptuous: 'Our treatment of the Basarwa dictates that they should be elevated from a status where they find themselves ... We all aspire to Cadillacs and would be concerned with any tribe to remain in the bush communing with flora and fauna.'[sic][74] Eric Molale, permanent secretary in local government, told the BBC when the second wave of the removals from the CKGR was beginning, that perpetuating 'a nomadic prehistoric way of living [was] outrageous', and the minister for local government, Margaret Nasha,

---

[72] Good (2002), pp. 61–2 and CMI (1996), xiii–xiv.
[73] Quoted by Suzanne Daley, 'No room in the desert for "human dodos"', the London *Guardian*, 16 July 1996. In actuality, the dodos did not 'die out' inevitably, but were rather killed off methodically by gun-carrying hunters.
[74] See Good (2003), *Bushmen and Diamonds*, p. 27.

declared rhetorically: 'You know the issue of Basarwa? Sometimes I equate it to the elephants. We once had the same problem when we wanted to cull the elephants and people said no.'[75] The ACHPR's working group noted a general contempt for Basarwa expressed 'even in top political leadership'.[76]

The removals from the CKGR since 1997 are different from what has gone before, despite the government's determination to disguise their actions. When Alice Mogwe began to study the human rights situation of the San in 1991, she noted immediately the 'great sensitivity on the part of central government and council officials' on the issues.[77] Thapelo, Wily and Scanlon's findings were broadly similar. Secrecy surrounded the RADP for good reason, and when new San leaders like John Hardbattle and Roy Sesana emerged nationally in the early 1990s, their aims and motives were immediately attacked and traduced in threatening and lordly terms.

When Hardbattle first spoke on San problems to the Botswana Society in Gaborone in 1992, 'it was like a bomb going off'. He was summoned with other leaders to meet officials at police headquarters, where he was told: 'We own you. Don't think the donors will be here forever, and when [they] leave, it will be just you and us.'[78] They were supposedly only advancing 'their own personal interests', and their views were those of 'people who are opposed to any form of development of Basarwa', as Masire declared in June 1996.[79] Hardbattle and Roy Sesana set up the First People of the Kalahari (FPK) in 1991 to express Bushman rights, and it became the leading national organisation in the region run by and for the San.[80]

Presidentialist secrecy exists in this arena because the government knows it has a lot to hide about the suppression of the San. It is a unique issue that goes to the core of Botswana's elitist dysfunctional democracy. The contemporary CKGR is different because of all the removals preceding it, the scale and intensity of this new action, and the scrutiny directed at it lately by the high

---

[75] BBC News Online, 'Botswana Cuts Bushman Services', 23 January 2002, and George Monbiot, 'Who really belongs to another age: bushmen or the House of Lords?', *Guardian*, 21 March 2006.

[76] ACHPR (2005), *'Report of the working group'*, p. 14.

[77] Alice Mogwe (1992), *Who Was (T) here First?*, Botswana Christian Council Occasional Paper no.10, March, p. 1.

[78] Quoted in Nora Boustany, 'The Bushmen's advocate', *The Washington Post*, 18 December 1995.

[79] See Good (2002) *The Liberal Model*, p. 46.

[80] Sesana became chairman of FPK in 1995, 'Roy Sesana – Biography', Survival International, Press Release, 26 February 2007.

court of Botswana, CERD, the ACHPR, and other international bodies. The CKGR is different because this time the government's obscurantism and lies are being penetrated authoritatively.

The CKGR: the first removals

Covering more than 52,000 square kilometres, the CKGR is the country's largest reserve. Established in 1961, its original purpose was to provide land where the San could pursue hunting and gathering; in the words of the Fauna Conservation Proclamation, 'to protect wildlife resources and reserve sufficient land for traditional use by hunter-gatherer communities'. Named as a game reserve for political convenience, the area was effectively reserved for those whose 'primary subsistence was derived from wild plants and animals'. Regulations in 1963 governing entry into the reserve extended the legal protection offered to San. 'No person other than a Bushman indigenous to the [CKGR] shall enter the said reserve without having first obtained a permit in writing from the district commissioner in Ghanzi.'[81]

At its inception, the population of the CKGR was around 4,000, whose ancestors, Pedder (n.d.) considered, had probably occupied the area for around 2,000 years. By the mid-1980s, the number of residents had dropped to around 1,300, most of whom were concentrated in a few settlements/communities in the south. At Xade there were around 860 people, at Gope 200, and at Mothlomelo perhaps 150 residents. Xade acquired a borehole and other facilities, and permanent water saw its population rise to 1,200 in 1995, when Mothlomelo's population was 350.[82]

In 1986 the government decided that social and economic development at Xade and other settlements in the CKGR was to be frozen; sites would be found outside the reserve where existing residents would be 'encouraged to relocate'; and the Department of Wildlife and National Parks (DWNP) would immediately begin to exploit the reserve's tourism potential. Recommendations made by the government's own fact-finding mission of the previous

---

[81] Though not named as a Bushman Reserve, that was what it was intended to be and what it effectively became. High Court of Botswana, 'Roy Sesana et al. and the Attorney General', Misca. No. 52 of 2002, Judgement, Justice Unity Dow, pp. 145–6.

[82] Emily Pedder (n.d.), 'Report on the [CKGR]', mimeo; the government's *Fact-Finding Mission, Report of 1985*, and Lin Cassidy (2001), 'District socio-economic data on San in Botswana', appendix in Good, et al. (2001), *An assessment of the status of the San in Botswana*, Windhoek: Legal Assistance Centre, April, pp. A8 and A17.

year, that San should continue residing in the reserve in association either with community-based tourism activities, or as game guards employed by DWNP, were rejected.

Implementation was initially variable, as official intentions mixed firmness with ambiguity and obscurantism. Minister Patrick Balopi told parliament in December 1995 that building schools and clinics inside the CKGR 'would not be compatible with maintaining the pristine environment of the [Reserve]'. He and another minister announced soon after that tourism could become a big income earner if wildlife was conserved and game reserves made attractive to tourists.

Official attitudes hardened as John Hardbattle and other San representatives successfully sought international support against the relocations. Political awareness was rising among San in Ghanzi and in the reserve.[83] When Balopi met some CKGR residents on 17 February 1996 he told them: 'I have not come to address any other question with you except that you must move ... you must be out by June.' The Ditshwanelo mission learnt that what the government had effectively said to the residents was: 'If you do not move, you will have to look after yourselves – you will be denied water and medical care – and you will remain with the [BDF] soldiers' on patrol in the area. According to residents in Metseamanong: 'the soldiers ... spread fear amongst the people – it is fear which is making the people move.' In the words of another person: 'Those who are moving are doing so because of government policy ... they are not doing it freely.' They detailed cases of assaults on San residents at the hands of game wardens. A supposed resettlement package – typically five cattle, eight donkeys, 15 goats and ploughing implements per household – was being offered to residents. But there was, said Ditshwanelo, 'no indication from the government that it is seriously considering the issue of compensation in both its narrow and broad definition.'[84]

The director of DWNP, Sedia Modise, affirmed in June 1997: 'There is no future for Basarwa. They must join the modern world now.'[85] The relocations were underway, involving initially perhaps 1,200 people. Xade was quickly emptied of its residents, moved to a 'wasteland' outside the reserve, 60 kilometres west, which slowly

[83] In 1994 at Xade 92 per cent of adults were registered voters, at Gope 21 per cent, at Molapo ('one of the older and more established settlements') 29 per cent, and at Mothlomelo 44 per cent. Cassidy (2001), A4 and A17.
[84] Ditshwanelo (1996), *When Will This Movement Stop?*, pp. 14, 17–9, 24–6.
[85] Quoted in the *Johannesburg Star*, 19 June 1997.

evolved into the new settlement of New Xade.[86] Some 500 others were moved to another new place, the future Kaudwane settlement, on the opposite side of the CKGR. According to Samora Gaborone, the government had speeded up the relocations following the sudden death of John Hardbattle on his return from international consultations in 1997. Contrary to the false claims of ministers, FPK had indeed written to Minister Balopi and his successor at local government, Margaret Nasha, seeking consultations, but their letters were neither acknowledged nor responded to. Gaborone believed that the responsible ministry 'did not want to enter into negotiations with Basarwa.' No consultations had occurred with residents – if there had been, he believed, no one would ever have moved.[87]

Estimates indicated that some 1,200 had been relocated at New Xade, and 500 at Kaudwane, during 1997 and 1998. But, against official claims that the relocations had been voluntary, large numbers of people had soon moved back into the reserve of their own volition.[88] Mobility was a basic part of the culture of the people since the formation of the reserve. They were, as Judge Unity Dow recognised, 'a highly mobile people', travelling frequently within the reserve and to places outside, 'linked to [the] availability of drinking water'. Movement in search of water was further inter-linked, prior to 1997, with the possession of 'clearly defined territories' or family homes. Here they grew crops, such as melons, beans and maize; 'reared livestock, notably goats, donkeys and horses'; 'hunted for meat' on horseback and with traps and bows and arrows; and relied over some forty years, on services provided by government. Except for places like Xade and Mothomelo, where there were boreholes, many were particularly reliant on water brought in regularly by truck, as essential supplement to occasional, seasonal rainwater.[89]

Surviving on such limited resources, the residents were extremely poor, 'most of them' officially classified as destitutes. They thus

---

[86] Christian Erni (1997), 'Resettlement of Khwe Communities Continues', *Indigenous Affairs*, July–December, and Paul Weinberg and Tony Weaver, 'The Bittereinders of the Kalahari', *Mail and Guardian*, 2 July 1999.

[87] Gaborone was an adviser to CKGR residents and to FPK, and he was presenting a statement, which he had addressed to the then vice-president designate, Ian Khama, to a meeting of UB's Basarwa Research Committee, May 1998. He soon came under vehement attack from government officials for his insights, depicted as unsound and non-academic.

[88] DWNP (1999), *Second Draft Management Plan*, Gaborone: Protected Areas Development Unit, May, pp.16–18. Some 90 people had walked to Mothomelo carrying their belongings on their backs. Personal interview with Jumanda Gakelebone, FPK, Ghanzi, 6 May 1999.

[89] Judge Dow (2005), 'Judgement', pp. 157–59. She recognised that a few residents may have reared cattle outside.

received meagre food rations and, under RADP structures, transportation of their children to boarding school. When the court visited the CKGR in 2004 they saw one wintry night a group that resembled people at a refugee camp – 'bare-footed, poorly clad ... obviously without sufficient water for proper hygiene'.[90]

Tshokodiso Bosiilwane and Amogelang Segootsane were men whose personal circumstances were fairly typical of the average male applicant before the high court. Bosiilwane was born at Metsiamanong (or Metseamanong) in the CKGR, as was his wife, and his parents and grandparents too. He did not know his date of birth. At the time of the relocations in 2002, he had nine huts in the family compound at Metsiamanong, where they grew crops and reared small livestock. He received food rations, and the RADP transported his children to and from boarding school. Opposed to relocation, he associated himself with FPK because he believed they would represent his interests. When he came to know that the government was 'planning to "take away what is theirs"', he decided he would 'continue to live in the CKGR even without the services'.

Segootsane had a similar story to tell, said Justice Dow. Born not far outside the CKGR in Salajwe, he had come to live at Gugamma along with his wife and children. His parents had historical ties with the reserve. He possessed three huts, donkeys, goats and a horse; he grew crops, gathered veld foods, and hunted for food. He too was involved in FPK, and he was a member of the negotiating team, established earlier by concerned civic groups, and he had 'no intention to relocate from the reserve'.[91]

The so-called negotiating team had come into formal existence in 1997, when representative and civic groups – FPK, Ditshwanelo, the Council of Churches (BCC), BOCONGO and MISA – established a consultative group to try to hold discussions with government on the future of the CKGR and its residents. They had a brief meeting with President Masire in June 1997, but negotiations 'proved futile', as the government pursued a unilateralist line and accused the team of being influenced by 'outsiders'. After the second relocations were underway, the residents decided, in April 2002, to go to the high court to assert their rights to reside in the CKGR, and the case began two years later.[92] Their claims derived

---

[90] Dow (2005), p. 159.

[91] Dow (2003), pp. 160–4.

[92] The residents claimed that they had occupied or used the reserve uninterruptedly since time immemorial, and argued that ILO Convention No. 169, the Draft Declaration on Indigenous Rights and other international documents accorded them rights to the CKGR. ACHPR (2005) , The Working Group, pp. 15–16.

from their rights as the indigenous inhabitants, colonial laws and the constitution of Botswana, and overall on one fundamental issue: 'Is it for the government to tell the Basarwa how and where they should live their lives, or are the Basarwa to be allowed to make those decisions for themselves?'[93]

2002 and the deepening dispossessions

Dow's judgement helps to untangle the thicket of government policies and actions that culminated in the intensified relocations of 2002. When the government rejected the findings of its own fact-finding mission in 1986, and immediately terminated all development work within the CKGR, it also decided, she notes, to discontinue all water deliveries to the settlements, even as a temporary measure. In 1994, this was taken further, through a decision in cabinet directing the relevant ministry to accelerate the development of relocation sites. Nevertheless, the government in fact continued to deliver water to those settlements. They had little choice. To have done otherwise, says Dow, before relocation sites had been properly prepared, would have led to a large congregation at the boreholes of Xade and Mothomelo with consequent depletion of wildlife resources there.[94]

The government's overall strategy towards relocations, Dow appears to accept, was to 'persuade but not force' the residents to leave. By the time the San case came before the high court, that is after the event of the relocations, the government agreed that water, welfare rations, and healthcare were 'basic and essential'.[95] Earlier it had offered repeated and firm assurances to that effect to concerned foreign governments. On 22 May 1996 the government told British, American, Norwegian and Swedish representatives that 'social services to people who wish to stay in the reserve will not be discontinued', and the minister of local government made a similar statement in June. In a written statement in September 1997, the government's position was affirmed as being that services will continue being provided 'for so long as there shall be a human soul in the CKGR'.[96]

---

[93] Gordon Bennett, 'Summary of issues in court case', *Survival International News Release*, 26 February 2007.
[94] Dow (2005), pp. 168–73.
[95] Dow (2005), pp. 171–72.
[96] Dow (2005), pp.176–77.

Meanwhile, the resistance of residents to relocation was demonstrably rising, as people associated themselves with FPK, Ditshwanelo and the Negotiating Team, and in boycotting the government's registration exercise of September 1996 – not one household at Metsiamanong or Gope and only one at Molapo registered to relocate. The government, furthermore, presented alternative proposals to relocations, such as the creation of Community Use Zones (CUZs) within the CKGR, and it promulgated regulations in 2000 that suggested it accepted the feasibility of continued human residence within the reserve. So-called management plans went through numerous drafts, specifically stating that 'resettlement is completely voluntary', and those who did not wish to move could remain within designated CUZs.[97]

DWNP produced a third draft management plan which, it is claimed, had gained approval from both Ghanzi and Kweneng district councils by the end of March 2001, and which had been discussed, in open and constructive meetings, with FPK, Ditshwanelo and related civic groups. The plan's unpublished proposals were referred to in the *Mail and Guardian* as follows: 'San and Bakgalagadi people are`set to be given usage rights over 24,000 km of the [CKGR] and Khutse Game Reserves ... They will be allowed to carry out subsistence hunting on a quota system, will be free to gather veld food, [and] will be actively involved in environmental monitoring.' But in 2003 the DWNP produced a so-called 'final' draft plan which rejected CUZs for any residents of the CKGR, and proposed instead a complete ban on hunting, livestock, and the cultivation of crops therein. It effectively deprived residents of any means of subsistence and made it impossible for them to remain.[98]

Sesana's case before the high court said essentially the same: 'For two years the Basarwa negotiated with the government about a management plan for the reserve. These ... were close to producing an agreement under which the settlements inside the reserve would have had their own Community Use Zones, could have continued to hunt and gather ... and could have launched projects to generate much-needed revenue. The government's unilateral decision to withdraw basic services brought these negotiations to a grinding halt.'[99] This amounts to the fact that after almost 40

[97] Dow (2005), pp.179–83.
[98] Letter from Phil Marshall, 'Government ignored the Wildlife Department's advice on CKGR', *Mmegi Online*, 1 November 2006.
[99] Bennett, 'Summary of issues in court case'.

years, the government had failed to produce a definitive, acceptable management plan for the CKGR, and what it had done, 1997 to
2002, had negated the original concept for the reserve and the
rights of its inhabitants.

Government moved to implement the relocations through 2001,
a decision to terminate all services in the CKGR having been made
at the Ghanzi District Council in the first week of April.
Equivocation nevertheless continued, when Minister Nasha stated
that services would be maintained for a while but gradually phased
out. But inside the reserve, government agents began to destroy
existing water supplies and seal boreholes such as that at
Mothomelo. People's huts were dismantled whether or not they
had agreed to be relocated. Bosiilwane had notified officials that
he did not wish to relocate, but they dismantled his huts nonetheless, those belonging to his wife and daughter and, he claimed,
took his wife away by force. At Gugamma, as Segootsane experienced things, officials removed the settlement's water tank in
2002, and vital water was thrown out.[100]

As individual residents were pressured into registering for relocation, 'hut dismantlement was a key feature' of their removal, as
officials took apart people's huts and loaded their goods on to
waiting trucks. Dow notes that the exercise 'involved twenty-nine
big trucks and seven smaller vehicles', attendant drivers and officials, representing altogether 'a significant and overwhelming dis-
turbance' in the settlements. Police were also present; one officer,
for example, commissioning the oaths of two of Sesana's wives in
a letter they wrote asking to be relocated. The government nevertheless maintained a 'persistent denial ... that there was [a] police
presence'. Families, especially husbands and wives, were separated, and there was considerable 'pestering', as Dow puts it, of
individuals to leave. No opportunities were offered, however, for
negotiations on compensation for homes and property lost.[101]

The government ignored the fact that the residents 'lived in
families, compounds and small settlements', and that people were
interlinked by blood, marriage and interdependence. True consent
for relocation was neither solicited nor obtained, and processing
people as individuals necessarily forced family members living
with a supposedly consenting individual to relocate. 'Wife was

[100] Dow (2005), pp. 161 and 163, and 185–6. People re-located to New Xade told the working
group (2005) that government agents had destroyed water pumps and emptied storage tanks in
February 2002, p. 39.
[101] Dow (2005), PP. 186–9.

pitted against husband and child against parent', in some instances, and family unity and community cohesion was undermined. As the huts were taken down and residents boarded trucks and, for example, the 'village of Molapo literally disappeared around them', people 'had no choice but to request to be relocated.'[102]

The size of the relocation exercise, and the diversity of departments and personnel involved, indicated that the government anticipated that the termination of services would precipitate the final removals. This emerged out of what Dow calls a welter of 'confusing and unclear policy', and the negation of the principle that regularity and predictability are fundamental to the rule of law.[103]

The termination of the issuance of Special Game Licences (SGLs), on 17 January 2002, was another key element in the stoppage of government services. The DWNP issued a blanket instruction that no more SGLs would be issued and that all existing ones be simultaneously withdrawn. The motivation for this important step could not have been wildlife conservation, disease control, nor anything that residents had done, for then DWNP could have dealt with individual offenders. DWNP's decision meant that Bosiilwane's existing licence was rendered useless and he could no longer hunt. The plan, said Dow, was that by the end of January 2002, 'there would be no water, no food, and no hunting, within the reserve. Life would simply be very hard, if not outright impossible.'[104]

Dow emphasises the people's resistance to what was being done to them. They refused to consent to their enforced relocation. 'Most of the residents in the smaller settlements [were] consistent in their reluctance to relocate.' Some reluctantly relocated to Xade in 1995 'only to go back to their settlements later'. Others relocated to Kaudwane and New Xade during the 1997 relocations 'only to go back to the reserve' soon after. Many people vacated the reserve not because of a personal decision to do so, but because a family member had registered for relocation and the hut/s had been taken down – 'family members had no option but to get into the truck.' The evidence is that 'they did not consent to the 2002 relocations.' The evidence was further that 'they were dispossessed of the land they occupied wrongfully and unlawfully and without their consent.'[105]

---

[102] Dow (2005), pp. 227–31.

[103] Dow (2005), pp. 226–7.

[104] Dow (2005), pp. 162, and 251–3.

[105] Dow (2005), pp.254–5, 268–9.

According to the working group's findings: There was 'sufficient evidence' that 'physical force was used' to remove the residents from the CKGR: they were not consulted; children and/or spouses were separated; people's belongings including their huts were dismantled and taken away to the new settlements; and water pumps and other services were destroyed.[106]

BBC world affairs editor, John Simpson, told the BBC World Service in 2005 that he had witnessed that 'the wells the Bushmen had used were broken up and concreted over', and he noted 'the disgusting beatings and torture' which accompanied the forced removals. Barnaby Phillips, then Southern Africa BBC correspondent, reported on Molatwe Mokalake, an old man probably in his 70s, still seething with anger three weeks after he was forced out of his home village of Molapo. 'The police came with guns', he said. 'They did not allow the women to collect firewood, and we were not allowed to bring water from outside the reserve. This went on for two weeks ... It felt like a war against us,' Mokalake stated.[107]

The issue of compensation for lives and property wrongly destroyed, and the further issue of the right to return to one's homeland, were closely related. In monetary terms, government policy had moved on from the resettlement package of a few donkeys and goats, previously offered in 1997, but at further costs to the people. Mogae had issued a presidential directive (CAB 38a) on 30 October 2002, that all those who 'relocated and were compensated should not be allowed to resettle in the CKGR'. In the case of Kaingotla Kanyo and his wife, Mongwegi Tihobogelo, who had both registered to relocate and moved to New Xade after he had received compensation of P66,325, five cattle and land to settle, they then moved back to Molapo leaving the cattle in New Xade. Questioned in court as to why she and Kanyo did not go to Molapo before receiving the supposed compensation, Tihobogelo replied: 'How could we go back to Molapo before we received that *which caused* us to go to New Xade?' (Dow's emphasis). Kanyo and some ten other former residents were subsequently charged with re-entry into the reserve without a permit. A similar case involved Roy Sesana and his family. He 'ordinarily lives outside the reserve and had two wives and six children at Molapo'. Accepting relocation, his wives, Gaotihobogwe and Roy, received compensation respectively of P36,347 and P7,708. Subsequently,

---

[106] Report (2005), p. 44.
[107] *BBC News Online*, 2 May and 24 November 2005.

WHAT DOES IT TAKE
TO LET THESE PEOPLE LIVE IN PEACE?

| ARRESTED & BEATEN | ARRESTED & BEATEN | ARRESTED & TORTURED | ARRESTED & ASSAULTED | ARRESTED & TORTURED |

| ARRESTED & TORTURED | ARRESTED & BEATEN | ARRESTED & ASSAULTED | ARRESTED & ASSAULTED | ARRESTED & TORTURED |

Last year, the Bushmen of Botswana won an historic victory.

Expelled from their ancient homeland, the Bushmen took the government to court – and won.

Botswana's High Court ruled that the Bushmen have the right to return to their land, and to hunt and gather there. That's all they've ever wanted.

But since then, the government has:

ARRESTED MORE THAN 50 BUSHMEN FOR HUNTING TO FEED THEIR FAMILIES.

BANNED THE BUSHMEN FROM USING THEIR WATER BOREHOLE DURING ONE OF THE FIERCEST DROUGHTS IN YEARS.

BACKED PLANS FOR A MASSIVE DIAMOND MINE WORTH $2.2 BILLION ON THE BUSHMEN'S LAND.

Meanwhile, hundreds still languish in resettlement camps, unable or too scared to return home.

The Bushmen don't want your money, but they do need your help if they are ever to live in peace on their own land once more. To see what it takes, go to **www.survival-international.org/bushmen**

We help tribal peoples defend
their lives, protect their lands
and determine their own futures.

info@survival-international.org

Founded 1969. Registered Charity 267444.

Survival

5.2 Survival International campaign poster
Source: courtesy of Survival International

in early 2002, the government refused to allow Sesana to re-enter the CKGR on at least one occasion.[108]

Dow felt that the government's policy on the issue of re-entry after compensation was 'far from clear'. Was the government's policy 'to persuade [as it had claimed] or to prosecute?', as it was doing. It could not be both. It was only after the government had set up a relocation task force in November 2002, to enquire into 'Why People are Going Back to the CKGR', that 'returns were visited with punishment'. If the government's position was that in relocating and accepting compensation a resident had extinguished their rights to return without permit, that then constituted the government's implicit acceptance that prior to the relocations the people were fully entitled to live in the reserve. The social consequences of what was happening – possible permanent division and disruption within families – were also profound.[109]

This left unaddressed the question of the true measure and value of compensation, and the inadequacies of the government's position. The government saw the issue only in developmentalist terms – it offered those who relocated a paper offering title to a piece of land, typically 40 metres by 25 metres, and a choice between 15 goats or 5 cows. It also directed that 'all those relocated be classed as temporary destitutes', recipients of monthly rations. They would have access to health services and schooling. But residents of the reserve had enjoyed 'access to a much larger area' of land, and the proffered cows and goats, even if they had none before, were 'clearly not enough to pull them out of the need to receive rations in the short term'. And access to health and schooling had been theirs before inside the CKGR. The judge felt that a resident might well have decided that it was 'better to be poor at home, than to be poor in a new and unfamiliar place'. [110] Compensation for the right to live at home in the reserve was ultimately incalculable.

The government had simply assumed that residents would accept whatever was offered them in the above terms, and 'no attempt was made' to explain to 'any of the residents' how compensation was being calculated and what they individually could expect. There were in fact, 'no compensation negotiations, only a one-sided decision process'.[111]

[108] Dow (2005), pp. 264–5 and 271–2.
[109] Dow (2005), pp.266–73.
[110] Dow (2005), pp. 240–42.
[111] Dow (2005), pp. 249–50.

Aside from the talk of persuasion, the government had actually relied on forceful demonstration, the 'pouring out of water', the overturning of storage tanks, as a dramatic and clear statement, intended to cause the residents to register to relocate. The dismantlement of huts was similarly intended to assure the residents that 'nothing remained that could possibly entice people back'.[112]

The 'relative powerlessness' of the people, as Justice Dow described their relationship to the government, was totally ignored, not for the first time. The average resident, illiterate, impoverished and dependent on government services, was in no position to give genuine consent to the government's intended policies. When they looked to advocacy groups for advice and support, these were denounced by the likes of Sidney Pilane, legal advisor to the president and leader of the government's case before the high court, as interfering outsiders who 'would not leave Botswana alone' – supposedly even the real cause of the problems facing the court. The weaknesses of the San people extended into the closely related issue of the meaning of development. Dow saw this as the government's big unacknowledged and on-going problem. The case was ultimately about 'a people demanding dignity and respect', and the government had reacted to this, simply on the evidence before the court, with ignorance and contempt.[113]

When the case started, Pilane, Dow noted, was 'full of talk about how the services belonged to the [government]' and how it had the right to 'do what it wished with them'. Later, when one of the applicants before the court explained that she did not relocate because she wished to be near the graves of her ancestors, 'Pilane burst out laughing.'[114] His behaviour here was not unlike the belligerence he displayed towards the ACHPR,[115] and suggested to Justice Dow how the government's developmentalist views 'fail[ed] to take into consideration the knowledge, culture and ideologies of the [San].' It was 'unable to appreciate the reasons

---

[112] Dow (2005), pp. 247–8.

[113] Dow (2005), pp. 231 and 274–6.

[114] In the resulting silence in the Court, Pilane explained that, in Dow's words, 'he had not been aware that they buried their dead but assumed that they collapsed a hut over their dead and moved on'. Dow (2005), p. 244.

[115] The ACHPR's Mission visited the Special Adviser on 17 June 2005; but 'even before the delegation could introduce the purpose of the mission', he asked whether any African state had ratified the ILO Convention No. 169 on Indigenous Peoples, 'then went further to say that the Commission must make itself relevant to Africa … and warned that if the [ACHPR] were to allow itself to be led by the UN bodies, it would make itself irrelevant.' He said that the ILO Convention was 'separatist', and urged the ACHPR to 'prioritise its activities'. Report (2005), pp. 20–21.

behind the persistent resistance to relocat[ion]', and then 'explained it away' as the result of bad advice by meddling outsiders.[116]

Justice Dow recognised that the residents of the CKGR belonged to a group internationally recognised as 'indigenous peoples', and the ideas and conventions associated with this status were intended to compensate them for the powerlessness which CKGR residents and other San experienced. By refusing to recognise them as an indigenous community, the government was refusing to accord them their corresponding rights, the ACHPR also noted.[117]

Dow expressed appropriate support for the role of Survival International, as well as FPK, Ditshwanelo and the negotiating team, in 'giving courage and support' to an historically powerless people. The residents had full right to associate with these groups in their efforts to resist relocation. That the government's attitude is the opposite was recognised too by the ACHPR: 'persons deemed to be sympathetic with the Basarwa cause are regarded as traitors or unpatriotic'. Local NGOs that had worked with Survival were 'forced to withdraw their support and denounce [the London-based group]'.[118]

Coordination with key policy issues was being strongly promoted by the government, as noted in Chapter 3. Some needed little encouragement to remain in step with government, with Rev. Braam le Roux of the Kuru Family of Organizations in Ghanzi, affirming that 'We're afraid of [Survival International]', adding: 'I think there's a general fear amongst NGOs and everyone out here about Survival,' without bothering to explain the content and causes of this fear. Alice Mogwe also dissented in the name of Ditshwanelo from what she called Survival's confrontational tactics, claiming that this approach 'is not one which African governments react to positively'.[119] This ignored the fact that Reteng is a local group which practised confrontational tactics around the emotive issue of cultural genocide, and FPK and the BNF were also ready to use strong language at times. Moreover, the Treatment Action Campaign (TAC) in South Africa has achieved outstanding success on the big problem of HIV-AIDS, precisely through tough

---

[116] Dow (2005), pp. 244–5.
[117] Dow (2005), pp. 201–2 and Report (2005), pp. 48.
[118] Report (2005), p. 48 and Dow (2005), p. 238.
[119] Quoted by Paul Kenyon, 'Row Over Bushmen "Genocide"', BBC News Online, 6 November 2005.

name-and-shame tactics against President Mbeki and his health minister. Ditshwanelo is recognised by the government as its partner in development, and accepts a usually subordinate role therein. Towards others the government continues its coercive tactics, with President Mogae 'hardly deliver[ing] any speech without saying something about [Survival], its hostile campaigns and its meddling in our affairs'.[120]

After the relocations and judgements

Government policy towards the San is imbued with lies and pre-varication at all levels and stages. When the working group had visited Kaudwane settlement, in June 2005, residents stressed the failed promises of the government, the inadequate facilities, the lack of employment and gainful activities, and police assaults. Only 16 households had been given cattle or goats, and most of those had been killed by wild animals. Food was scarce and people 'went for days without food.' Residents were assaulted when they went to hunt, and two persons reported torture by officials. Drunkenness and other social ills were rampant, and Basarwa had no representation on the settlement's management committee.

At New Xade they found a 'population of more than 3,000' most of whom had come from Xade in 1997 and 2002. The settlement supposedly possessed a clinic, school and poultry factory, but there was 'no telephone communication' and 'the only way to reach the outside world' was through radio owned and used by the police.

The delegation held a fruitful meeting with residents, and the participants were chiefly 'young adults', unlike in the other places. They said that 'they had become destitutes and beggars [who] could no longer provide for their families', dependent entirely on irregular government handouts. There were no income-generating activities at New Xade. Hunting was prohibited and 'they were restricted from leaving the settlement'. Poverty and misery were the results.

The delegation also visited West Hanahai, the oldest in the set-tlement system. A small number of residents said that the govern-ment 'had not met any of its promises' regarding incomes, jobs and social services. After thirty years in the settlement 'there had been

---

[120] Dan Moabi, 'Whither Botswana', *Mmegi Online*, 23 November 2006.

no improvement in their lives'. Basarwa in the CKGR had resisted relocation in their turn, they believed, because of the 'constant humiliation' which they had experienced. .

The working group spent nine days collecting information on indigenous issues in Botswana, and their conclusions were firm, detailed and very critical. While the government claimed that relocated San were given land, 'only a few' in fact had legal title over what were small arable plots, and 'few, if any', had grazing or water rights.

While new government buildings were highly visible in Kaudwane and New Xade, they were 'widely regarded by most NGOs as white elephants': there were few teachers in the schools, the clinic in Kaudwane had one non-resident nurse, and the agricultural project in New Xade and leather-making factory in Kaudwane had been shut down. Overall the settlements looked like 'abandoned mine camps', with little sense of hope. After 40 years of independence, Basarwa faced 'complete exclusion' from the economic and political structures of the country.[121]

Justice Dow's judgement and the findings of the ACHPR testify to the illegalities and injustices perpetrated by the government in their approach to the CKGR, and the international and African human rights conventions which were flouted. Accountability and openness were absent and all semblances of democratic consultation subordinated to presidential fiat. The proposals of San leaders, the suggestions of a small and dependent civil society, and the peaceful resistance of the residents were all ignored. The Mogae government remained unready to recognise the severity of the judgements against it, to express regret for its mistakes and make restitution for them.

Policies of denial and vindictiveness prevailed throughout 2007. Residents of the CKGR continued to be denied access to their land. In a petition to the government on 20 November, the FPK stated that 152 letters had been signed by people protesting against the government's refusal to let them use the water boreholes at Mothomelo in the Reserve; as Roy Sesana and Jumanda Gakelebone declared, 'without water, no person can survive'. Basarwa had also signed letters asking the department of wildlife to issue them with hunting licences. This right was as basic as that of water: 'Without the right to hunt we must die of hunger', the FPK said.[122] Despite the high court's ruling that residents had been evicted

[121] Report (2005), pp. 31–2, 38–41, and 43–8.
[122] Oliver Modise, in *Mmegi Online*, 21 November 2007.

illegally, wrongfully and forcibly, the government was insisting that only a limited number of people could return, and refusing to provide transport home. FPK and Survival had detailed information that more than 50 San had been assaulted and tortured for endeavouring to hunt for food – men were beaten and kicked, forced to run through sandy soil for hours, handcuffs were tightened round their wrists and rubber tubes around their throats.[123]

On the anniversary of the high court's decision, as the FPK prepared to return to court to gain an enforcement order against the government, FPK wrote to President Mogae who was about to retire: ' Let us use our borehole. Let us hunt, as we are legally allowed to do. Let everyone who wants to go home be allowed to go without needing a permit. Investigate the wildlife officers at Khutse gate and prosecute the ones who are guilty of torture.' They noted that 'we have been given no assistance to fund our return home, even though the government spent hundreds of thousands of pula to evict us.' They concluded: 'When you leave government, let it be on a positive note.'[124]

The issue of diamonds in the CKGR also remained unaddressed by the government, although Gem Diamonds' plans for mining at Gope could not be realised without governmental permission and support. Gem, unlike De Beers, had declared their readiness to discuss plans with the community, but meaningful discussions seemed difficult while the San remained excluded from their land. Important unaddressed issues were reactivated involving royalties from mining. Keineetse was a lone voice in 2006 arguing the need for positive discrimination in favour of Basarwa. Reparations for deep past and present wrongs were involved: 'Everybody in this country is implicated by our collective silence over the years and the reluctance to talk about the slavery that takes place in our midst.' Basarwa have long occupied the lowest rung in our class divided society, and Botswana should use 'some of the largesse accrued from mineral extraction' for their overdue development.[125] South Africa has shown what could be done in according land and mineral rights to San, but there was scant reason to believe that Botswana might act similarly.

[123] Survival International Press Release, 31 October 2007 and advertisement, *Independent*, 5 November 2007.
[124] FPK, Open Letter to President Mogae, 12 December 2007.
[125] Keineetse Keineetse, Opinion/Letters, 'Basarwa Must be Given Royalties From Mining Rights', *Mmegi Online*, 15 September 2006.

Conclusion   Facing the Realities

Botswana is in a deep trough of its rulers' making, from which no easy or quick escape is foreseeable. The country is caught between an autocratic and increasingly powerful presidency and vision-less, stultified ruling party, on the one hand, and a disorganised people and divided opposition, on the other. Underlying all is diamond dependency, set to deepen even further with the estab-lishment of sorting and aggregation functions in the DTC Botswana and the corresponding responsibility for 'maintaining the integ-rity' of the inherently fraudulent commodity. This was the special role of the secretive, monopolistic De Beers private corporation. But it is an impossible task for a democracy. Skills and some jobs may be acquired in jewellery manufacture, but accountability and openness are set to worsen.

As a directorate of intelligence services, and enhanced elec-tronic surveillance systems become realities, the over-empower-ment of the rulers increases, with no likely reduction in their existing arrogance. Instead, the gulf between the ruling elite and the people will widen further. There are no indications either that the rulers will turn away from the established growth-first strategy of economic development which maintains poverty and inequali-ties at critical levels.

The political duopoly of presidentialism and predominance gained the support of less than a quarter of the electorate in 2004, but maintains a slough of stasis and complacency. The ruling party is bereft of new ideas, but blocks the electoral change that could produce them. Predominance promotes low turnout in the discriminatory first-past-the-post system, and presidentialism stifles debate on the issues. The task of winning a parliamentary majority by a weak opposition appears almost Sisyphean.

But the foundation and need for it is there. Elections in 1994 and 2004 indicated that, against the odds, people want change. Since almost 50 per cent of the population live in poverty, the need to escape from that is manifest. Forty-eight per cent of voters in 2004 supported the two main opposition parties, a level of support far greater than the 12 per cent gained by the main opposition party in South Africa then.

Structural barriers are huge. The undiversified economy deprives the people of the physical and human resources for the development of popular organisations. An independent civil society is the great absent member, and it is unlikely to grow without broad economic development and extensive political reform. Change is inevitably for the long-haul, and the abandonment of all illusory notions is a vital first step down that road.

A quick survey of essential reforms is indicative of the problems ahead. Constitutional reform must be extensive. A basic need is for sovereignty to be placed in the hands of the people. The powers of the president must be reduced across the board – locating executive powers in the cabinet collectively, restricting the president's appointment powers, and providing for his/her popular election on the basis of 50 per cent or more of votes cast. The legislature must be greatly strengthened, recognised as being the servant of the people, and accorded broad powers of scrutiny on that basis. Namibian constitutional arrangements offer exemplars here. It is possible that support for such reforms would attract support in parliament, and an electoral programme on these issues could attract strong popular response; the BNF's campaign slogan in 1994 was 'Time for a Change', and its need now is much greater.

It is of course certain that strong resistance would quickly arise from the presidency, utilising prevarication, propaganda and coercion. General Khama will be president in 2008; he is pleased to be known as an authoritarian, likes 'decisions to be made quickly and carried out properly', and prefers his democracy imbued with 'discipline' (quoted by Christina Lamb, *The Sunday Times*, London, 3 July 2005); he is contemptuous of parliament and uninterested in discussion. This would have to be faced by a reformist constituency, and the people could learn from that overt opposition and confrontation.

Change within the judiciary must also be extensive, to establish openness and uniformity, and to scrutinise the role of the attorney general and the circulation of positions between that executive office and the high court. South Africa provides important models for law reform. Human rights provisions must be extended, modernised, institutionalised and strengthened: the concept of a living wage should be introduced and minimum wages and pension provisions improved in accordance with it. The right of free speech must be transformed and freed of all presidential dominations.

Political reforms in many areas are vital. New and improved institutions to promote accountability and clean government; enactment of freedom of information and of whistleblower protections; the introduction at last of an effective register of members' assets, with enforcement powers in law, and accessibility to the public. The DCEC and the ombudsman must be empowered and required to enforce strict conflict of interest provisions, to sever the linkages between power and wealth.

Other dimensions of reform include the party, electoral and voting systems: introducing either a proportional or a preferential voting system, while retaining the liberal-democratic constituency foundation, with a threshold (or filter) requirement for parliamentary representation; and introducing state funding for all parties, based on their share of the popular vote over a chosen period.

Only when most of these changes had been introduced would the country be in a position to determine, on a sound non-elitist and deliberative basis, future economic strategies for reducing diamond dependency, for diversification, and the reduction of poverty and inequalities. The rise of an active civil society, and a participatory democracy, would accompany and strengthen structural change.

The subordination of the San within the gulag of special settlements constitutes an enormity long unaddressed by the rulers and scandalously unmentioned in the 'miracle' story. No movement forward has occurred since the episode of the early 1990s.

A brief survey indicates the extent of the work required for the achievement of democracy and development in Botswana. It must also be recognised that Botswana is at present poorly equipped in most ways other than in the wealth of the UMC for realising these advances. It is more poorly placed than many of its neighbours, South Africa especially. The point is that diamond dependency and presidentialism have been co-joined and mutually supportive over the life of the country, and their debilitating effects are scorched into Botswana society. The range of the necessary reforms attests to the inherited problem, not to the impossibility of the tasks ahead. Change is destined to be slow. But the incentive for confronting the barriers lies in the great needs and unchannelled capacities of the people. Youth after all have been in inchoate rebellion against remote and repressive authority since 1995. The potential constituency for change is large – the San and other remote people are about ten per cent of the population, overlapping ethnic minorities constitute at least one-third of the population, and the poor are half the total.

Appendix

A Case of the President, High Court & Public Opinion

Matters arising

I arrived in Botswana from Kaunda's Zambia, attracted by the country's multi-party democracy and relative efficiency. It already had a large political literature, and I soon settled into serious research and writing. My first published article of early 1992, 'Interpreting the Exceptionality of Botswana', reflected my enthusiasm.

On Friday 18 February 2005, soon after I returned home from work around 5pm three men appeared at my door. The apparent leader announced without preamble that he had a message from the president; I had been declared a prohibited immigrant, and had 48 hours in which to leave.

I needed a lawyer and raced over to Dick Bayford's office. A night of feverish activity followed, with Joao Salbany and Duma Boko. Bojosi Otlhogile, Vice Chancellor at UB, expressed his shock, and said he had known nothing of the impending PI. He offered constitutional advice to Dick throughout the evening. The immediate task was daunting. Papers had to be prepared to call out a judge of the high court on Saturday, when they are usually unwilling to appear in Lobatse 80 kilometres from Gaborone. The PI order effective on Sunday night had to be stopped and arguments to substantiate this assembled. On Dick's suggestion, we decided to fight on the constitutional guarantees of freedom of speech. The essential documents were prepared and faxed to the court. A hearing could be gained.

The first high court hearing

The court, on the northern outskirts of Lobatse, was almost empty that Saturday evening. Justice Moatlhodi Marumo seemed friendly and informal and immediately invited all of us, with accompanying journalists and students into his chambers. The attorney general was unrepresented, indicative perhaps of the government's expectation that I would be shocked into mute compliance. Marumo listened to Dick's submission, which included reference to my active record of scholarly and media work, asked a few explanatory questions, and quickly delivered his order.

He agreed that the matter was clearly an urgent one and that normal court rules had to be set aside. He directed most crucially that it was within 'the Court's jurisdiction to hear and determine this application', which was 'not ousted by Section 11 (b) of the Immigration Act', prioritising the presidential prerogative. He proceeded to set aside the PI order for being 'irregular and null and void'; he further declared that Section 11 (6) of the Immigration Act was '*ultra vires* Section 3 of the Constitution of Botswana' upholding the fundamental rights and freedom of the individual; and he declared that 'the Applicant's Constitutional Rights enshrined under Section 11 and 12 of the Constitution [protecting freedom of conscience and expression] ... have been infringed'. Pending the final determination of the issues, I was permitted to remain in Botswana on the same terms and conditions as prevailed before 18 February. Marumo's order could hardly have been improved upon.[1]

But my thoughts were focused on the apparent malevolence of the state's actions towards me. The serving of the order on a Friday evening, Michael Dingake, an experienced observer believed, was intended to frustrate any possible court interdict on my part. Proclaimed as being a presidential decree, but initially signed only by an immigration officer, it was intended to be beyond the jurisdiction of the courts. The hour on Friday was also convenient for keeping the event under wraps. The first media publicity of my deportation was likely to have been with *Mmegi Monitor* on Monday, after I had gone. The attorney general's chambers was apparently confident of its impregnable case and procedures and left for their weekend as normal.[2]

As court hearings occurred in quick succession, the community reacted to the events. Otlhogile issued a brief email announcement

[1] In the High Court of Botswana held at Lobatse, *Kenneth Good and the Attorney General, MISCA No. 90 of 2005*, pp. 1 and 2.
[2] Michael Dingake, 'As I See it', *Mmegi Monitor*, 1 March 2005. There are only two daily newspapers, the government's own, and free, *Daily News*, and *Mmegi*; all other independent newspapers are weeklies. In the event, the *Sunday Standard* acted quickly with a short piece, 'OP give Prof Good 48 hrs to pack and go', on 20 February.

to staff and students on 19 February, stating merely that I had been 'PI'd' that no reasons have been given, and that he was in touch with me. The academic staff association held an emergency meeting on Monday 21, and called on the vice chancellor to state clearly the position of UB management on academic freedom. They also unanimously agreed to march to the president's office to present a petition on Tuesday morning, and go to the high court that afternoon 'to show solidarity with Prof Good'.[3] Nothing was forthcoming from management about academic freedom. The acting Vice Chancellor B.S. Mguni, stated on Tuesday 22 that 'management like you [does not] have the reasons for the [PI] decision to be able to comment competently and rationally'.[4]

Some were less circumspect. Elmon Tafa in educational foundations declared that he had 'always admired [my] critical and independent mind ... something sadly missing in this university'; Ishmael Masesane in chemistry said it was 'fundamentally wrong for the whole might of government to come crashing down on a man whose weaponry is centred on a pen and critical thinking'; Mpho Molomo in my own department declared that 'a Tsunami has hit our shores ... today it's Ken Good, tomorrow it may be me or you ...': and Taolo Lucas in social work (and senior member of the Botswana Congress Party) made perhaps the most serious observations:

> Prof Good has been declared a [PI]. No reasons given. I find this absurd and unacceptable. We read in the laws of this country that every person shall be presumed innocent until proven guilty. We are also told about the 'due process of the law'. The [guiding philosophy] makes reference to a tolerant nation ... The expulsion ... is not a good example of any of these.[5]

In a statement to the press, Ditshwanelo, the human rights centre, strongly condemned the order. 'Good was not given any official reasons for his deportation, violating the basic principle that anyone accused of an offence has the right to present his or her side of the story.' The Media Institute of Southern Africa similarly noted that I had on a number of occasions expressed divergent views from the government on various issues, including the

---

[3] Email of Secretary General of the Association, 21 February 2005.
[4] There were no arrangements for the VC to address staff either. Email of Dr B.S. Mguni, 22 February 2005.
[5] All the above were emails to the UB mailgroup of 21 February 2005. A press cartoon some weeks earlier had shown a huge Tsunami looming over a fleeing Batswana man and woman, the wave inscribed 'automatic presidential succession'.

removal of San/Basarwa from the CKGR, ethnic inequalities and automatic succession to the presidency. Free speech and academic freedom were clearly involved and the case had already created a lot of apprehension among the public.[6]

Dumelang Saleshando, prominent BCP parliamentarian, noted correctly that I had been critical of both the ruling party and the opposition parties, and that such criticisms should be accommodated in a democracy. The problem was with the law as it stood. Laws which allowed the head of state to take predjudicial action against any citizen or non-citizen without giving reasons were archaic and primitive.[7]

Harassment and insinuation swirled. Duma Boko, who also represented the San/Basarwa in their case before the high court, stated publicly that he had received an anonymous death threat on Monday 21, and had informed the police. Batlhalefi Leagajang reported sources close to the office of the president which claimed that I had committed a crime that would shock the nation if it were revealed. The point was made in the middle of a long story and not enlarged upon.[8] But it was echoed elsewhere; a diplomatic source suggested that a member of the cabinet had stated privately that Good had circulated subversive documents.[9]

As part of my professorial responsibilities, I had organised my department's seminars since soon after my arrival. The politics seminars had grown over the years into a regular programme drawing on a range of speakers from on and off campus with active student participation. The emphasis was on open and lively discussion. I had made a point of always presenting my work-in-progress to the seminar, both to inform people of my research activities and profit from their criticisms. 'Interpreting the exceptionality of Botswana' was presented on 3 October 1991, and papers that followed addressed corruption, poverty, the San, and short-lived car assembly in Gaborone.

On 22 October 2003 I presented a seminar entitled 'Bushmen and diamonds: (un)civil society in Botswana' which attracted a huge response.[10] Participants included a number of bureaucrats who

---

[6] Both statements were in *Botswana Gazette*, 23 February 2005.
[7] Sello Motseta, 'Mogae in huff after stinging criticism,' *Business Day*, 23 February 2005. Point echoed by *Mmegi Monitor*, 21 February with its editorial entitled 'Barbarisms that belong to a by-gone era.'
[8] *Botswana Gazette*, 23 February 2005.
[9] From documents in my possession. Identity withheld.
[10] Papers were always circulated online before a seminar in order to attract a bigger turnout and to strengthen discussion.

criticised me for not having consulted them or specific government reports and invited me to withdraw the paper from publication. A purported debate followed on GabsFM, where a government representative pressed me to accept his views while I tried to enlighten the listeners on the issues involved. The paper was published soon after by the Nordic Africa Institute in Sweden.[11]

In 2004, South Africa's Human Sciences Research Council had embarked on a project studying presidential succession in Africa, and invited Ian Taylor and myself to write on Botswana. The proposed book was a comparative study of several countries aimed at persuading the Big Men – the bane of African politics in the view of many African intellectuals – to step down when their tenure was over. By February our paper on Botswana, which had already been exposed to criticism within the project, was ready for presentation at a politics seminar.

These were normally held in the faculty's committee room, seating some 20 people, but a crowd of more than a hundred assembled before the scheduled hour of 4pm, and we hurriedly relocated to one of the university's largest lecture halls, holding some 250 people. To a packed audience inside and more crowded outside I presented the co-authored paper on presidential succession to what *Mmegi* termed 'a hero's welcome'. Odubeng noted that there were a good number of MPs, and politicians from across the political divide, representatives of civil society, school teachers and diplomats, as well as lecturers and many students in the audience.

The issue of automatic succession merged with that of my expulsion. As Odubeng reported: 'The students and for most part the crowd ... shared sentiments that the deportation is unfair and proves that [as Good and Taylor] argue that 'Botswana is marching towards authoritarianism.'[12] The event was more like a rugby match than a seminar. When I quoted the admonition of Mamphela Ramphele that 'silence is a threat to democracy', the reaction of students, according to the *Botswana Guardian,* threatened to bring the roof of the auditorium down. In near chaotic circumstances, without a microphone, I summarised the argument that presidential succession occurred over the heads of parliament and people in

---

[11] Around this time my university office was broken into and my laptop stolen. The burglary was cleanly effected, nothing else was taken, and adjacent offices were untouched. A week later my house was burgled and a new computer removed. Cash and items of value nearby were ignored. Campus security and the Botswana Police were informed but neither machine was recovered. Diplomatic comment in Gaborone attributed the thefts to an arm of Military Intelligence.

[12] Maureen Odubeng, *Mmegi*, 24 February 2005. Her piece filled the entire front page.

Botswana, and that automatic transition was autocratic and elitist, and answered questions, including one from a top BDP official. The meeting concluded after some 75 minutes.[13]

In London earlier that week President Mogae had declared that 'freedom of expression is embedded in the cultural heritage of Botswana', while at home, as the media did not fail to note, a UB professor was in court challenging a deportation order that had come without causes stated.[14]

Church leaders voiced strong support. The vice-president of the Botswana council of churches, Reverend Cosmos Moenga, called the deportation wrong and immoral, while the principal of Kgolagono Theological College, Reverend Prince Dibeela, hoped that criticism would strengthen democracy, adding that I was echoing what Batswana were saying about automatic succession.[15]

Speaking for the First People of the Kalahari, Roy Sesana said that my eviction was an outrage, and that I had been training the people who tomorrow would be improving the democracy of this country. He agreed with me that presidents should be elected, not chosen by another president.[16]

Several students offered detailed assessments of my work. In 'A Professor Students Love to Hate', I was described as being a frank academic not willing to compromise his standards.[17] Elsewhere, Saleshando said that I was 'highly informed and well read and one of the very few disciplined lecturers at UB.' Paul Rantao, opposition MP, journalist and researcher, called me a 'real political scientist' who published only after thorough research: 'I took him as a model that we could emulate as emerging academics and scholars', he added. Boyce Sebetela, ruling party MP for Palapye, had played a lively role in my ethics and accountability course, and was quoted as saying that I was an enlightened and open thinker, and great scholar. 'His students were always on their toes exchanging ideas freely and I literally enjoyed him very much. Even today we still talk.' He held me in high esteem, he said, 'without fear or favour.'[18]

---

[13] Moabi Phia, *Botswana Guardian*, 25 February 2005. Thursday's *Mmegi* carried an abridged version of the paper, the *Guardian* offered excerpts and the paper was reported in Johannesburg's *Business Day* and accorded full-page coverage in the *Star*, 8 March 2005.

[14] The editor, *Botswana Guardian*, 25 February 2005.

[15] Stryker Motlaloso, 'Church Leaders Criticise Good's Deportation', *Mmegi*, 25 February 2005.

[16] Letters, *Botswana Gazette*, 2 March 2006.

[17] Moabi Phia, *Botswana Guardian*, 25 February 2005.

[18] Ryder Gabathuse, 'The incisive mind that cuts dictators down to size', *Mmegi*, 1 March 2005. When we met at an occasional workshop in Gaborone the former minister would address me as 'teacher'.

The Australian high commissioner in Pretoria, Philip Green, met Foreign Minister Merafhe in Gaborone a short time later. When Green expressed his concern about my deportation, the minister expressly denied accountability. As Merafhe was directly reported: 'People are entitled to speculate' about the reasons for the deportation. 'Let people speculate.'[19]

The second court hearing

Judge Marumo, who had had played such a vital role, was no longer presiding on 28 February, his place taken by Acting Justice Stanley Sapire.[20] At issue was the constitution as the law of the land, and presidential power versus individual rights. The attorney general was adamant that a presidential decree could not be questioned and that the court was misled in stopping that order on 19 February.[21] History had already been made, legal opinion suggested, in challenging the deportation and being a step ahead of the state for nine days. Debate had been opened on sweeping presidential powers.[22]

Judge Sapire's order was substantive. He noted my submission that it was the duty of a professor at UB to serve the community, and to make his knowledge and opinions available to groups or individuals who seek it. 'He claims to have diligently lived up to and satisfied this expectation.' He noted that I had 'consistently maintained an unblemished lifestyle'. He agreed that in keeping with my calling, I had occasionally commented analytically on the political issues of the day. 'His right to do so is protected by the constitution ... As a non-citizen ... he can have no aspirations for himself to political office. His interest in politics is, he insists, his calling, academic, and non-partisan.'[23] Sapire also noted that the

---

[19] Joel Konopo, *Mmegi*, 1 March 2005. Green saw Merafhe in company with the British high commissioner resident in Gaborone, and the minister implied that the diplomats were representatives of two large white nations interfering in the affairs of a small African country, and he referred to Australia's policies to exclude illegal immigrants.

[20] While we were decidedly sorry about Marumo's replacement, we had reason to be hopeful of Sapire. Previously chief justice in Swaziland, he had resigned after he and two other judges refused to drop their investigations into an abduction of a schoolgirl by King Mswati. Gideon Nkala, 'The men of law in Good's case', *Mmegi Monitor*, 28 February 2005.

[21] Batlhalefi Leagajang, 'Victory for democracy?', *Botswana Gazette*, 2 March 2005.

[22] Nkala, 'Crunch times in deportation case', *Mmegi Monitor*, 28 February 2005.

[23] In discussion the previous week Sapire had asked counsel why my PI came now after 15 years work in the country, and Bayford, apparently surprised, failed to say that it was because the political context had changed.

attorney general had not challenged my description of myself: 'There is no hint in the papers ... of any seditious conduct on his part.'[24]

Sapire described the arrival of the three officials at my home on 18 February, observing that the order had left me devastated. Having been resident in Botswana for over 14 years, and having had my residence and work permits re-extended for a further two years as recently as January that year, 'the Applicant found his plight inexplicable.' He noted my suggestion that my hurried deportation was intended to frustrate the planned seminar. This perception was reasonable, he admitted, and my claim for redress would therefore 'fall within the provisions of section 18 of the Constitution [on the derogation and enforcement of fundamental rights], which require only this to be alleged.'

Sapire continued that the attorney general had argued that the immigration act gave the president plenary powers to declare any non-citizen a prohibited immigrant, and that these powers are exercised 'on receipt of information from a source deemed reliable by the president.' Coupled with the provision of the act that 'no court shall question the adequacy of the grounds for any such declaration', the state had argued, effectively excluded the court from entertaining my application.

'On examination', declared Sapire, 'the fallacies of this argument become apparent'. The court's jurisdiction stemmed from section 18 which stated that where provisions of other statutes are in conflict with the terms of the constitution, 'it is the provisions of the constitution which prevail.' Further: section 47 of the constitution while vesting executive power in the president, stated that such powers were to be exercised subject to the provisions of the constitution. It might therefore be deduced that the 'president cannot validly exercise the powers vested in him under the immigration act to defeat the provisions of the constitution.' My perception that my constitutional rights have been contravened were not 'fanciful, frivolous, or groundless', and I was therefore entitled to be heard. To deny me this opportunity, he concluded, would constitute the disruption of my life and irreparable loss. Sapire confirmed Judge Marumo's decision, and he ordered the agencies of the state not to harass me in the interim.

---

[24] I had testified under oath that I was not a member of any political party or any organisation other than UB. All following are from the high court of Botswana at Lobatse, 28 February 2005, *MISCA No. 90 of 2005.*

The charge of defamation

Responses to Judge Sapire's declaration were broadly supportive and its significance recognised. The *Gazette* commented that upholding the supremacy of the constitution over presidential decree would be a positive step in rolling back the executive powers of the president.[25] Hostile opinion appeared in a decided minority in the independent press.[26] Dick Bayford was receiving strong support from both the legal profession and the public. Lawyers from the ruling and opposition parties and others were offering assistance. 'They give us citations and other information we could use in the case. Some members of the public have even contributed money', he said.[27]

The assault on my freedom assumed new form in the first week of March when Daniel Kwelagobe, secretary-general of the BDP, issued a writ of defamation against me, claiming damages of P1.2 million. He claimed that in the paper of 23 February I had set out with 'nefarious and sinful intent to damage [his] good name and his high standing in society.' Taylor and I had referred to Kwelagobe as a man deeply tainted with self-interest and described him as closely involved in factionalism in the ruling party – matters we believed of common cause throughout the 1990s, attested to by many and extensively documented. Duma Boko described the writ as part of an orchestrated campaign to harass, intimidate and victimise me.[28]

A threat to national security

In an unprecedented move, President Mogae filed a supporting affidavit dated 15 March at the High Court.[29] He stated that he had declared me a prohibited immigrant 'in the interest of peace, security and national security of Botswana'. He did this, he affirmed,

[25] The Editor, *Botswana Gazette*, 2 March 2005.
[26] See for example J.B. Gabaake, 'How good is Good?'. *Mmegi Monitor*, 14 March, and Boruru Okitlanye, 'We can take care of ourselves', Letters, *Mmegi*, 8 March, and Lesedi Moagi, 'Good riddance', Letters, *Mmegi*, 16 March, and Thomson Tshiamiso, 'To Australia With Good', *Botswana Guardian*, 18 March 2005.
[27] Gideon Nkala, *Mmegi Monitor*, 14 March 2005. He and Duma Boko were acting *pro bono* for me.
[28] Spencer Mogapi, in the *Sunday Standard*, 13 March, and Giedon Nkala, *Mmegi Monitor*, 14 March 2005.
[29] Dikarabo Ramadubu, 'Mogae comes out', *Botswana Guardian*, 18 March 2005.

on the basis of 'information received by me from sources I deemed to be reliable', acting on powers vested in him by the Immigration Act.

As I continued with my teaching and other duties, I formally addressed the board of my department of political and administrative studies about my deportation and the issues surrounding it. I informed my colleagues that since President Mogae was obliged to make a PI decision on the basis of reliable information, they were in a uniquely important position. They had greater knowledge about me than anyone else in the country. Three of them, including the departmental head, the Zambian Gervaise Maipose, had known me since we were together at UNZA in Lusaka, and a few others, including Mpho Molomo and the dean of FSS, Balefi Tsie, had been close colleagues since my arrival at UB. They knew as a matter of fact, from the daily interchange in the collegial, argumentative atmosphere of a university department, from what I had said and written over fifteen to twenty years, that I was no threat to national security. Was it possible that they had a responsibility to make this information – far more detailed and solid than the allegations of any immigration officer or the fantasies of an intelligence spook – known to the president? I then withdrew from the meeting so as not to constrain their discussion. Nothing resulted, as I had half anticipated.[30]

Many others were different. Some political science students had designed and produced T-shirts which were on sale in the main mall in central Gaborone. They were inscribed: 'Prof Good, Champion of Democratic Ideals: Freedom of Expression, Academic Freedom.' Then below, 'Declared a Prohibited Immigrant, August 1973, Ian Smith; February 2005, Ian Khama.' On the back, the T-shirt read: 'Information Helps to Empower People, While Secrecy Weakens Them.' The reporter said that most political science students were against the PI order, and the designer of the shirts, Lefoko Molebatsi, a UB tutor, said they were selling at a brisk rate.[31]

Gaborone is a small city, and people in the streets were warm in their greetings. Men and women, old and young, black, white and Asian, sometimes called out, 'We're praying for you, Prof', 'hang

---

[30] Some department members, like Molomo, had voiced support and sympathy, but the department head was a notable absentee, as Dean Tsie stressed in his email to all PAS staff on 25 February: 'I have already been to the head of PAS to express my disappointment at the way colleagues in that department have been aloof [and] detached as if they never knew Ken.'

[31] Duncan Kgangkenna, 'Prof Good made a hero', *Botswana Gazette*, 27 April 2005.

in there', and 'You're saying just what we're thinking.' Police who stopped me running a red light late to a lecture, checked my name and sent me on with a call to drive safely and get back to court. Even someone from the attorney general's chambers supported the relevance of my teaching when we chanced to meet one Friday afternoon at Riverwalk.

The third court hearing

In the first week of May the arguments became more focused at the high court. The composition of the bench was again changed by Chief Justice Julian Nganunu, close associate of President Mogae, to now comprise three judges, with John Mosojane and Stephen Gaongalelwe joining Sapire. Anton Katz, an advocate from Cape Town and a specialist in immigration law, had joined my defence. Attorney General Ian Kirby was present for the first time.

The hearing of Tuesday 8 May was fairly typical of the last stages of the case. A packed crowd, including lecturers, students and foreign journalists, sat all day in close attention to arguments between Katz and Attorney General Kirby. The former argued that clauses of the Immigration Act that empowered the president to expel foreigners without giving reasons were unconstitutional, and supported this with reference to the case of a Czechoslovakian woman, denied entry into the United States as a Soviet spy, when it later emerged that the information was the fabrication of a disgruntled ex-lover. Judge Sapire observed that a person in my position could have been reported by anyone, including a disgruntled student.[32] Advocate Katz submitted that Botswana was bound by international convention, including the Covenant on Civil and Political Rights (ICCPR), which it signed and ratified in 2000, expressly entitled a person facing expulsion to submit reasons against that expulsion and have the matter reviewed by competent authority.

Attorney General Kirby countered with an assertion of the uniqueness and conservatism of Botswana. The country's 39 years of peace, stability, and rule of law made it 'unique'; it 'represent[ed] our country's most precious asset'. Botswana did not support the avant garde rights to freedom of expression embraced by larger nations. The people of Botswana approved of and retained both the

[32] Rob Amato, 'Immigration Beyond Judicial Review', *Sunday Independent* (Johannesburg), 8 May 2005.

death penalty and corporal punishment. In these and many other penal offences, the law in Botswana was conservative, and should be kept so. He said that Batswana did not want Baader Meinhof or al-Qaeda in Botswana, without explaining this reference.

Katz conceded significantly that Mogae had not acted with malice towards me, though evidence and opinion strongly suggested the opposite. Kirby emphasised national security, an argument which had been expressly excluded from the court on and before 28 February, as Sapire had noted. President Mogae had decided that I threatened the nation, and he acted in accordance with the laws in Botswana. Nothing more needed to be said, Kirby insisted.[33]

On the eve of the final decision the *Sunday Standard* carried a lengthy statement entitled 'Our Academics are a Disappointment' for 'not interrogating issues of national interest to better inform the public' and of even being fearful of being quoted on record when approached by the media.[34] Mike Mothibi, chief editor of the *Guardian*, pointed to the context of events and to popular sentiments. The government had become very sensitive since the October 2004 elections. 'The professor authoritatively brings to the fore issues that worry all of Botswana. That leads to panic,' he suggested.[35]

The court room was packed on 31 May and I had difficulty finding a space near my representatives. Stanley Sapire was presiding and reading his judgement on behalf of his more senior colleagues, Justices Mosojane and Gaongalelwe.

Anton Katz had focused on section seven of the Immigration Act which defined a prohibited immigrant as any person who is declared by the president 'to be an undesirable inhabitant of or visitor to Botswana', and especially on the usage of the word 'or', and claimed that the president had acted capriciously and illogically in failing to distinguish between an inhabitant and a visitor. Sapire branded this an example of 'extreme legal sophistry' which could bring 'the whole legal system of justice into disrespect'. Katz's first challenge was based on 'a fragile and flimsy semantic premise [and] must fail.'[36]

Justice Sapire moved to the second challenge based on the proclamation in the constitution that every person in Botswana is

[33] Amato, *Sunday Independent*, 1 and 8 May 2005.
[34] Commentary, *Sunday Standard*, 29 May 2005.
[35] Interviewed by Bram Vermeulen, 1 March 2005, for the Dutch paper *NRC Handelsblad*.
[36] The account over the following pages is from the High Court of Botswana at Lobatse, *Miscellaneous Civil Application N0. 90 of 2005*, Judgement of 31 May 2005, pp. 7–12.

entitled to specific rights and freedoms, citizens and non-citizens alike. Sapire stressed that Katz had made clear 'disavowal of any allegations of bad faith or impropriety on the part of the president', and this 'implie[d] that the president's statement that he received information from a source which he deemed to be reliable ... is not questioned and must be accepted'.

What the president learnt from the source deemed reliable by him, the judge continued, 'may not be disclosed'. The Immigration Act provided that no court shall question the adequacy of the grounds for a declaration, but my team had argued that this exclusion of the deportation process from judicial review conflicted with constitutional rights (under section 3) to 'freedom of conscience, of expression and of assembly and association'. Sapire declared that 'fundamental rights so declared are not absolute' and are 'subordinated to public interest'. Moreover, matters relating to the control of entry of non-citizens to Botswana and their continued presence were of public interest. Although I had heard many people say that they hoped I could remain in Botswana, and others had made statements in the press to the same effect, Sapire accepted the overriding knowledge and responsibilities of the president. Speaking in Kirby-like terms, he said: 'The president exercises [the right to exclude or expel non-citizens] as the executive head of state in what he considers to be the public interest. The use of the word 'desirable' [as in 'undesirable inhabitant of or visitor to Botswana'] imports the concept of public interest. The word in its context c[ould] only relate to what the president considers to be in the best interests of Botswana.' Under the Immigration Act, 'the sole reason' for a person becoming a prohibited immigrant is the presidential declaration. That itself makes the individual concerned a prohibited immigrant, and further steps 'follow automatically'. His earlier belief in the primacy of the constitution appeared to have been abandoned.

In a brief intermission, I was startled to see a man associated with the security services seated prominently on the public benches immediately behind me; his jacket carried the logo, 'International Police Enforcement Academy'. Dick Bayford had said how much the police respected the sanctity of the court, and that they always approached it with care and diffidence.

Sapire continued. There was no limit, to the nature of the information which the president might receive concerning an individual. When Sapire himself had expressed concerns about the admission of dubious information emanating perhaps from disgruntled students, and I too had worried about the misrepresentation of correspondence in my stolen laptops, the judge declared that 'whether the source is in fact reliable, is not an issue. There is accordingly no room for debate, argument, or appeal. Only the president knows his own state of mind, which is manifested by his declaration.'

The judge was unrestrained in upholding presidential power over individual rights, and allowed for only a 'rare exceptional case', where a 'PI'd' person might allege that the president acted unconstitutionally, in bad faith or in abuse of the powers conferred on him. Such a case was foreshadowed in earlier argument, but expressly disavowed by Katz, he again noted. I was rendered silent in court throughout the long proceedings, but I strongly believed and had publicly said that mine was indeed this so-called exceptional case. President Mogae's portrayal of me as a threat to national security was a baseless fabrication on any objective test, and his actions on 18 February were deemed malicious by several observers.

My counsel also argued that denying me the right to be heard on the presidential declaration and subsequent steps, breached Botswana's obligations under international treaties and declarations to which it was a signatory. Katz referred specifically to the ICCPR.[37] Though Kirby claimed that international treaties adopted by Botswana did not have the force of law until incorporated in domestic law, the Interpretation Act allowed that international conventions could be used as an aid to the construction or interpretation of the Botswana constitution and statutes. Article 13 of the ICCPR provided that a person facing expulsion is entitled to submit reasons against deportation, and to have the matter reviewed by competent authority. Sapire affirmed that the provisions of domestic law made the president's declaration unassailable on the merits. One cannot, he further said, 'interpret domestic law to accommodate Botswana's [international] undertakings to avail deportees facing expulsion, with a hearing.'

Discrimination against me as a non-citizen was also upheld. Constitutional provisions for the protection of the law must include, my counsel held, the right to be informed on the allegations against me and to be heard thereon. But Sapire's view was

---

[37] Among other relevant human rights treaties to which Botswana is a party are CERD (1974) and the African Charter on Human and Peoples' Rights (1986). See Alice Mogwe, Maureen Akena and Timothy Curry (eds) (2006), *In the Shadow of the Noose*, Gaborone: Ditshwanelo, p. 119.

that the Immigration Act 'expressly allows for discrimination in the case of a non-citizen'. Further, to the extent that such sections of the act discriminated against persons from outside Botswana, the constitution 'permits such discrimination.'[38]

Katz had made reference to recent cases upholding free speech in Britain, but Sapire found that they were so completely distinguishable from the present that reference thereto was unhelpful.

Despite the findings of both Marumo and Sapire in February, there was no way forward for me within the Botswana judicial system. Acting Judge Sapire finally declared: 'the applicant has not established his basic allegation that his deportation is in breach of his rights under the constitution,' and it was dismissed with costs.[39]

The end came at midday, and further steps immediately followed. As I tried to talk with Joao Salbany in an annex of the court, I was approached by the person from the police enforcement academy already present in the chamber. Amid much confusion, as Bayford endeavoured to obtain a stay of execution from the attorney general, the security man pressed closer. Salbany remonstrated that the unknown official should respect his right to address his client, but I was pushed into an unmarked Volvo, with another non-uniformed man and a driver. No identification was offered.[40] We began a two-hour high-speed drive back and forth across country roads as the security men shook off my lawyers and reporters trailing behind. We waited for an hour in the grounds of the international police enforcement academy behind the police college at Ootse, as the people holding me appeared to await instructions as to what to do next with me. In mid-afternoon I was transferred to the back of a barred police wagon, which then speeded over rough roads for twenty or so minutes, while I was vigorously bounced around in the back. We arrived at Ramotswa police station around 4pm where I was treated as a prisoner.[41]

Peter Scott from the Australian high commission in Pretoria, eventually caught up with me after considerable misinformation

---

[38] He had specifically observed on 28 February that 'the president cannot validly exercise the powers vested in him under the Immigration Act to defeat the provisions of the constitution.'
[39] Justices Mosojane and Gaongalelwe 'agreed' with Sapire. *MISCA No. 90 of 2005*, pp. 13–23.
[40] 'The way in which the security forces came prepared for Good's deportation makes one wonder whether they were privy to the judgement ... The presence of [what were in fact] large numbers of security agents in court, sitting near Good amounted to intimidation.' Ndulamo Anthony Morima, 'Good's Deportation an Indication of Botswana's Dictatorship', *Mmegi Monitor* 6 June 2005.
[41] Botswana Police, 'Prisoners Property Receipt Book' no. 147798, 31 May 2005.

from the authorities.[42] I was to be put on a plane out of Botswana, in Scott's company, that very night.

I was accorded a few minutes at my house. I was unable to speak properly with my seventeen-year-old daughter, Clara, whom I had to leave behind, or to my lawyers or friends, and was allowed to put only a few underclothes in a bag. As Morima noted later, 'making [Clara] part with her parent in such a traumatic manner violate[d] her right to family life'.[43] The last flight out of Gaborone to Joburg, left in 30 minutes time. Air Botswana staff, who had seen Clara and me many times over the years, expressed their sympathy.

The dependency of the high court

My odyssey began at Philip Green's residence in Pretoria,[44] as I endeavoured to plan anew. Morima's analysis stressed the high court's lack of independence. Judges are appointed by the president acting on the advice of the judicial service commission, themselves all presidential appointees, save for one member from and nominated by the Law Society. The court's lack of independence, he believed, may have compromised justice in my case, considering that the case involved the president. The appeal court too, he noted, lacked independence. The president of the court of appeal is the chief justice. Both high court and appeal court judges have no security of tenure, and judges working on renewable contracts, are dependent on the goodwill of the executive. And the way in which I was 'whisked away' violated natural justice and 'confirmed [the executive's] bad faith against [me]'[45].

The Economist Intelligence Unit (EIU) noted the 'considerable public outcry that the government should use such [punitive] measures against its critics.' The government had demonstrated its intolerance, they said, and the costs of the negative publicity was mounting. The court's decision 'came as no surprise', and Ian

---

[42] He held consular powers and responsibilities for my physical safety.

[43] *Mmegi Monitor*, 6 June 2005. The African charter on Human and People's Rights upholds the unity and sanctity of the family.

[44] The high commissioner was concerned for my welfare and I was able to spend a week at his house. But I soon understood over conversations in the evening that he and his minister, Alexander Downer, were firmly guided by efficacy, and did not pursue issues which they judged unlikely to succeed.

[45] Ndulamo Anthony Morima, *Mmegi Monitor*, 6 June 2005.

Kirby's involvement 'again drew attention to the relationship between the government and the judiciary'[46]

Justice Moatlhodi Marumo had been appointed to the bench in late 2000, and his resignation just five years later was described as 'unprecedented' and a grave loss to the country's jurisprudence.[47] He too expressed subsequent concerns about the incompleteness of both the separation of powers and judicial independence in Botswana, and he took exception to the fact that 'the judiciary [was] a department in the office of the president.'[48]

The substantive issue of free speech within a university had been addressed in the Kampala Declaration on Intellectual Freedom of 29 November 1990. This resolved that every academic in Africa had the right to 'pursue intellectual activity, including teaching, research and dissemination of research results, without let or hindrance subject only to universally recognised principles of scientific enquiry and ethical and professional standards'. He or she also had the right to 'initiate and develop contacts with other intellectuals and communities, and to 'express opinions freely in the media'. An academic deserved to be supported in turn by the university when he or she acted in this socially responsible manner: 'the intellectual community is obliged to show solidarity and give sanctuary to any member who is persecuted for his or her intellectual activity', the declaration affirmed.[49]

However, the University of Botswana chose instead to augment my problems seriously. After having failed in February to recognise publicly that my academic freedom was at stake, it now stopped my salary on the very night of my expulsion. This action not only deprived my daughter and me of our only source of cash income, but also terminated our medical insurance. The university only responded to repeated questions from me about my pay, and the safety of my house and property, in late July, and then it endeavoured to uphold the fiction that normal work relations somehow prevailed. It stated that stopping my salary was 'in line with the policy of the university and the principle of "no work no pay"' [50] My contract with UB was current and not due to expire until the end of December 2006. No UB official expressed sympathy or regret at the treatment meted out to me on 31 May. No one

[46] EIU (2005), *Country Report; Botswana*, London: July, pp. 16–17.
[47] Gideon Nkala, 'High court judge resigns', *Mmegi Online*, 11 November 2005. Suggestions existed that he had been rusticated to Francistown after his decision of 19 February.
[48] Bashi Letsididi, 'The judge and the wheels of justice', *Mmegi Online*, 23 June 2006.
[49] Articles 5, 6 and 9 of the Declaration.
[50] Email from Mr D.O. Fani, Legal Officer, 23 July 2005.

saw it as their responsibility to ensure the safety of my property which I was forced to leave behind on the night of my expulsion.

In late June, when my approach to the appeal court in Botswana was underway, and I had just arrived in London, the university advertised my existing post.[51] I had proposed to fulfil my teaching responsibilities by distance methods, and that UB pay my salary abroad.[52] The university continued to insist that nothing untoward had happened, that a spurious contractual equality existed between the university and me, and that it had no responsibility towards me. As Legal Officer Fani insisted: 'since neither us nor yourself are responsible for your departure ... before your contract could be fulfilled, none of us have any claim against the other. We will not insist that you must come and fulfil the terms of your contract, neither should you claim payment'. [53]

Outside academic communities showed contrasting responses. The Senate Academic Freedom Committee of the University of Witwatersrand, Johannesburg, expressed deep concern at my situation and especially the summary manner in which I was forced out.[54] An important response came from the American Political Science Association, whose President, Margaret Levi, wrote to President Mogae on 27 June on behalf of the '15,000 US and international professors and students of political science'. She said that I appeared to have been singled out for practising 'what we would regard as basic principles of academic freedom in a university setting.' She hoped that Mogae would rectify an apparent patent injustice, thereby reclaiming Botswana's progressive reputation.[55]

Scott Pegg is an American political scientist whom I had met when he was doing research in Botswana in 2004. He published a broad assessment which said that I was 'by no means blind to Botswana's achievements'. He noted that my 'Bushmen and Diamonds' paper cited official maps with additional shading by

[51] 'Professor – Political Science, University of Botswana, Vacancy No FSS/PAS 1/2005', dated 28 June 2005. The department had an establishment of only one full professor of politics, and Maiopse, head of department, was already canvassing for people to apply for my position.
[52] When I asked Vice Chancellor Otlhogile about the advertising of my position he replied that there was 'no need for excitement', and that of course, if my appeal was successful they would 'have to take me back'.
[53] Email communication dated 10 April 2006.
[54] Letter from Chairperson Prof Yunus Ballim, *Mmegi*, 1 April 2005.
[55] The APSA letter specifically noted that 'individuals like Professor Good depend upon the protection of international agreements' such as the ICCPR, the Universal Declaration of Human Rights (Art 19), and the Human Rights Defenders Declaration (Art 6a,6b and 6c), the latter in particular declaring that 'everyone has the right ... freely to publish, impart or disseminate to others views, information and knowledge', and noted that 'both our countries are signatories to the[se] covenants.' 'APSA response to Good deportation', *PS Online*, October 2005.

Survival International, and observed further that 'Good's critiques long predated SI's interest in Botswana'. He said that I 'spoke truth to power and paid a heavy price for doing so'. His deportation painfully confirms the validity of many of his arguments about the nature of democracy in Botswana. Pegg also condemned 'the complete and utter failure of the University of Botswana to defend one of its professors or academic freedom more generally'.

In Pretoria in June I had met with Bayford, Katz and his legal academic colleague, Max du Plessis, and was aware that Katz harboured no illusions about the outcome of my appeal before the Appeal Court of Botswana. It was a matter of exhausting all avenues open to me within the domestic judicial system. In July my case was before a five-judge bench of the appeal court, with advocate Brian Spilg, representing Ditshwanelo, having joined as *amicus curiae.*

As international interest continued, the BBC's Sue Lloyd-Roberts interviewed Mogae for the programme 'Newsnight'. The president described me as an outlaw and a rogue and a vagabond, and he said on camera that 'no matter what the court might say', he would 'never let me back'. Shocked by this summary dismissal of separation of powers principles and his contempt for the integrity of the judiciary, she failed on the moment to respond.[56]

Christina Lamb was also reporting on Botswana, and was accorded a rare interview with Vice-President General Ian Khama. She remarked that many people saw him as authoritarian, and he replied: ' I don't shy away from that description.' He went on: 'Some say I'll be a dictator. If making decisions means I'm going to be a dictator, they can call me that. I like decisions to be made quickly and carried out properly.'[57]

On 27 July the appeal court upheld the decision of 31 May, under legislation that permitted me no hearing, on the grounds that peace, order and national security required that the president possess and exercise powers to deport me as he did.

At the end of August I arrived in Sweden as a guest researcher at the Nordic Africa Institute (NAI) in Uppsala. I was acquainted with Henning Melber, the director of research. Henning organised an appeal urging President Mogae to rescind his PI order,[58] and

---

[56] I was in London and receiving mail through my daughter Hannah. Email from Ian Taylor quoting the Botswana government website, and my conversations with Lloyd-Roberts in London, 12 and 13 July 2005.

[57] Christina Lamb, 'In sickness and in wealth', *Sunday Times* (London), 3 July 2005, pp.57–59.

[58] The Act, under Section 12, specifically empowers the president to revoke an order, under identified conditions. Additionally PI status is not something permanent, and it is supposedly reviewed in the light of changing circumstances.

allow me to return to complete my contract, based on moral and humanitarian grounds and academic freedom. In the week of 8 to 15 September, this call attracted 150 supporters from scholars in 20 countries, but won no evident response from the president.[59]

The office given to me at the NAI had been previously allocated to Teedzani Thapelo, a scholar from Botswana with interests similar to mine. Like other guest researchers, he had been expected to give a public lecture at the end of his stay, and his chosen topic was 'A world of fancy figures and ugly facts: The political elite and democratization in Botswana.' The lecture was scheduled for 12 May 2005, and widely advertised. But within a few hours of the delivery time, Thapelo received a phone call from the Botswana embassy in Stockholm, and abruptly departed.[60]

To pursue all avenues, I wrote a personal appeal to President Mogae on 2 November, which stressed the difficulties I faced in caring for my daughter. I emphasised that I viewed criticism as a positive and necessary factor in societal development, and that my work was concerned more with systems and institutions than personalities. I apologised for any unintended offence I might have given to him personally, and I appealed to him to permit me to return and complete my work at UB until the end of 2006, when my daughter's matriculation would be finalised.

Henning and my colleague, Roger Southall, were in Gaborone in December for the launch of our book *Legacies of Power*, and they sought an opportunity to present my letter formally to the president. He met them in company with the new attorney general, Athaliah Molokomme.[61] Mogae said that it was quite normal for Batswana parents to be separated from their school-age children at boarding school. On the same date, 7 December 2005, his senior private secretary, Oteng Tebape, wrote to inform me that my 'appeal on family grounds has not been accepted. The appeal is too late, coming as it does after protracted and abusive court battles.'

The president's attitude remained vindictive, as indicated at a *kgotla* meeting in Kanye on 23 June 2006. He told this rural audience that I had 'appealed to the international community to reject our diamonds and tourism yet he stayed with us here. He even lied

---

[59] Henning Melber, 'Appeal to H.E. Festus Mogae', September 2005, NAI, Uppsala.
[60] Amin Kamete of the NAI was to be the chair. Personal communication with the convenor of the NAI's public lecture programme, October 2005, and flyer for the lecture.
[61] She was a former law lecturer at UB where we had been active together in the staff association, and we had occasional contact thereafter. I felt then that she sympathised with my work and criticism.

with his compatriots, Survival International, that we were killing Basarwa like animals.' He had 'PI'd' me after the government realised that I threatened the country's livelihood.[62]

Dick Bayford spoke up noting that I did not have any relationship with any organisation that might be regarded as in any way predjudicial to Botswana. Instead of expressing unsubstantiated assertions to a gullible rural audience, Bayford wrote, the president should tell the nation 'how he intended to revamp the country's battered international image occasioned by the Good case', and when his government intends to repeal that suite of archaic and oppressive laws that facilitated my deportation.[63]

When the UN's Committee on the Elimination of Racial Discrimination (CERD) met in Geneva, 20 February to 10 March 2006, it noted with concern that the decrees by the President of Botswana declaring a non-citizen as a prohibited immigrant, 'cannot be effectively appealed before a judicial body, as demonstrated in the decision of the court of appeal in the case of *Kenneth Good*.' [64]

By the end of 2005 my case was before the African Commission on Human and Peoples' Rights (ACHPR), supported by Interights, the International Committee for the Legal Defence of Human Rights, based in London, and advocates Katz and Max du Plessis. During its thirty-eighth Ordinary Session in Banjul, from 21 November to 5 December 2005, the ACHPR decided to be seized by the matter.[65] The commission meets only twice a year, and for just two weeks on each occasion. Hearings on the admissibility of my case were held in May and November 2006. The Botswana attorney general used various ploys and technicalities to obstruct proceedings on both occasions.[66] Judith Oder, legal officer at Interights, however, was of the firm opinion that our arguments 'on violations of due process guarantees, freedom of expression, sanctity of the family and the right to property [we]re strong and convincing'. She believed too that 'the commission will most likely find violations against Botswana.'[67] In Accra in May 2007 the ACHPR recognised the merits of my case. The process continues.

[62] Tuduetso Setsiba, 'Good was terrible – Mogae', *Mmegi Online*, 26 June 2006.
[63] Dick Bayford, 'This is Mogae's dirty tricks on Good', *Mmegi Online*, 30 June 2006.
[64] CERD, sixty-eigth session, concluding observations Botswana, paragraph 17.
[65] Letter from Omari Holaki, officer-in charge, to Judith Oder, Interights, 13 January 2006.
[66] As they had previously done many years before the existence of ACHPR in the case of John Modise.
[67] In her email to me of 21 November 2005.

BIBLIOGRAPHY

Acemoglu, D., S. Johnson and J. Robinson, 2001. 'An African Success Story: Botswana', mimeo, July 11.

—— 2002, 'An African Success Story: Botswana', CEPR Discussion Paper 3219, February.

—— 2003, 'An African story: Botswana' in D. Rodrik (ed.), *In Search of Prosperity: Analytical Narrative on Economic Growth*, Princeton University Press: Princeton.

ACHPR, 2000, 'John K. Modise v. Botswana', Comm. No. 97/93, Human Rights Library: University of Minnesota.

ACHPR, 2005a, *Report of the Working Group on Indigenous Populations/ Communities in Africa Mission to the Republic of Botswana.*

ACHPR, 2005b, *Report of the African Commission's Working Group of Experts on Indigenous Populations/Communities*, Adopted by the ACHPR at its 28th ordinary session.

Afro Barometer, 2005, 'Public opinion on presidential selection in Botswana', *Botswana Briefing*, 30 August.

Bannon, I. and P. Collier, 2003, *Natural Resources and Violent Conflict*, World Bank: Washington DC.

Bar-On, A., 1998, 'Poverty amid plenty', Paper presented to Ccomparative Research Programme on Poverty, Bergen, Norway (CROP) conference, University of Cape Town.

—— 2001, 'Providing so little for so few' in F. Wilson, N. Kanji and E. Braathen (eds), *Poverty Reduction,* NAEP and Zed Books: Cape Town and London.

Bennett, G., 2007, 'Summary of issues in court case', *Survival International News Release*, 26 February.

BIDPA, 2003, *Report on the Review of the Remote Area Development Programme (RADP),* Gaborone, 19 December.

Breytenbach, B., 1998, *Dog Heart: A Travel Memoir*, Human and Rousseau: Cape Town.

Campbell, Main and Associates, 1991, *Western Sandveld Remote Area Dwellers: Report*, Gaborone, April.

Cassidy, L., 2001, 'District socio-economic data on San in Botswana', in K. Good, I. Mazonde, L. Cassidy and R. Rivers, *An Assessment of the*

Status of the San in Botswana, Legal Assistance Centre: Windhoek, April.

CERD, 2005, 'Reports Submitted by States Parties Under Article 9 of the Convention: Addendum Botswana', 23 March.

—— 2006, 'Consideration of Reports Submitted by States Parties … Botswana', 20 February–10 March.

Childers, G. W., 1976, *Report of the Survey/Investigation of the Ghanzi Farm Basarwa Situation*, Republic of Botswana: Gaborone, September.

Childers, G., J. Stanley and K. Rick, 1982, *Government Settlement or People's Community?: A Study of Local Institutions in Ghanzi District*, Republic of Botswana, Ministry of Local Government and Lands, Applied Research Unit: June.

Chr. Michelsen Institute, 1996, *NORAD's Support of the [RADP] in Botswana*, a report submitted to the Royal Norwegian Ministry of Foreign Affairs: Bergen, February.

—— 1996, *NORAD's Support for the [RADP], Evaluation Report*, Bergen/Oslo.

Clover, J., 2003, 'Botswana: Future prospects and the need for broad-based development', African Security Analysis Programme, *Situation Report*, Institute for Strategic Studies: Pretoria.

Cullis, A. and C. Watson, 2003, 'Winner and losers: Privatising the commons in Botswana', Briefing Paper, International Institute for Environment and Development and RECONCILE, December.

Dale, R., 1995, Botswana's Search for Autonomy in Southern Africa, Greenwood Press: Westport, Conn.

Danevad, A., 1993, *Development Planning and the Importance of Democratic Institutions in Botswana*, Chr. Michelsen Institute, Bergen.

Ditshwanelo, 1996, 'When will this moving stop?', Report on a Fact-finding Mission to the CKGR, Gaborone: 10 April.

Ditshwanelo, 2006, 'Shadow Report to CERD', 68th Session, Geneva, 3–6 March.

Dow, Justice U., 2005, 'Judgement', in the High Court: Lobatse, 13 December.

DWNP, 1999, *Second Draft Management Plan*, Protected Areas Development Unit: Gaborone, 16–18 May.

Economic Consultancies Pty Ltd, Environmental Services Pty Ltd, Data Handle Pty Ltd and Maendeleo Botswana Pty Ltd., 1991, *A monitoring programme for the settlements at Thankane, Kokotsha, Inalegolo, Monong, Ngwatlhe and Groot Laagte*, Ministry of Local Government and Lands: Gaborone, May.

Economist Intelligence Unit, 2005, 'Botswana', *Country Report*, London, July.

Egner, E.B. and A.L. Klausen, 1980, *Poverty in Botswana*, National Institute of Development and Cultural Research: Gaborone.

Erni, C., 1997, 'Resettlement of Khwe communities continues', *Indigenous Affairs*, July–December.

Farmer, P., 2003, *Pathologies of Power: Health, Human Rights and the New War on the Poor*, University of California Press: Berkeley.

Fawcus, P. and A. Tilbury, 2000, *Botswana: the Road to Independence*, Pula Press and the Botswana Society: Gaborone.

Feinstein, A., 2007, *After the Party*, Jonathan Ball Publishers: Johannesburg & Cape Town.

Financial Times, Special Report Botswana, 2006, 'An Exception but not Quite a Model', London: 20 June.

Global Witness Report, 2005, *Making it Work: Why the Kimberley Process Must do More to Stop Conflict Diamonds*, November.

Good, K., 1992, 'Interpreting the exceptionality of Botswana', *Journal of Modern African Studies*, 30, 1.

—— 1993, 'At the ends of the ladder: Radical inequalities in Botswana', *Journal of Modern African Studies*, 31, 2.

—— 1994, 'Corruption and mismanagement in Botswana: A best-case example?', *Journal of Modern African Studies*, 32, 3.

—— 1996a, 'Towards popular participation in Botswana', *Journal of Modern African Studies*, 34, 1.

—— 1996b, 'Authoritarian liberalism: A defining characteristic of Botswana', *Journal of Contemporary African Studies*, 14, 1.

—— 1997, *Realizing Democracy in Botswana, Namibia and South Africa*, Africa Institute of South Africa: Pretoria.

—— 1999, 'The state and extreme poverty in Botswana: The San and destitutes', *Journal of Modern African Studies*, 37, 2.

—— 2002, *The Liberal Model and Africa: Elites against Democracy*, Palgrave: London and New York.

—— 2003, *Bushmen and diamonds: (Un) civil society in Botswana*, Nordic Africa Institute, Uppsala, Discussion Paper 23.

—— 2004, *Realising Democracy and Legitimacy in Southern Africa*, second edition, Africa Institute of Southern Africa: Pretoria.

Good, K., I. Mazoude, L. Cassidy and R. Rivers, 2001, *An Assessment of the Status of the San in Botswana*, Windhoek: Legal Assistance Centre, April, pp. A8 and A17.

Good, K. and S. Hughes, 2002, 'Globalization and Diversification: Two Case Studies in Southern Africa', *African Affairs*, 101.402, January.

Good, K. and I. Taylor, 2006, 'Unpacking the model: Presidential succession in Botswana', in R. Southall and H. Melber (eds), *Legacies of Power*, NAI and HSRC Press, Uppsala and Cape Town.

Good, K. and I. Taylor, 2007, 'Mounting repression in Botswana', *The Round Table*, 390, June.

Gordon, R., 1986, 'Bushmen banditry in Namibia', in D. Crummey (ed.), *Banditry, Rebellion and Social Protest in Africa*, James Currey and Heinemann: London and Portsmouth.

Guenther, M., 1976, 'From hunters to squatters', in R. Lee and I. DeVore (eds), *Kalahari Hunter-Gatherers*, Harvard University Press: Harvard, MA.

—— 1994, 'Lords of the desert land: Politics and resistance of the Ghanzi Bushmen of the nineteenth century', paper presented to the conference, *People Politics and Power: Representing the Bushman People of Southern Africa*, 4–7 August, Rock Art Research Unit, University of the Witwatersrand.

—— 1996, 'From 'lords of the desert' to "rubbish people', in Pippa Skotnes (ed.), *Miscast: Negotiating the Presence of the Bushmen*, Cape Town University Press: Cape Town.

Gulbrandsen, O., 2007, 'Popular reactions to the hidden exercise of political power: Botswana and Italy Compared', Social Anthropology Seminar Paper: University of Bergen, 19 March.

Gulbrandsen, O., M. Kalsen and J. Lexow, 1986, *Botswana: Remote Area Development Programme*, Report Submitted to the Royal Norwegian Ministry of Development Cooperation: Bergen/Gaborone/Oslo.

Harvey, C. and S. Lewis, 1990, *Policy Choice and Development Performance in Botswana*, St Martin's Press: New York.

High Court of Botswana, 2002, 'Roy Sesana et.al. and the Attorney General', Misca. No. 52 of 2002, Judgement, Justice Unity Dow.

Hillbom, E. C., (forthcoming), 'Diamonds or development? A structural assessment of Botswana's forty years of success', *Journal of Modern African Studies*.

Hitchcock, R.K., 1988, *Monitoring Research and Development in the Remote Areas of Botswana*; Report, Bergen/Gaborone/Oslo.

Hitchcock, R. K. and J. D. Holm, 1993, 'Bureaucratic domination of hunter-gatherer societies: A study of the San in Botswana', *Development and Change*, 24: 313.

Holm, J. and P. Molutsi, 1989, (eds), *Democracy in Botswana*, Macmillan, Gaborone.

Holm, J. D., P. Molutsi and G. Somolekae, 1996, 'The development of civil society in a democratic state: The Botswana model', *African Studies Review*, 39, 2, September.

Hope, K. R., 1996, 'Growth, unemployment and poverty in Botswana', *Journal of Contemporary African Studies*, 14, 1.

House of Lords, 2006, Debate on Botswana, 13 March.

Huntington, S. P., 1991, *The Third Wave: Democratization in the Late Twentieth Century*, Oklahoma University Press: Norman, OK.

Illife, J., 1987, *The African Poor: A History*, Cambridge University Press: Cambridge.

Iyanda, O. and B. Keakesitse, 2005, 'Making HIV/AIDS prevention campaign more acceptable among teenagers and young adults in Botswana', *Pula*, 19, 1.

Jefferis, K. 1998, 'Botswana and Diamond Dependent Development', in W. Edge and M.H. Lekorwe, (eds), *Botswana: Politics and Society*, Van Schaik: Pretoria.

Kekic, L., 2007, *The Economist Intelligence Unit's index of democracy*, *Economist* Intelligence Unit: London.

Le Roux, W., 1999, *Torn Apart*, Kuru Development Trust and WIMSA.

Le Roux, W. and A. White (eds), 2004, *Voices of the San: Living in Southern Africa Today*, Kwela Books: Cape Town.

Leith, J. C., 2004, 'Why Botswana prospered', paper presented to the Politics Seminar, University of Botswana, 3 March.

Leith, J. C, 2005, *Why Botswana Prospered*, McGill-Queen's University Press: Montreal and Kingston.

Levellers, The, 2007, (presented by Geoffrey Robertson in) *The Putney Debates*, Verso: London and New York.

Limi, A., 2006, 'Did Botswana escape the resource curse?'. *IMF Working Paper*, Washington, June.

Lodge, T., 2006, *Mandela: A Critical Life*, Oxford University Press: Oxford.

Makgala, C. J., (n.d.), 'Arrested Development: Some Notes on Ambition and Marginalization in the Botswana Democratic Party', mimeo, University of Botswana.

—— 2004, 'Calling a spade a spade: New dimensions in internal democracy in the BDP, 1991–2003', Paper presented to the Politics Seminar, University of Botswana, 11 February.

—— 2005, 'The relationship between Kenneth Koma and the Botswana Democratic Party, 1965-2003', *African Affairs*, 104.

—— 2006, *Elite Conflict in Botswana: A History*, Africa Institute of South Africa: Pretoria.

Masire, K., 2006, 'Democracy in Botswana: Challenges and motivations since 1996', Lecture at the University of Botswana, 20 September.

Masire, K., 2006, *Very Brave or Very Foolish?: Memoirs of an African Democrat*, Macmillan Botswana: Gaborone.

Matsheka, T.C. and M.Z. Botlhomilwe, 2000, 'Economic conditions and election outcomes in Botswana', *Pula*, 14, 1.

Maundeni, Z., (ed.) *40 Years of Democracy in Botswana, 1965–2005*, Mmegi Publishing House: Gaborone.

Mda, Z., 2000, *The Heart of Redness*, Oxford University Press: Oxford.

Mfundisi, A., 2005, 'Civil society and voter education in Botswana: 1965–2004', in Z. Maundeni (ed.), *40 Years of Democracy in Botswana*, Mmegi Publishing House: Gaborone.

Miers, S. and M. Crowder, 1988, 'The politics of slavery in Bechuanaland: Power struggles and the plight of the Basarwa in the Bamangwato Reserve, 1926–1940' in S. Miers and R. Roberts (eds), *The End of Slavery in Africa*, Madison, WI.

Mogalakwe, M., 1986, *Inside Ghanzi Freehold Farms*, Ministry of Local Government and Land, Applied Research Unit: Gaborone, April.

Mogwe, A. 1992, *Who Was Here First?*, Botswana Christian Council Occasional Paper no.10, March.

Mogwe, A., M. Akena and T. Curry (eds), 2006, *In the Shadow of the Noose*, Ditshwanelo: Gaborone.

Molomo, M., 2000, 'Democracy under siege: The presidency and executive powers in Botswana', *Pula*, 14, 1.

—— 2001, 'Civil-military relations in Botswana's developmental state', *African Studies Quarterly*, 5, 2.

Molomo, M. and W. Molefe, 2005, 'Voters and electoral performance of political parties in Botswana', in Maundeni, (ed.), *40 Years of Democracy in Botswana*, Mmegi Publishing House: Gaborone.

Mosca, G.,1939, *The Ruling Class*, McGraw-Hill: New York.

Mpabanga, D. 1997, 'Constraints to industrial development', in J. S. Salkin, D. Mpabanga, D. Cowan, J. Selwe and M. Wright (eds) (1997). *Aspects of the Botswana Economy: Selected papers*, Leutswe La Lesedi and James Currey: Gaborone and Oxford.

Ndozi, C. and E. Toteng, 1989, *A Socio-Economic Survey of Selected Central District Remote Area Settlements*, Ministry of Local Government and Lands, Applied Research Unit, December.

Ombudsman, 2001, Report in Terms of Section 8 (1) of the Ombudsman Act of 1995, Government Printer: Gaborone.

Otlhogile, B., 1998, 'The president: his office, functions and powers', in W. A. Edge and M.H. Lekorwe (eds), *Botswana: Politics and Society*, Van Schaik Publishers: Pretoria.

Pallister, D., S. Stewart I. and I. Lepper, 1987, *South Africa Inc: The Oppenheimer Empire*, Simon and Schuster: London.

Parsons, N., W. Henderson, and T. Tlou, 1995, *Seretse Khama, 1921–1980*, Macmillan and Botswana Society: Gaborone.

Pempel, T, (ed.), 1980, *Uncommon Democracies*, Cornell University Press: Ithaca and London.

Picard, L. (ed.), 1985, *The Evolution of Modern Botswana*, University of Nebraska Press: Lincoln, NE.

—— 1987, *The politics of Development in Botswana: A model for success?* Lynne Rienner: Boulder, CO.

Polelo, M., 2005a, 'Inside undemocratic schools: Corporal punishment and physical abuse in Botswana schools', *Journal of Sociology and Education in Africa,* June, 4, 2.

—— 2005b, 'School dropout among the remote area dwellers of Botswana', *Pula*, 9, 1.

—— (forthcoming), 'The state and education policy in Botswana', Doctoral Dissertation, University of Melbourne.

Raditlhokwa, L., 1994, 'Time to break the passive cycle', *HEDU Bulletin*, Higher Education Development Unit UB, 11 October.

Randall, W., 2005, *Botswana Time*, Abacus Books: London.

Republic of Botswana, 1990a, 'The Revised National Policy on Incomes, Employment, Prices and Profits', draft white paper.

—— 1990b, The Report of the Presidential Commission on the Review of the Incomes Policy, Republic of Botswana, March.

—— 1991a, *Report of the Presidential Commission of Inquiry into Problems in Mogoditshane etc*, 13 December.

—— 1991b, *Report of the Presidential Commission of Inquiry into the Supply of School Books etc*, 16 April.

—— 1992, *Report of the Presidential Commission of Inquiry into the Operations of the BHC etc.*, 30 November.

—— 2003. *Botswana Statistical Yearbook* Vol. 28, No. 64, Central Statistics Office, Gaborone.

—— 2004, *Report of the Judicial Commission of Inquiry into State Land Allocations in Gaborone* (the Lesetedi Commission), Gaborone, July.

Republic of Botswana: Gaborone, 2004, *Budget Speech*.

Republic of Botswana: Gaborone, 2007, *Budget Speech*

Reteng, 2005, 'Alternative Report Submitted to [CERD]', Gaborone, January.

Revelli, P., 2007, 'Brazil: the squatters won't go away', *Le Monde Diplomatique*, November.

Ross, M., 2003, 'The Natural Resource Curse: How Wealth can Make you Poor', in Bannon and Collier, (eds), *Natural Resources and Violent Conflict*, World Bank: Washington DC.

Russell, M., 1976, 'Slaves or workers? Relations between Bushmen, Tswana and Boers in the Kalahari', *Journal of Southern African Studies*, 2, 1.

Samatar, A., 1999, *An African Miracle: State and Class Leadership and Colonial Legacy in Botswana's Development*, Heinemann Press: Portsmouth, NH.

Saugestad, Sidsel, 1998, *The Inconvenient Indigenous*, Faculty of Social Science: University of Tromso.

—— 2005/4, 'Improving their lives: State policies and San resistance in Botswana', *Before Farming*, 1, 2.

Scanlon, C., 2002, 'Educating for peace: Politics and human rights in Botswana', paper presented to the Politics Seminar, University of Botswana, 27 March.

Siphambe, H.K. (n.d.) 'Minimum wages in Botswana: Should they be increased?, *Barclays Botswana Economic Review*, 3, 4.

Siwawa-Ndai, P. D., 1997, 'Industrialization in Botswana: evolution, performance and prospects', in J. S. Salkin, D. Mpabanga, D. Cocran, L. Selwe and M. Wright, (eds), *Aspects of the Botswana Economy: Selected Papers*, Lentswe La Lesedi and James Currey: Gaborone and Oxford.

Steadman, S. J., 1993, *Botswana: The Political Economy of Democratic Development*, Lynne Rienner, Boulder, CO.

Thapelo, T., 2002, 'Nomads no more: Public policy and San (Bushman) displacement in liberal democratic Botswana', paper presented at the International Conference on Democracy and Liberation in Southern Africa, Windhoek: 11–13 July.

Thumberg-Hartland, P., 1978, *Botswana: An African Growth Economy*, Westview Press: Boulder, CO.

United Nations Conference on Trade and Development (UNCTAD), 2005, *Economic Development in Africa: Rethinking the Role of Foreign Direct Investment*, New York and Geneva.

United Nations Development Programme (UNDP), 2004, *Human Development Report 2004.*

—— 2005, 'Country Reports on Human Rights Practices – 2005', Released by the Bureau of Democracy, Human Rights and Labor, 8 March 2006.

—— 2005, *Human Development Report 2005.*

—— 2006, 'Country Reports on Human Rights Practices – 2006', Released by the Bureau of Democracy, Human Rights and Labor, 6 March.

Vengroff, R., 1977, *Botswana: Rural Development in the Shadow of Apartheid,* Associated University Presses: London.

Werbner, R., 2004, *Reasonable Radicals and Citizenship in Botswana: the Public Anthropology of Kalanga Elites*, Indiana University Press: Bloomington, IN.

Wilkinson, R. G., 1996, *Unhealthy Societies: The Afflictions of Inequality*, Routledge: London and New York.

Wilkinson, R. G., 2005, *The Impact of Inequality*, Routledge: London and New York.

Wilmsen, E., 1989, *Land Filled With Flies: A Political Economy of the Kalahari,* University of Chicago Press: Chicago, IL.

Wilmsen, E. and R. Vossen, 1984, 'Labour, language and power in the construction of ethnicity in Botswana', *Critique of Anthropology,* 10, 1.

Wilson, F., N. Kanji and E. Braathen, 2001, *Poverty Reduction*, NAEP and Zed Books: Cape Town and London.

Wily, Liz, 1980, *Land Allocation and Hunter-Gatherer Land Rights in Botswana: The Impact of the TGLP*, The Anti-Slavery Society, Working Paper No. 4: London.

—— 1982, 'A strategy of self-determination for the Kalahari San (The Botswana government's programme of action in the Ghanzi farms)', *Development and Change,* 13.

World Bank, 2000, *Can Africa Claim the 21st Century?* Washington, DC.

World Bank, 2004, *African Development Indicators*, Washington, DC.

Wylie, D., 1990, *A Little God: The Twilight of Patriarchy in a Southern African Chiefdom*, University of Witwatersrand Press: Hanover, NH and London.